T0240783

Palm Programming
in Basic

JON KILBURN

Apress™

Technical Reviewers: Hody Couch, Carl Ganz, George Henne, Frank O'Brien
Editorial Directors: Dan Appleman, Peter Blackburn, Gary Cornell, Jason Gilmore, Karen Watterson
Marketing Manager: Stephanie Rodriguez
Managing Editor: Grace Wong
Project Manager: Tracy Brown
Development Editors: Tracy Brown, Valerie Perry
Copy Editors: Tom Gillen, Ami Knox
Production Editor: Sofia Marchant
Compositor: Impressions Book and Journal Services, Inc.
Indexer: Nancy A. Guenther
Cover Designer: Tom Debolski

Distributed to the book trade in the United States by Springer-Verlag New York, Inc., 233 Spring Street, 6th Floor, New York, NY 10013 and outside the United States by Springer-Verlag GmbH & Co. KG, Tiergartenstr. 17, 69112 Heidelberg, Germany.
In the United States, phone 1-800-SPRINGER, email orders@springer-ny.com, or visit http://www.springer-ny.com.
Outside the United States, fax +49 6221 345229, email orders@springer.de, or visit http://www.springer.de.

For information on translations, please contact Apress directly at 2560 Ninth Street, Suite 219, Berkeley, CA 94710.
Phone 510-549-5938, fax 510-549-5939, email info@apress.com, or visit http://www.apress.com.

The source code for this book is available to readers at http://www.apress.com in the Source Code section. You will need to answer questions pertaining to this book in order to successfully download the code.

This book is dedicated to my loving wife, Brett, who spent many nights sleeping without me while I toiled.

Contents at a Glance

Contents

About the Author

Jon Kilburn graduated from Penn State and has been actively involved in the programming community since 1988. He's written articles and taught seminars all over the world and is president of Vivid Software, a Texas-based consulting firm that specializes in developing Internet solutions that use VB, PDAs, and SQL Server. You can learn more about Jon by reading his VB @ 10 essay posted on the Apress Web site http://www.apress.com.

Preface

This book is written with a slightly different approach than those taken by a majority of books that are currently on the market. My goal was to give the Visual Basic programmer the tools to be productive building applications in the Palm OS world.

To that end, you may notice that there is overlap between the chapters. What do I mean by this? Specifically, I demonstrate building the same application across three similar, yet different compilers. Each of these compilers requires something different, but the basis for the application remains the same. In every instance, I try to explain exactly how to do something, such as creating a menu, in each compiler.

The goal is for you, the programmer, to be able to open the book to any of the chapters about these compilers and read that section, and, when you're finished, feel confident that you could write an application using that compiler.

Some of you may notice that in chapters for each compiler I restate information. This is by design. This book is designed to help a programmer learn each of these compilers. You may decide that you wish to learn NS Basic or CASL, but do not intend to learn AppForge. As such, you can open this book to the "Introduction to NS Basic" and begin. If you come back later to learn CASL, you will discover that I discuss the database design and the GolfPro application in much the same manner as I did for NS Basic. Database design concepts are constant, and must be applied in the context of each compiler so you, the programmer, can learn the ins and outs of each language.

Along the way, I try to cover every aspect of Palm OS application development, encompassing application design principles, compilers, conduits, and even Web Clipping.

Who Should Read This Book?

This book is written with the Visual Basic programmer in mind. Visual Basic is the world's largest and most widely used development tool, and this book targets those Visual Basic developers who want to begin developing Palm applications without the hassles of learning C.

This book was written assuming that the reader has little or no Palm programming experience. In fact, I assume that the Visual Basic programmer has no knowledge of C or C++, but this does not mean that C and C++ programmers cannot use this book.

How to Use This Book

This book can be used in two ways: you can read it as a beginning-to-end tutorial about programming for the Palm OS environment using a variety of compilers, or you can simply pick the compiler you want to use and follow the information about building applications using that compiler from beginning to end.

I recommend reading Chapters 1, 2, and 9 regardless of which compiler is to your liking. The design principles in Chapter 1 are sound throughout any hand-held programming environment. Chapter 2 provides a good understanding of how to use the Palm OS Emulator (POSE), and Chapter 9, well, odds are that when you build a Palm application you will need a conduit. Chapter 9 covers building conduits using the tools that come with each of the compilers as well as the Palm Conduit Developers Kit (CDK) and EHAND's PalmAccess custom OCX for conduit development.

The primary sections of the book (Chapters 3 through 8) are separated into two chapter blocks, each covering one of the compilers (AppForge, NS Basic, and CASL) in both an introductory and application development mode.

You will notice that I try very hard not to compare each tool to the others in the book. This is done on purpose. It was my wish that you would learn the capabilities of each compiler and then decide for yourself which tool best fits not only your wallet, but your project.

If you have questions or need some general advice, you can feel free to contact me at Jkilburn@vividsoftware.com.

Acknowledgments

Many special people helped me write this book.

Ric Aarlan has been a mainstay of the AppForge group and provided tons of help with the conduits section of the book.

Colin Allen is one of the many contributors to this book. He helped with the CASL conduit sections and has proofed and conferred with me on many items throughout this book.

Hody Crouch is one of the many talented people at AppForge. He has lent his hand by providing technical editing and has proofed many of the chapters.

Carl Ganz has been a mentor for many years. He helped me get started writing and has continued to be a colleague and friend. You'll notice his hand in the appendix on data compression, and he provided technical editing throughout the book as well.

George Henne provided valuable assistance with NS Basic in many ways: first in helping me learn the product and then by helping make sure that the chapters covered many of the items that the NS Basic programmer would need.

Frank O'Brien has helped immensely with the sections on CASL. When the decision was made to add CASL to the book, Frank stepped up and wrote the GolfPro for CASL application. He also lent a hand penning Chapter 8 on building the GolfPro application using CASL.

Matt Ridge provided help with many aspects including proofing chapters and writing the installation sections of Chapter 9.

Gary Stark ("the redback") penned both Chapters 1 and 11. He is an excellent author and is a well-spoken individual; it has been a pleasure knowing him.

Without Karen Watterson's help and guidance, I might never have taken the step from penning columns for *Visual Basic Developer* to writing a book. She has been a guide, an editor, and a friend.

Application Design– Desktop versus Handheld

Writing applications for a handheld system requires you to think a little differently than if you're writing for a desktop platform. I cannot stress too strongly here how important good design is. If one takes the time and effort to design an application with care and forethought, much unnecessary work and frustration can be avoided. Objects and functions can be overloaded, and interfaces simplified, if you take a few minutes to think through the entire process that you're working with.

You should also be looking beyond the pure development process. No application is free of bugs, nor do I believe that there is any such thing as a fully completed application. It's a safe bet to assume that maintenance will be required at some time in the future, and you should always write your code with the presumption that you are the one who will be performing that maintenance.

This chapter will discuss the importance of good design and how it applies to your applications. Whether you're using AppForge, NS Basic, CASL, or any other development tool, the use of sound design principals in your application will reap rewards in many diverse areas. Real benefits can be achieved in the areas of screen design, code reuse, database design, and, of course, maintenance.

Application Design–What's It All About?

The specific design of any application that you're going to produce is always subject to many considerations. The primary purpose of the application should be obvious, but there are many other issues to consider as well. For instance, if your users are entering data from a form that their clients have completed, it might be prudent to look to that form's layout for clues to your screens' designs. Or it might not. Seventeen pages of handwritten essays, for example, won't be exactly easy to enter into a handheld system (or any other system for that matter).

Looking at how your end users actually work with the data that they're using is always a good idea. This permits you to gain an appreciation for the physical task of gathering the data. You also need to look at your application to see if there are ways in which you can simplify the task at hand for those end users. Issues such as the nature of the data captured as well as the ease in which the data is captured need to be considered at this point. Consider also the structure of the data, and where and how you need to store it.

Frequently, your selection of tools may be forced upon you by the choice of the platform that you have targeted your application for. There is simply no point in selecting a development tool that does not target your chosen platform. Which tool is chosen by you to satisfy your needs will depend upon which of these products you feel comfortable using, as well as which of them you feel will meet the needs defined by your application's specifications.

Finally, there are the questions of what tools you can and do use to create your masterpiece. These are all questions that can be solved with proper attention to application design.

System Specifications

A good set of system specifications and good design concepts are two of the most important parts of a successful development project. The system specification should be used as a roadmap that tells you where you're going with the application. It should define a number of components that include the following:

- The application's defined purpose
- How the application will be developed
- The data sources needed by the application
- The application's input requirements
- The application's output
- Factors that are outside of the scope of the application and specification, and are therefore explicitly excluded
- The testing regime that will be used

With a good specification to work from, you can confidently commence the development of an application knowing exactly what it should look like and what results are expected.

Microsoft eMbedded toolkit and Metrowerks CodeWarrior

Until recently, the only usable tool for development of applications on the Pocket PC platform was the Microsoft Embedded toolkit, in its various guises. Similarly, much development for the Palm OS platform needed to be done using the Metrowerks CodeWarrior product. Each of these products provides a very robust C environment, and for those comfortable programming with the C language, the choices were relatively easy.

The Microsoft Embedded Toolkit also provides a version of VB scripting that is quite viable. It uses a Visual Basic integrated development environment (IDE) within which the forms are drawn, and code is attached to the form in the usual VB manner. Compilation and debugging is performed within the IDE while the application is being executed either within the (supplied) emulation environment, or else directly on a connected handheld device.

AppForge and NSBasic

Today that situation has changed, and there are a number of other very usable tools available that permit development of applications for a variety of platforms using some common products. Satellite Forms, Pendragon Forms, KVM (Java), CASL (Compact Application Solution Language), Visual CE, AppForge and NSBasic all provide different ways of getting to a particular point. All have their pros and cons, and some might suit the way that you work, whereas others might not.

 NOTE *CASL also offers the ability to write code for both the Palm OS and Windows CE, but only for Windows CE version 2.0. Windows CE version 3.0 support is forthcoming.*

The AppForge and NSBasic products both offer facilities that permit you to develop for the Palm OS and Windows CE platforms using a form of the Visual Basic language, and each of them now promise some form of cross-platform capabilities. Whether you wish to develop applications across the different platforms is another question altogether, but the tools are now becoming sophisticated enough to permit this to happen.

Different Development Paradigms

Obviously, developing an application for a desktop system imposes certain constraints. When the target platform becomes a Palm OS or Windows CE device, you will encounter different sets of constraints. These constraints will need to be considered when writing your code, but a wise programmer will look to his or her application's design and start to give consideration to these issues much earlier in the development process.

Color

Consider, as a simple example, the use of color in your applications. The use of color can be a great aid to differentiating between various items on a form presented to an end user. Credit values on an account can be displayed in red, for instance. Serious errors in data input might be similarly highlighted in red, whereas less serious ones might perhaps be highlighted in some other color.

When you are developing an application for a desktop system, it can be safely assumed that your end users will have access to a color monitor. The only issue to contend with here will be the number of colors that they might have available to them.

By way of contrast, if you are developing applications for the Palm OS environment, it may frequently be the case that your end users will be working with a monochrome display. The use of colors to highlight values, errors, or other items of note is really not a workable solution when you are restricted by such a display.

An alternative means of directing the attention of your end users to these items will need to be found when there is a reasonable likelihood that your end users will not have a color system. Displaying text in an inverse format might be needed to direct your users' attention to the problem. The use of message boxes can also be considered, but in doing so, remember to take into account the possible effect that interruptions to the workflow can have on your users as well. One or two interruptions might be okay, but many more should probably be avoided.

Storage

Storage imposes different constraints upon you and your users. Although desktop systems today have virtually unlimited storage, this is not the case for handheld systems. While current Palm systems might have between 2MB and 8MB of RAM available, earlier systems were limited to just 512KB. Newer devices, such as the Sony Clié, Handera 330, and Palm m500/m505, support even more RAM through the use of memory sticks or expansion cards. The Handera also supports the IBM MicroDrive, providing up to 1GB of storage. Windows CE systems will range from 8MB of storage to in excess of 1GB, with the use of add-ons such as compact flash cards or a MicroDrive.

 NOTE *There will be little point in designing a system that requires 4MB for data storage if there is no way for your users to retain that amount of data online.*

Consider carefully the way that your data will be stored within your handheld device, as well as how it will be backed up, stored, and viewed on the desktop system. Should the data be permanent or transient? In either case, what should its layout be—structured, freeform, or something else of your own design?

How will the data be transmitted between systems? Standard synchronization techniques are useful and practical, but what are the real needs of your users, and what is the topology of the environment? Will infrared or wireless transmission work, or are you restricted to just the physically hard-wired layout?

Different Form Factors

The different form factors available impose a whole new way of thinking about your applications' designs. On your desktop, you have a system with 1024×768 pixels typically available to you. Within this video area you not only use applications that take advantage of this size, but also design the windows that your end users will be using to communicate with your applications. In terms of real estate, that provides you with a great expanse of screen within which you can place your controls and the data that is represented by those controls. Handheld systems are, by their very nature, handheld. That means small.

Recall that a desktop system you might be working with provides users with an area of perhaps 1024×768 pixels. On a Palm device, that size is reduced to just 160×160 pixels. A Windows CE Pocket PC will give you 240×320 pixels, while a Windows CE Handheld PC might give you 640×240 pixels.

It should be somewhat obvious to a developer that there is no way that you can fit a similar number of controls into the smaller display of a handheld system. Less obvious perhaps is the fact that as well as being different sizes, the actual screen layouts can also be very different. The Windows CE Handheld PC will be, like the desktop system, formatted for a landscape view of the data, but it will at best be just half the apparent height of a typical desktop system.

A Pocket PC, like a Palm OS system, is formatted for a portrait view of data. Note again that although the Pocket PC and Palm OS devices might share a similar perspective, their sizes—and available real estate—are different. Different screen sizes means that control layouts will also tend to be different.

Users might not always recognize that level of detail, and so you may need to take them by the hand and gently walk them through some of the changes that the different form factors within which you're working will impose.

Form/Screen Design

The screen layout and placement of controls within each of your applications' windows is directly affected by the very nature of your target devices' physical characteristics. If you're not careful about this aspect of your design, you may find that certain information will be hidden from your end users' view. This could lead to errors or omissions in data capture, or to incorrect reading of the data you are displaying.

Recall the target systems that you are developing for can have very different physical characteristics, and that these characteristics can and should have an impact on how you design your screen layouts. Because the area of real estate available is significantly reduced, techniques such as the use of tab control pages or individual forms should be considered to break up data entry and display groups in logical subdivisions. This permits the simplification of the data capture and display process. Users will find smaller groupings of information easier to deal with and assimilate. Keeping it simple is of the essence.

Use of Controls

You also need to review the manner by which data input is actually made. When you're developing for a desktop system, you probably take it for granted that users will have access to a keyboard and a mouse as common input devices. These are tools that are generally easy to learn to use for most people, and are quite efficient for most data input tasks. This is not quite the case when it comes to handheld devices. Users of handheld devices will generally have access to some form of pointing device; even a fingernail is effective in a difficult situation.

However, although it's true that portable keyboards are starting to become more common for handheld devices, they are still considered by many to be a burden. Do not take for granted that your end users will have access to a keyboard at their point of data input. Consequently, your screen design should take into account that intensive data input of any sort should not be anticipated or expected. Tools such as Transcriber (on Windows CE systems) and the Graffiti scripting application (on Palm devices), and onscreen keyboards remain prevalent, but for prolonged sessions of data input these are to be avoided.

This means that, as a general guide, input of a textual nature should be avoided, and where possible designs using point-and-click controls, preloaded with valid data selections only, should be promoted.

Text Controls

Due to the need to reduce input of a textual nature, the use of text controls should be discouraged. I will accept that their use is frequently unavoidable, but thoughtful design of your application can and should lead to minimizing their use. Although information such as client and street names will need to be directly captured, consider whether there is perhaps some way that this data could initially be captured on another device and then transferred to the handheld in a synchronization process.

Using Alternative Methods of Data Capture

Be sure to consider alternative methods of data capture. In one medical-based application, I had a situation whereby certain actions needed to be initiated by the practitioner. At first glance, it appeared that I needed a free-form text field to permit the practitioner to enter whatever action he or she felt appropriate for that patient. Upon closer review, however, it appeared that the various types of actions being recorded fell within a narrow range of items that were easily defined.

It was a trivial task to provide an interface on the desktop companion application to permit practitioners to define their own customized list of actions that they deemed appropriate to their needs. The data that made up this list was then formatted and synchronized with the handheld system, and loaded into a list box within my handheld application.

The practitioner was then able to select a valid item from his or her predefined list of choices, thereby reducing the data entry task from a complex handwriting recognition or hunt-and-peck keyboard one to a simple point-and-tap operation.

Combo Boxes and List Boxes

As you have just seen, it may be possible to consider the replacement of simple data entry fields with data selected from a prefilled combo or list box. I would encourage you to examine carefully the nature of each element of data that your users will be feeding to your application. Consider whether the data in question is really freeform in nature, or can be distilled down to a finite set of options.

Lists are very useful here. Consider that sizes, colors, brand names, models, days of the week, or even choices of a fast food restaurant's menu can all be reduced to lists. State and ZIP codes can always be provided in the form of a list of some sort, and if you think that the list might be too big, reduce it by creating subgroups. State, ZIP, and area codes are all easily related to one another. If you know that the customer is in Florida, why bother giving them California ZIP and area codes?

Use a process of progressive selection if necessary. How did you know that your customer was in Florida? The first selection you provided for your users might have been a state selection drop-down combo box. Once a valid selection was made—and note that with a list box or combo box the only selections that can be made must be valid—you could then go on and display a list of only those ZIP codes that are valid for that state.

Here you truly have a win-win situation available to you. The task of your end users is reduced to a series of point-and-tap operations. From their perspective, this is quick and easy. They don't even need to think! Given that this is a natural situation for many users, you are indeed doing them a service.

From your perspective, you have not just simplified the process of data capture, but also of data validation. You have already established the parameters for the data being entered by the user. The only data that can be captured is valid data. You reduce the need to provide error checking or validation routines when you are already providing prevalidated data.

Every player wins a prize.

Checkboxes and Radio Buttons

Often you will find that much of the data that your users enter can be reduced to not just a list of items, but to a choice of two or three items. Yes or No (or Yes, No, or Cancel), True or False, Male or Female, Present or Absent, Operable or Faulty are but a few examples of these sorts of choices. In these circumstances, you can look to using either a list or combo box, as noted previously, or perhaps a checkbox or radio button.

If you elect to use a checkbox, be careful to ensure that your understanding of the checkbox's meaning (when either checked or unchecked) is the same as that of your users. Consider whether, for example, the simple act of checking a box to indicate gender is really meaningful within that context.

Figure 1-1 shows a single checkbox with the label Male. Does checking this box indicate that the subject of it is male? More significantly, does leaving this box unchecked indicate that the subject of it is female, or is simply not male? The two might not necessarily be the same thing.

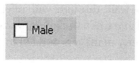

Figure 1-1. A simple but possibly ambiguous checkbox

Figure 1-2 displays a pair of radio buttons labeled Male and Female. In this instance, you have a much clearer indication of intent, and the selected choice will be obvious. The fact that in such cases you choose to use radio buttons as the user interface also adds to the functionality you provide to your users. This is because, if one option is selected, all alternate options are automatically de-selected. Only one selection may ever be made.

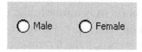

Figure 1-2. A pair of radio buttons

 NOTE *Please be aware that not all development platforms provide all of the tools that I'm describing. Where a tool is not available, such as radio buttons in NSBasic, you will need to use an alternative control, such as a checkbox, and write the logic that deselects the alternative buttons yourself.*

Figure 1-3 displays a portion of a checklist for an apartment walk-through application. As you can see, it clearly displays the intent of both the programmer and the end user. Data capture from the perspective of the end user is extremely simple; he or she simply needs to check one box against each category. Completion of an apartment walk-through using this sort of application takes just a few moments, and a hard copy version will be available for verification by the users—and the tenants—within just a short time after synchronization.

Curtains	☐ Good	☐ Bad
Blinds	☐ Good	☐ Bad
Carpets	☐ Good	☐ Bad
Light Fittings	☐ Good	☐ Bad

Figure 1-3. A simple checklist

A modified version of the walk-through, with references to the data collected upon move-in, is made available when the tenant vacates the property, thus simplifying the process for property managers and tenants alike.

Spinners and Numeric Data

Numerical data, like textual data, is often subject to the rigors of manual input by your users. And as with textual data, this can be a tedious and unreliable means of gathering the data that your clients need to record. The use of either spinner boxes or drop-down combo boxes should be seriously considered. This can simplify the means of capture and, again, increase the accuracy of the data captured. For some applications, the use of a barcode reader might be a feasible approach.

Some will propose the use of a calculator control for input of numeric data. I would contend that if the data is truly numeric and calculable, then this might be an appropriate metaphor for data input. However, I would caution you that not all data consisting of numbers is, in fact, numeric. A good example of this might be a phone number, where the data looks to be numbers, but it's really just textual in nature.

To my mind, using a calculator style of control for entry of this sort of data is not quite correct. The use of a calculator control can—and probably should—imply that calculations can (or might be) performed using this data. Clearly, in the instance of a phone number this will not be the case.

The indications that you are giving to your users in this instance may well be misleading and confusing, and I suspect that there are more than enough confused users already running around out there without you adding more to the mix. My advice is that the choice of controls that are utilized is yours, and yours alone. Choose wisely.

Graphics

It has been said that a picture is worth a thousand words. Therefore, the use of graphic elements within your application should be carefully considered. Branding of your applications is one area where the use of graphics might be considered. If your application uses a splash screen or other identifying graphics, these can be employed within the handheld application to both identify the application and also help relate it to and identify it with its companion application on the desktop.

But the use of graphics on a handheld system can go far beyond just the simple branding and identification of the application. Consider that in an apartment walk-through program, a simple graphic of each room might be presented to your users so that they can clearly indicate where a particular item of specific interest, such as perhaps a carpet stain or a hole punched through a wall, might be. Consider too the use of graphics in incident report forms. I can see benefits in the use of this technology for reporting anything from apartment security to traffic accidents.

Figure 1-4 illustrates one element of an optometry practice management system written for the Pocket PC. Within this particular window, a practitioner can draw directly on his handheld unit irregularities that he or she has observed within a patient's eyes. The image is saved back to the desktop system within the patient's clinical record, and is available for subsequent retrieval, either on the desktop or on the handheld.

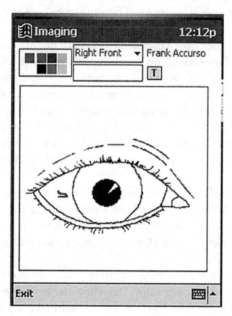

Figure 1-4. Graphic functionality within an optometry practice management system on the Pocket PC

 NOTE   *The issue of storage needs to be raised when considering graphic images. If you've done much work with graphic elements on desktop systems, you are probably aware of the size that graphic files can attain. Whomever it was that said that size doesn't matter was clearly not concerned with storing graphic images on PDAs.*

My purpose here is not to deter you from using graphics. Rather I wish to encourage you to think seriously, intelligently, and creatively about their use, and their impact upon both your users and the systems within which they will operate.

Data Capture Issues

Earlier in this chapter, I discussed the issues of data capture, and how important it is to try to use controls that are relevant to the nature of the data being cap-tured as well as easy for your users to interact with. If you are choosing your controls wisely and prefilling them with relevant selections where appropriate, many issues related to data capture will become more benign than you might be accustomed to.

I have also described how a prefilled combo box might be used to capture a customer's state of residence, and how you can then use that data to filter out ZIP and area codes that are not relevant to that state. That discussion indicated how you might use checkboxes or radio buttons to capture data whose selections might best be represented within very short option lists. In cases such as these, simple encoding of the data for storage may be desirable and viable. Although the M = Male, F = Female, and CA = California, TX = Texas concepts are quite obvious, you may wish to consider using similar techniques for other, less obvi-ous choices.

The advantages of using these sorts of techniques may be quite subtle, yet could be manifold. Where there is a large volume of information that needs to be stored, placing the encoded data can bring savings in memory used, and data transfer times between handheld and desktop systems can be signifi-cantly reduced.

Consider the savings if a descriptive string that might need 50 bytes can be stored as a one- or two-byte key value. Decoding that key value at either end of the system is a trivial task, but the savings in storage and potential performance gains might be significant.

Data Display Issues

Although you're concerned with the process of gathering data, you also need to concern yourself with the process of also retrieving and displaying data that has been captured. If you're now displaying data for your users to view, consider whether that data should be displayed in a manner that permits them to modify and then store the modified version, or whether the data should be displayed in read-only mode. While in both instances you can easily overload the forms that you've designed, you need to be aware that many controls will automatically enable the modification of the data being displayed. If you need to only display (but not modify) the data in question, then the use of such controls is not just dangerous, but probably stupid.

If you're reading data to a set of read-only controls, good programming practice dictates that you should try to accomplish this task within just the one function, subroutine, or method within your application. (Similarly, writing of your data should also be controlled from a complementary function, subroutine, or method, but I'm probably getting a little ahead of the discussion.)

When using read-only controls, ensure that where appropriate they can be used to access all of the data available. Consider that a disabled list box within Visual Basic is exactly that—disabled. If a selected option is outside of the disabled control's default view port, it will not be able to be seen by your user; that is probably not a good thing. If the control that you have selected is not set up for displaying of the items only, then you may need to write your code defensively, to prevent changes occurring unless the user specifically authorizes those changes.

Managing Storage

The issues associated with the storage of your data are too frequently not given adequate consideration. Working on desktop systems, the issue is often simply addressed by adding more disk capacity, or perhaps, when working within a client/server architecture, the problem is disposed of by delegating it to the database administrator. Recall that handheld systems don't have the same virtually unlimited capacity when it comes to storage, and if you're not careful, you can—you surely will—bump into issues that require some lateral thought processes to enable them to be overcome.

The primary question I wish to address in this area is that of *data latency*. How long does your end user really need this data hanging around on his or her handheld system? Too frequently, I see systems where the application designer simply ensures that all of the data exists on both systems—the handheld as well as the desktop—all the time. This approach is perfectly acceptable as long as it can be justified. If you look at the typical PDA Address Book applications, one can readily see the need for taking this approach.

You always want—need—to have access to your complete list of contacts, and in its most current form. You're in Dallas, your PC's not, and Bill just changed his phone number; what is his new number? More importantly, where is that new number stored? Case closed.

Let's now look at a different style of application, a stock ordering system. Here, you have a need for several different types of data in order to accept an order. You need to have client data. Who is placing the order? Where is that person located? To where will that person's orders be delivered? And let's not forget the user's credit status. It seems to me that in this instance you have a need, similar to the Address Book's need, to maintain an up-to-date client database on the handheld system.

I accept that you also need to have a current stock database available at all times. You don't wish to be placing orders for items flagged as in stock, when in fact they're not. That leads to frustration on the part of both your users and their customers. This is something that's best avoided, especially if your users' customers are anything like me.

Finally, you have a need for the data that represents the order itself. Looking at a simple order entry system, this could comprise a data set as simple as an Order Header record and a group of Line Item Detail records, which would be linked to the Order Header record.

You already know that the client and stock databases need to be available and current in order to enable orders to be captured. But what about the actual orders that have been placed? You need to consider whether there is justification to maintain this data within the handheld system beyond the point of transference to the primary system. Can you (or more importantly, your users) accept that this data is transient in nature? Should the order records be deleted from the PDA once they have been sent to the primary system? Is there a need for your users to recall those orders—on the handheld device—once the orders have been processed?

It doesn't take a rocket scientist to see that the data within the client database, while somewhat volatile, will be relatively static. Likewise, the stock database will display some minor volatility within its data, but it will also over time display moderate growth.

In an active and healthy business, it is hoped that orders will be frequent and large. This can lead to significant and swift changes in the storage needs of the orders database, and this aspect needs to be seriously reviewed before committing to any particular storage strategy.

Transfer of Data

In considering the design of your application, you need to always consider when and how the data can be transmitted between the various components of the complete system. Traditionally, the physical act of data transfer between the handheld system and its companion desktop system will occur through a synchronization process, be that HotSync for the Palm OS systems, or Microsoft's ActiveSync for Windows CE systems.

Within this traditional approach, you would expect to be using these processes to send updated information from either device to the other, and maintain both sets of data in a state of harmony. Typically, these processes utilize the desktop systems' serial or USB ports to enable communications to occur. The use of conduits, delimited text files, or any other form of data transfer that is deemed appropriate can be used to service the needs of ensuring that all systems maintain true data integrity.

Today, however, different methods of communications exist between the various devices we use. Local area networks (LANs) have been around for years, and infrared technology has been with us for some time now as well. Wireless transmission of data through the radio spectrum, either through the 802.11b or Bluetooth standards, is starting to make inroads here also.

We have now reached the point whereby real-time data updates on a desktop server can be achieved through the use of techniques that rely on client/server or Web Clipping technology and a wireless LAN topology. A handheld device can now pass requests for data via a wireless LAN to a local server, which can then answer that request and return responses to the client in real time.

NOTE *If you're writing applications with wireless technology as a target, you need to remain alert to the limitations imposed by the technology. Typical wireless LANs will be good for up to 300 feet from an access point when situated indoors, and perhaps up to 1000 feet from an access point when located outdoors. Bluetooth technology imposes similar constraints and limitations, and both can be expanded with additional hardware. However, all of these options offer greater flexibility than being fixed to a desktop location.*

Within this topology, it is possible that very little application-specific data will, in fact, need to be stored on the handheld device. Client lists can be accessed through a simple query; with a client's key information, the rest of that client's information can be requested and transmitted within a reasonable timeframe. Similarly, current product lists and inventory information will be readily available.

Any new data can be built up on the handheld device and transmitted back to the base, for addition to and inclusion in the primary databases; subsequent queries will not actually be handled locally (on the handheld), but again will be passed back to the server for processing and response. Many small business locations are ideally suited to this sort of setup, in fact.

Consider a small shop in a mall or a typical medical practitioner. Don't forget your apartment complex's management office, or your realtor's office either. Engineering, architectural, and small manufacturing businesses seem to me to also be potential prospects for the implementation of this technology. It may be that you should look to this area for a solution to some of the data transmission issues that you will encounter. This will have the effect of improving the convenience that your users will enjoy through the use of your product, as well as the perceived performance and data availability that your system provides them with.

Conclusion

In this chapter, I've briefly shown you why application design is an important factor to consider in your development work. You have seen how design concepts differ between some of the disparate environments within which probably you work, and how those environments can affect the way that your application looks and the way that your users will interact with your application.

It is up to you to try to incorporate those elements of design into your products, giving your end users applications they will not only find easy to use, but also be compelled to use.

#### CHAPTER 2

Introduction to the Palm Operating System Emulator (POSE)

So you've decided to take the plunge and start developing software for the Palm OS, running on all those nifty little handheld organizers, but maybe you don't actually have a Palm Pilot, or you're unsure which device you want to write programs for. Well, before you jump right in, let's review a little bit about the Palm operating system, and the core of Palm development, the Palm OS Emulator (POSE). First, a brief history of Palm Computing, and how this company (first as US Robotics, and later as 3Com) has single-handedly set the standard for an entire market, and created a phenomenon that is even now a target of many big players, including Microsoft.

The Story of Palm Computing

Palm set the standard with its PalmPilot and the Palm III organizers. People love them, and use them in ways we probably never would have imagined just a few years ago.

So, why did Palm succeed when so many have failed? The answer is very simple, and it involves just a few items.

- Palm figured out exactly what the customer wanted.

- Palm figured out just how much each customer was willing to pay.

As you can see, there was no magic, no special overpowering features, just a simple-to-use, cost-effective solution. Frankly, that's a formula for success, no matter what service or product you are providing to the end consumer.

The Palm platform consists of the core Palm operating system, a set of applications included with each Palm device, and related hardware and software tools.

Palm Devices

Of course, no discussion of Palm would be complete without a brief rundown of the Palm devices in use in an attempt to alleviate some of the confusion over the names of the various generations of devices. Why has Palm Computing used the names Pilot, then PalmPilot, and now simply Palm for its devices? What do other manufacturers of Palm OS–based devices use?

The short of it is this: Palm Computing has released several generations of devices. Almost everyone on the planet refers to the Palm devices as Palm Pilots, or just plain Pilots. This is because when 3Com first introduced the Palm Pilot, the company received a rather nasty phone call from the lawyers at Pilot Corporation, a well-known pen company. Pilot Corporation was upset at Palm for using the name "Pilot," and threatened legal action against 3Com for infringement upon its name.

Anyway, things were just starting to heat up, as Palm's name troubles were not over yet. Along came Microsoft, which saw the emerging market and decided that it should go after a piece of the pie. So what did Microsoft choose as the name for its new device? The PalmPC. Eventually Microsoft stopped using the name PalmPC, but by that time the damage to the name "Palm" had already been done.

So 3Com has gone to great lengths to refer to its products as Palm devices, opting instead to pursue the approach that Palm is an operating system platform rather than a single device.

In any event, I will refer to all of 3Com's Palm handheld devices, as well as those of the various other companies that have licensed and used the Palm OS to build their own devices, as *Palm devices*. I will refer to the Palm OS and its related tools collectively as the *Palm platform*.

The generations of Palm Computing's own devices have so far included the following:

- Palm Pilot 1000, Palm Pilot 5000

- PalmPilot Personal, PalmPilot Professional

- Palm III (in many variations, such as III, IIIe, and so on)

- Palm V (with a sleeker case than those of previous generations, plus a rechargeable battery and recharger built into the docking station)

- Palm VII (similar in form to the Palm III, but with hardware and software to access Palm.net wireless Web Clipping services[1])

---

[1] I'll discuss Web Clipping and Palm Query Applications (or PQA's) later in Chapter 10.

- Palm m100 (smaller screen for price-sensitive customers)

- Palm m500 (similar in form to the Palm V, with a faster processor and expansion slots)

- Palm m505 (color version of the m500)

For a complete comparison of all the Palm devices and some of their major differences, please check out http://www.palmos.com/dev/tech/hardware/compare.html.

One gotcha to note here is that the release of a new generation of Palm devices does not preclude the continuing sale of previous generations. Palm III, V, and VII series devices are all currently available from Palm Computing.

Other Palm Platform-Based Devices

Users pick the model they want based on features and, of course, cost. In general, each new generation of Palm Computing devices has brought an increase in retail price for the new device along with steadily decreasing prices for previous generations.

Here is a list of some of the other Palm platform–based devices on the market:

- IBM WorkPads

- Symbol Barcode Scanners

- QUALCOMM's pdQ smartphones (which include a built-in Palm connected organizer and some custom applications that link the organizer functionality to the phone—you can tap on a phone number to dial it, for instance)

- Handspring's Visor devices, including the Springboard expansion modules

- HandEra devices, including the 330 model, which features a 240×320 display and a virtual Graffiti area

- Kyocera's QCP 6035 Smartphone

- Sony CLIÉs

One of the beauties of the Palm platform is that Palm Computing has expended a lot of effort to ensure the compatibility of new devices: Palm applications that run on one generation of devices should (with few exceptions) run unchanged on later generations.

This brings you up to date on the history of the Palm. If you would like to see a full timeline of the evolution of Palm devices, go to http://www.palm.com/about/corporate/timeline.html.

Palm Core Development Tools

At the Palm Web site (http://www.palmos.com/dev/tech/tools/core.html) you'll find a fairly comprehensive and complete list of development tools (see Figure 2-1). Now by this I don't mean languages—I'm referring instead to some of the more common support tools, such as the Palm SDK, the Web Clipping tools, PRC tools, and the conduit development kits. From this page, you can also find a complete list of all the development tools registered at Palm by clicking the Browse all tools link.

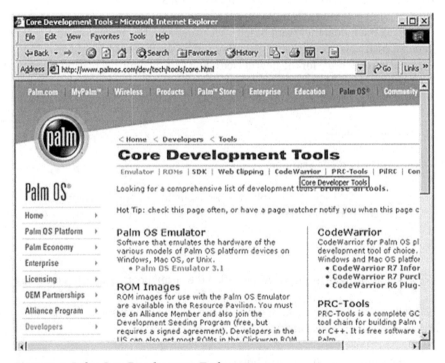

Figure 2-1. Palm Core Development Tools page

The Pocket PC vs. the Palm Device

There is a long tradition of user interface design that dates back to Xerox PARC and the pioneering work done on the Apple Lisa, the Mac, and Windows, that has, for better or worse, established certain standards. For example, the Palm OS, Windows, the Mac, and most other graphical operating systems always use an ellipsis (. . .) to indicate an option requiring further input. All menu items with an ellipsis on these platforms always include an option to exit out of a decision, usually a Cancel button. Thus, a Windows or Palm user may select a menu option such as Save As. . ., knowing full well that no immediate action will be taken.

Windows CE 3.0, probably to save screen real estate, seemingly does away with this behavior some of the time. There is an ellipsis after the Options. . . command and an OK button. No ellipsis appears after the Delete Page option in the Edit menu of the task launcher screen, but this option *does* give you the ability to cancel the deletion. Elsewhere, the Find. . . command includes the ellipsis (which of course makes sense), but no OK or Cancel buttons to confirm or cancel the command. The ellipsis in this case signifies that there will be an option to input a word. Shouldn't there be a way to cancel or at least confirm this option?

Here's another example: Apparently, the OK button is used to close documents in Windows CE 3.0. Although not exactly conventional design, this makes a reasonable amount of sense. But then why is there an OK button in the main Options dialog box, but not one in the main Settings dialog box? And, if OK is used to signify the status of a document, why don't open Media Player documents and the like have an OK button?

It is hard to deny that the latest generation of Pocket PCs, with processors running at speeds greater than 130 MHz (Compaq's new iPAQ runs at 206 MHz), vastly outpaces anything currently on the market that runs the Palm OS. Palm's machines typically run at 20 MHz. The difference in speed is clearly noticeable when scrolling through pages of text, and when performing certain other functions.

Indeed, certain aspects of the Palm user experience "feel" better than their counterparts on the Pocket PC platform. Although the Pocket PC's ActiveSync feature is nice—and totally automatic, if you want it to be—the ability to push the button on the base of the Palm's desktop cradle (battery charger) and have it synchronize all the data between the desktop and the handheld organizer is, in my view, less confusing than the behind-the-scenes activities of Microsoft's ActiveSync or the act of pushing an onscreen button instead. Palm also provides direct—albeit optional—support for serial- or USB-based Macintosh clients, something that is achievable with a Pocket PC only by running Windows-emulation software (a clumsy workaround at best).

There's no question about which platform has a better-quality display. The Pocket PCs win by a mile, with 320×240 resolution and thousands of colors. In contrast, the Palm IIIc supports only 256 colors at a paltry 160×160 resolution, on a screen that looks noticeably grainier. (Monochrome Palm units also support a 160×160-pixel display and are technically able to use four levels of grayscale, although such functionality is not officially supported.)

The forthcoming Palm OS 4.0 promises support for 16-bit color, Bluetooth wireless connectivity, and wireless telephony. And it may seem like old hat for

Pocket PC advocates (and Mac owners, who've been increasingly inconvenienced by Palm's stubborn persistence in supporting only old-fashioned serial connections not available on Apple's new models), but the new Palm OS will support universal serial bus connections for easier Palm-to-PC synchronization.

One of the biggest differences between the Palm OS 3.5 and Pocket PC (Windows CE 3.0) platforms is what you see on your computer's screen.

Microsoft has elected, for better or worse, to tie the Pocket PC closely to its Outlook mail and scheduling client. Outlook provides a calendar, an address book, e-mail capability, task scheduling, note-keeping features, and a to-do list. Palm provides its own application for these functions that is remarkably speedy and efficient. Several third-party products further enhance the ability for Palm users to exchange data with desktop computers. Looking ahead, products based on the emerging SyncML standard should make such data exchanges virtually seamless.

Each OS has its own share of flaws and features not found on the other. For the moment, they each exist, but a victor must emerge sometime, vanquishing the other to the technology graveyard to go the way of DOS and CPM.

Expectations of Performance

Desktop applications users usually won't mind waiting a few seconds for a program to load because they plan to use the application for an extended period of time, and they will often have other applications open at the same time. This is *not* true for typical handheld users.

If you think about it, this is logical. Handheld devices were created for users on the go. You should try to bear in mind that the average handheld user is often searching for some piece of data that he or she needs to find quickly (such as a phone number) or spending only a few seconds making a couple of notes in the middle of a meeting before quitting the device (generally speaking).

Two key elements you should always keep in mind when developing a Palm application are speed and efficiency. Writing fast code that performs well is only half the battle.

A few other items to make note of are that Palm devices have a small screen size (160×160 pixels). Compare that with the minimum resolution running on a standard windows machine of 640×480, and you'll see that I'm talking about a tiny area. Forms must be designed so that the user can navigate easily and find data with a minimum amount of effort. Requiring users to scroll to find information will often frustrate them.

The other important item is RAM as permanent storage. Available memory on Palm devices can range from 128KB on the Pilot 1000 to 8MB on the Palm Vx. This kind of limited storage dictates that your applications should be as small as possible. A good rule of thumb to follow is this: if a feature will be used by less than 20 percent of your users, then leave it out.

 NOTE *If you're a bit new to this whole Palm thing, I suggest that you take a few moments to read over some of the frequently asked questions (or FAQs) that can be found at the Palm Web site (check out* http://oasis.palm.com/dev/kb/*). Here you'll find a pretty good knowledge base posted and maintained by Palm. The only drawback is that much of the information is geared toward development using CodeWarrior. You will find other useful information there as well, but be advised you should brush up on your C.*

Palm Operating System Emulator

Now before you can begin to write programs for the Palm (or any other OS for that matter), you need a platform on which to test. The developers at Palm are one step ahead of the rest, creating a special emulator for just this use. The emulator is essentially like having a virtual Palm on your desktop. POSE allows you to debug and run the programs you develop on your computer, instead of performing a HotSync every time you make a new build. You definitely need the emulator, unless you enjoy resetting your Palm device several times a day while writing your software (see Figure 2-2).

Figure 2-2. The Palm OS Emulator (POSE)

NOTE *For the most part, much of the information provided in this chapter is part of the documentation that comes with POSE, and some of the information has been compiled from various Web sites.*

POSE is based on the CoPilot emulator, written by several different developers, principally Greg Hewgill. Palm enhanced the earlier emulator with new features, debugging support, and support for more recent ROMs. The core of the CoPilot emulator, in fact, is still available as open-source code and is a central piece of many other emulators available on the Web.

POSE is, as far as I know, the only emulator supported by Palm Computing, so your mileage may vary if you use one of the others. I will be using POSE version 3.2 for this book, unless otherwise noted.

Obtaining the POSE

In order to make sure that you get the most recent version of POSE, it is probably a good idea to go to `http://www.palmos.com/dev/tech/tools/emulator/` and read carefully through the page and the relevant links.

Before you can download the POSE emulator, you must sign an agreement (for legal reasons) with Palm to download ROM images. To obtain the Prototype License and Confidentiality Agreement, you must be a member of the Alliance Program.

After you join the Alliance Program, it is recommend that you join the Developer Seeding Program, which requires that you return a signed agreement to Palm. This agreement allows you to access ROM images and other valuable prerelease information. If you are based in the USA, you may also obtain images using a "clickwrap" agreement, which does not require a signed agreement.

Here are the steps to follow for signing up to get the POSE (note that this information is also available at the Palm Web site):

1. Join the Alliance Program, by filling out the online application (you can get more information by going to `http://www.palmos.com/alliance/`).

2. Next, you wait for Palm to review your application, which usually takes less than a day. When you've been approved, Palm will send your username and password via e-mail, which you use to enter the Resource Pavilion.

3. If you are located in the US and you do not want to join the Development Seeding Program, click the ROM Image Clickwrap Area link to start downloading ROMs.

Follow these steps to join the Development Seeding Program:

1. When Palm has received and reviewed you application, you'll get an e-mail announcing new Resource Pavilion access. After you get this notification, enter the Resource Pavilion. Once in the Members area, click the Development Seedling Program link in the section Apply for Programs.

2. An online form appears, which you need to fill out and submit.

3. Download the Acrobat format agreement, print it, sign it, and send the license to Palm as indicated on that page.

4. When Palm has received and reviewed you application, you'll get an e-mail announcing your new Resource Pavilion access.

ROM Images

One of the major advantages of the POSE is that users can load ROM images. What are ROM images? Well, imagine that you are developing an application, and you want to test this application on a variety of different devices. Currently there is a wide range of devices you can test on, including Palm IIIs, Vs, and VIIs, as well as Sony CLIÉs, Handspring Visors, and Symbol devices. Now unless you've got really deep pockets (or an overwhelming urge to have every handheld device out there), you will probably only own one (maybe two) of these devices.

 NOTE   *I personally have a Palm Vx, which I received as a gift, and a Symbol 1500. The Symbol devices (models SPT 1500 and SPT 1700) are quite nice, as they come with an integrated barcode scanner, and the new models will come with wireless capabilities built in. For more information on the Symbol devices, check out* http://www.symbol.com.

Enter ROM images. You can install any ROM image (with just about any memory configuration you wish) into the POSE. This little trick allows you to test on a variety of different platforms, memory configurations, and even skins (which handle the appearance of the POSE—more on that later).

The emulator software does not include ROM images. It is like a computer without an operating system. You can get your ROM images from one of two sources: ROM image files downloaded from the Resource Pavilion, or a ROM image uploaded from an actual device. There are also two types of ROM image files: debug and nondebug versions.

Because a Palm ROM image contains the actual Palm OS, Palm Computing does not bundle a ROM with POSE; instead, Palm tracks its usage with a separate download, which requires a more intricate license agreement.

ROM images for OEM Palm devices (those from Handspring, Sony, Handera, Symbol, and so on) may only be available from the device manufacturer. If you are unable to find the ROM images you need, you may want to join the particular manufacturer's developer program.

Whereas you can click through the POSE license and download the emulator immediately, you have to agree to a more stringent set of stipulations and wait for Palm Computing to process your ROM license request before you receive your ROM image to enable POSE.

Luckily, developers who already own a physical Palm device have a way around this hassle and delay. You can simply download the ROM image from your Palm device and use it in POSE.

To download a ROM image from your own Palm Device, follow these steps:

1. Load ROM Transfer.prc on your Palm device using the Palm Install tool.

2. Start POSE.

3. Select the option to download a ROM from the Palm device.

4. Follow the downloading instructions (select the COM port, speed, and so on) and save the ROM on your development system.

If using your own ROM is so easy, why doesn't everyone simply do it? Two reasons:

- Not everyone has a Palm device handy when they want to start using POSE.

- Palm provides a debugging-enabled ROM when you sign its license agreement. Some POSE debugging features will not be available if you do not use the debugging ROM from Palm.

POSE Development History

Although Palm Computing has assumed responsibility for maintaining and upgrading POSE, the program has been available for a number of years due to the programming efforts of several developers, including Greg Hewgill (who created CoPilot, the original POSE); the creators of PERL, Larry Wall et al.; and a few others, listed in Table 1-1.

Table 2-1. POSE Development Contributors

PERSON	DESCRIPTION
Greg Hewgill	Created CoPilot, the original Palm OS emulator
Craig Schofield	Ported CoPilot to the Mac OS
Bernd Schmidt	Created the UAE Amiga Emulator, which provided the 68000 CPU emulator that is used in the core of CoPilot
John C. Daub	Created CURLPushButton (for the Mac version of the POSE)
Quinn "The Eskimo," Peter N. Lewis et al.	Created Internet Config, which is used in the Macintosh version of POSE
Matthias Neeracher	Created the GUSI library for NetLib redirection on the Macintosh
Larry Wall et al.	Created PERL

ROMs transferred from a device (and nondebug ROM image files) are designed to cover up errors. Although appropriate for convincing users that applications work, they may interfere with developing truly reliable software. Debug ROMs are created to reveal programming errors and techniques that may not work in future versions of Palm OS.

Release ROMs perform fewer tests to confirm that software is operating properly. Debug images specifically check for common issues that may cause your program to be less reliable. For example, a debug image enables the Palm OS Emulator to report improper memory access, direct hardware access, and stack problems.

Palm strongly recommends that developers use debug ROMs.

 NOTE *When a developer sees a problem using a debug ROM but not a device-transferred ROM, this is nearly always a sign that the extra instrumentation in the debug ROM is working, as opposed to being a sign of a defect with the debug ROM. Developers should find the code that is triggering the report and make the appropriate changes.*

Palm OS Emulator Runtime Requirements

The Palm OS Emulator requires one of the following runtime environments:

- Windows 98

- Windows 95

- Windows NT

- MacOS 7.5 or later

- Unix (some versions, including Linux)

Standard Device Features of the Palm OS Emulator

The Palm OS Emulator includes the following features:

- An exact replica of the Palm device display, including the silkscreen and Graffiti areas

- Emulation of the Palm stylus with the desktop computer pointing device

- Emulation of the Palm device hardware buttons, including the following:

  - Power on/off button

  - Application buttons

  - Up and down buttons

  - Reset button

  - HotSync button

- Ability to zoom the display for enhanced readability and presentation

- Ability to capture handheld display images and save them as graphic files

- Communications port emulation for modem communications and synchronizing

Additional Device Features

Some OEM providers include additional device features through a custom version of the Palm OS Emulator. For example, Sony provides a custom POSE to support the jog-wheel controls on CLIÉ devices.

Extended Emulation Features

POSE also provides the following capabilities on your desktop computer to extend the standard Palm device interface:

- Capability to enter text with the desktop computer

- Configurable memory card size, up to 8MB

Debug Features

The Palm OS Emulator provides a large number of debugging features that help you to detect coding problems and unsafe application operations, some of which are listed here:

- Detection of applications that perform handheld accesses that may be incompatible with different versions of the Palm OS

- Availability of an automated test facility, consisting of components called gremlins, which repeatedly generates random events

- Support for external debuggers, such as PalmDebugger, the Metrowerks CodeWarrior debugger, and dbd

- Monitoring of application actions, including various memory access and memory block activities

- Logging of application activities, including events handled, functions called, and CPU opcodes executed by the application

- Profiling of application performance

Skins

Although it may sound silly, one of the coolest things about the POSE is you can actually change its appearance to mimic that of a number of different devices. When you download the POSE, you will find a number of .skin files included. If you create a directory underneath the POSE directory named Skins, the emulator will recursively load any .skin files it finds so that you can change the look of your POSE session (see Figure 2-3). Skins are especially useful for generating screen shots for use in promotional materials (or for making really cool-looking figures in a book).

Figure 2-3. Palm OS Emulator Japanese Skin

Getting Started with the POSE

The first time that you start the Palm OS Emulator, it does not display an image of any handheld device. What it does is asks you to create a new session. To create a session, you need to specify the OS version, the type of device (for example, III, V, VII, and so on), the language, and the RAM size (see Figure 2-4).

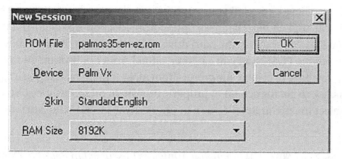

Figure 2-4. Creating a Palm OS Emulator session

After you have defined a session configuration, the emulator creates a new session based on those settings when it launches.

Now by right-clicking the POSE, you can access the standard menu that allows you to open other saved emulator sessions, create new sessions, change the skins, transfer ROMs, and turn on or off debugging (see Figure 2-5).

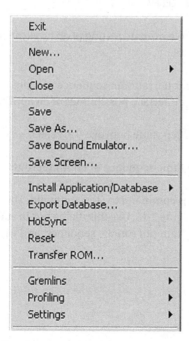

Figure 2-5. The Palm OS Emulator pop-up menu

When you have compiled your applications, you can install them by choosing the Install Application/Database option from this pop-up menu and then finding the files you want on the hard drive. Once you select the files, they are transferred to the POSE, and you can then launch your application. In some instances, you have to change the groups from All to something else (such as Games) and then back to get the screen to properly refresh. In other instances, you may need to select the menu Reset option to physically reset the POSE attributes.

NOTE *When using AppForge (discussed in detail in Chapter 3), you will have to manually reset the POSE (by selecting the Reset menu option). When installing AppForge via HotSync, Booster (the AppForge runtime engine) automatically prompts the user to reset the Palm OS device. The POSE does not tell you when a reset is needed.*

Debugging with Gremlins

You can use gremlins to automate testing of an application. Each gremlin has the following characteristics:

- It generates a unique, random sequence of stylus-and-key input to step through the user interface possibilities of an application.

- It has a unique seed value between 0 and 999.

- It generates the same sequence of random events whenever it is run.

Select the Gremlins command to start a gremlin. The New Gremlin Horde dialog box displays (see Figure 2-6). Use this dialog box to specify which gremlin (0 to 999) to run, how many times to run the sequence, and which application to test.

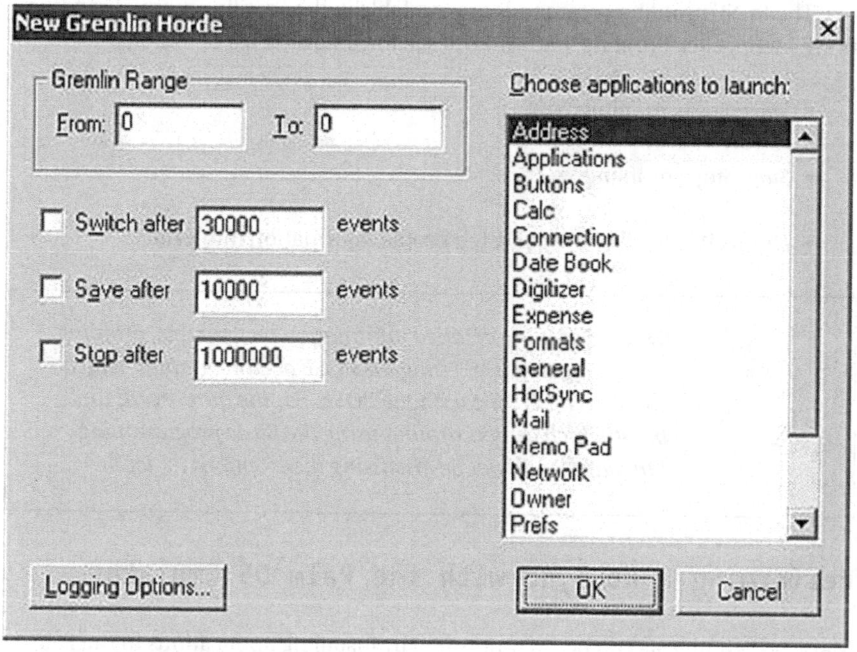

Figure 2-6. Launching a gremlin

You can then stop, resume, or step into a gremlin, allowing a more controlled method for debugging.

POSE does provide an interface that external debugger applications can use to debug an application. For example, Metrowerks (makers of the CodeWarrior C/C++ compiler) have developed a plug-in module that you can use to debug an application that POSE is running, in exactly the same manner as you would debug an application running on the handheld.

The Metrowerks plug-in module began shipping with release 5 of CodeWarrior. Updates for this module can be found on the POSE seed page.

Profiling

POSE provides a profiling mechanism that allows you to collect timing information about an application. The profiling facility monitors which system and application functions are executed and how much time is spent running each.

You can toggle profiling on and off with a menu command. And you can examine the profiling information from within POSE or save it to file.

The POSE profiling commands are available in the Profiling menu. From the POSE menu, click Profiling, and you will see the following list of options:

- *Start:* Starts profiling

- *Stop:* Stops profiling

- *Dump:* Writes all of the collected profile information into a file

NOTE *For more detailed information on gremlins, profiling, and debugging, see "Using the POSE documentation" which comes as a PDF file with the POSE. For the purposes of this book, which centers around using the Basic programming language, I will not be discussing these options in depth.*

Performing a HotSync with the Palm OS Emulator

Many tasks and tests can be accomplished by installing applications in the Palm OS Emulator. However, to accurately test your applications, especially if they use a conduit to transfer data (more on that topic in Chapter 9), the emulator should communicate through HotSync.

If two simple hardware requirements are met—the PC must have two available COM ports and you need a null modem cable on hand—with a few simple steps, the POSE will support a serial HotSync:

1. Install Palm Desktop using the first COM port for HotSync.

2. Open Settings | Properties within POSE, and set the serial port to the second available port.

3. Connect the two serial ports together using a null modem cable.

4. Trigger HotSync operations using the HotSync application within the emulator.

Recent versions of Palm OS also support Network HotSync. Network HotSync is enabled through a few simple steps, and requires that the PC have a network card with an IP address.

1. Open Settings | Properties within POSE and select the Redirect NetLib calls to host TCP/IP checkbox option.

2. Launch the HotSync application within POSE.

3. Open Menu-Modem Sync Prefs and select Network.

4. Open Menu-LANSync Prefs and select LANSync.

5. Open Menu-Primary PC Setup and enter your IP address.

6. Click Select Service under the Modem Sync icon and click Done (no actual settings are needed).

7. Enable Network HotSync within HotSync Manager on your PC by right-clicking the HotSync toolbar icon and selecting the Network checkbox option.

8. Trigger HotSync operations using the HotSync application within POSE by clicking the Modem Sync icon.

Other Emulator Resources

The links and information listed in this section can all be found at the Palm Emulator home page (http://www.palmos.com/dev/tech/tools/emulator/), and all were developed and are currently supported by Palm.

HostFS for Palm OS 4.0

HostFS implements a file system on Palm OS that works with the Palm OS Emulator's Host Control API to mount a local directory on the desktop as a volume or card in Palm OS. This program, available for both Windows and the Mac OS, requires a ROM that has the expansion manager, which includes all Palm OS 4.0 ROM images labeled "full."

Trace Utilities

A trace utility available from Palm, Palm Reporter, is used in conjunction with the POSE. Applications running inside the POSE send information to Palm Reporter, which can help you pinpoint problems that are hard to troubleshoot.

Please note, at this time I have not been able to use the trace utilities with any of the Basic compilers reviewed here as they all run on virtual machines (more on VMs in Chapter 3).

Third-Party Emulator Resources

The following products were developed by third-party vendors, and as such are not supported by Palm:

- *Debuffer:* A fully scriptable, assembly-level debugger for the emulator that runs under Windows 95/NT and Mac OS.

- *EZAsm & Debug:* An assembly debugger in Java that talks to the POSE version for Mac OS and Unix.

- *Posenet:* A utility that fixes application category placement in emulated Palm VII sessions.

- *Posedbexport:* A utility that saves databases within the POSE to your disk.

- *KProf:* A utility that parses and displays profiling results generated by profilers on Unix, including files generated by POSE.

Emulator Links

Check out the following Web sites for more information on and support for the POSE:

- *The Emulator Forum:* http://www.palmos.com/dev/tech/support/forums/

- *The Support Page:* http://www.palmos.com/dev/tech/support/

Conclusion

This chapter provided a brief introduction to the Palm OS Emulator and the basic history and use of the product. The next step of the journey is to begin learning more about the actual development tools you'll be using in this book to develop programs through the Basic language.

CHAPTER 3

Introduction to AppForge

WHEN I STARTED WRITING code for the Palm platform a while ago, I found it to almost be a step backwards for me at first. I say this for a number of reasons, not the least of which is the step back from using SQL to using flat files. Perhaps it was because I had lost touch with my C programming side, but I think the real reason it took so long to get my software running on the Palm was because I found the resources (books, example code, documentation) available for developers either confusing, contradictory, or just plain poor.

AppForge

AppForge is a whole new way of programming for the Palm. Okay, maybe it's not entirely new in some respects (I'll cover what those points are later), but it's a darn good start. What is AppForge? Well, AppForge is a compiler written for Visual Basic that integrates into the VB IDE and allows you to compile from within the Visual Basic environment directly to a Palm device program file (or PRC file).

At last, VB programmers now have a compiler that (in some fashion) works using a familiar language. AppForge offers a great way to get up to speed on Palm application development.

That's not to say that AppForge is the perfect solution, but it brings the term Rapid Application Development (RAD) screaming into the Palm world. Before I jump right in and start talking about using AppForge in conjunction with Visual Basic to develop software for the Palm operating system, let me be clear on something. Doing development with Visual Basic for a different platform (in this case, the Palm OS) simply gives you the ease of a language you are familiar with, but in no way does this indicate that you can continue to write programs in the same manner that you do for Windows applications.

For example, consider that you have memory constraints within the Palm models themselves. Some Palm devices come with 2MB of memory, and some come with up to 8MB of memory. So the development (and what you can or cannot do) can be limited by the memory in the device. With these limitations of the environment also come some limitations of the compiler. Make no mistake, AppForge is *not* an add-in or a library—it is a compiler (more on this later). Most of the supported functions are listed in the documentation, but there are a few hiccups you should be aware of (see the sidebar "AppForge Limitations").

AppForge Limitations

Here are a few of the limitations (and the reasons for some of them) that I've found with using AppForge:

- Standard API calls don't work, and if you think about it, this makes complete sense. API calls are direct programming interface calls to an underlying subsystem (in this example, I'm referring to Windows), so API calls to such functions as GetPrivateProfileString won't work, simply because the functions don't exist.
- The AppForge MsgBox function does not support the Title parameter. This parameter is determined by the severity of the message box displayed, and is set to either Error, Warning, Information, or Confirm. If a severity level is not specified via the Buttons parameter, the message box defaults to Information, unlike VB, which defaults to no icon.
- There are currently no pop-up forms. You can only have one window visible at a time.
- Use of the With clause is not supported. So you cannot use With [object] and End With.
- Use of For Each [object in collection] Next is not supported. This is most likely due to the fact that collections are not supported.
- Dynamic arrays are unsupported.
- Optional parameters are not supported. Presumably this is because the AppForge compiler tries to resolve all parameters and their types at compile time.
- The use of the vbModal parameter with Show is not supported. In this case, it appears that the use of vbModal would halt program execution until such time as the new form is unloaded, which would require maintaining a state within the calling form.
- The Format function is not supported. You instead have all the individual functions, such as FormatCurrency.
- The use of variant data types is not supported.
- Automatic data conversions are not supported by the compiler. By this I mean that when you assign an integer value to a string variable type, the AppForge compiler complains conversions of <type1> to <type2> may be potentially unsafe. Note the use of the word potentially. The compiler doesn't say, "Don't do this"—it says it's potentially unsafe, and then it pre-

vents you from compiling until you do explicit conversions using CStr(), CBool(), CLng(), and so on.

- When using the Palm Database (PDB) files, I could not find a method for filtering. You must search for records that match your condition, and then you must process the records and compare each one.
- Only ascending indexes are supported.

Check out the "Supported Visual Basic Functions" and "Unsupported Visual Basic Functions" documents in the online AppForge User's Guide (http://www.appforge.com/dev/usersguide.html). These documents give you a complete list of the functions that are supported and unsupported.

Okay, I know there will be some limitations, but this is not surprising. After all, this is a compiler for a different operating system (which has limited memory and uses flat files), so many of the restrictions imposed are there to help improve performance.

AppForge supports a very large subset of VB.[1] You will find that most of the more common Visual Basic functions are available and work identically to their desktop PC counterparts. Differences in language support are generally a result of limitations imposed by the Palm OS and represent decisions made by the AppForge compiler team when designing the AppForge compiler.

You will find that, for the most part, AppForge attempts to mirror Visual Basic, so much so that AppForge even has a comparable equivalent to the IntelliSense feature within Visual Basic.

NOTE *For most up-to-date articles about specifics of Visual Basic support, including techniques for optimizing your software using AppForge, you should visit the Developer Sector at* http://www.appforge.com.

AppForge was designed specifically to meet the special programming needs of the mobile devices. Speed, efficiency, and reliability are critical when writing software for these types of devices.

---

[1] For a complete list of the supported commands, you should take the time to review the "Supported Commands" section of the AppForge help file. It should be noted that with each release, AppForge adds new supported functions. In some cases, you will find function libraries on the AppForge Web site (http://www.appforge.com) under the Developer Sector Knowledge Base, such as the Format function library (the use of the Format function is not currently supported).

Beware!

There are a few things about AppForge that you need to be aware of, and I have
listed them here.

- *Limited RAM:* Reading and writing to RAM requires power, which reduces
  battery life. As a general rule, it is advisable to reduce RAM usage wherever
  possible. Programming styles that are less RAM intensive will translate well
  to the mobile software environment. For example, the use of Public variables when not needed should be minimized; instead, include local
  variables to reduce the amount of memory in constant use.

- *Slower execution:* To minimize per-unit costs and maximize the life of small
  batteries, low-speed processors are often used (the current Palm processors are running at between 16 and 33 MHz). Because of this, certain more
  CPU-intensive features may not be available.

- *In-the-field updates are difficult:* Hence, mobile applications should be as
  reliable as possible. Preventable errors, such as those related to type safety,
  should be identified at compile time, rather than after deployment to
  a mobile device. For this reason, AppForge does not do some things at
  compile time that you might be used to getting away with. For an example,
  see Listing 3-1.

Listing 3-1. Code That Will Generate an AppForge Compiler Error

```
Dim cCharString As String
Dim nValue As Integer

cCharString = "12"

' Assign this value to a numeric, this thows an error in AppForge
' This works fine in VB because at runtime VB will resolve the
' value to an Integer doing an "on the fly" conversion.
nValue = cCharString

' To make it work in AppForge
nValue = Cint(cCharString)
```

All of AppForge's design decisions were made in an attempt to balance the issues
in such a way as to present a useful and efficient subset of Visual Basic.

Virtual Machines

Now, I said I'd tell you a bit more about the AppForge compiler, so I'll do that here. AppForge is a compiler, but it also requires a virtual machine. This is similar to Java in that you need a runtime interpreter (or virtual machine) to execute your code. In older compilers such as Clipper (a DBase compiler), the runtime interpreter was actually compiled into the final EXE. You will also discover that several of the compilers available for the Palm (but not necessarily reviewed or explained in this book) also use this technique.

So what exactly is a virtual machine? The term *virtual machine* has been used to mean either an operating system or any program that runs on a computer.

A running program is often referred to as a virtual machine—a machine that doesn't exist as a matter of physical reality. The idea of a virtual machine is itself one of the most elegant in the history of technology, and is a crucial step in the evolution of ideas about software. In order to come up with it, scientists and technologists had to recognize that a computer running a program isn't merely a washing machine doing some dirty laundry. On the contrary, a washing machine is a washing machine no matter what kind of clothes you put inside, but when you put a new program in a computer, presto, by virtue of the new program it is also a new virtual machine.[2]

In the most recent computer usage, virtual machine is a term that was first used by Sun Microsystems (the developers of the Java programming language and runtime environment), to describe software that acts as an interface between compiled Java bytecode and the microprocessor (or hardware platform) that actually performs the program's instructions.

Once a virtual machine has been written for a particular platform, any program written to run within the specifications of that virtual machine will now run on that platform. Java was designed to allow application programs to be built that could be run on many platforms without having to be rewritten or recompiled by the programmer for each separate platform.

For example, take the Windows OS and Macintosh OS. Both are operating systems with their own very specific instruction sets. The goal behind Java is that a program written and compiled with the Java compiler could be ported from the Windows OS to the MAC OS by simply moving the code.[3]

Virtual machines are what make all this possible. The Java virtual machine has a specification, which is defined as an abstract, rather than a real machine (or processor), which specifies an instruction set, a set of registers, a stack, a garbage

---

[2] This discussion on virtual machines is based on the David Gelernter article, "Truth, Beauty, and the Virtual Machine," *Discover Magazine*, September 1997.

[3] Of course, this is the scenario played out as the ideal. In reality, there are so many steps to port an application written in Java for the Windows OS to the Macintosh OS, it would take another book to explain them all.

heap, and a method area. The real implementation of this abstract (or logically defined processor) is done in other code that is recognized by the real processor. The output of "compiling" a Java source program is called bytecode. A Java virtual machine can either interpret the bytecode one instruction at a time (mapping it to a real microprocessor instruction) or the bytecode can be compiled further for the real microprocessor using what is called a just-in-time compiler.

AppForge has taken the virtual machine approach and applied it to handheld devices. AppForge already exists for Palm OS and Pocket PC devices. In the case of AppForge, the virtual machine is called Booster. Before any AppForge application can run, Booster must be installed on the target device.

Using the Palm OS Emulator with AppForge

In a small aside here, I figured I should explain a few simple things about the Palm OS Emulator (POSE). First, Booster is required in order for any AppForge Palm application to run. Booster is a virtual machine, as it runs your compiled bytecode application. So, before you can test your application in the emulator, you must first install and run the POSE

When POSE has been installed and configured, you can then right-click the emulator to view a pop-up menu of choices. Once you select the Install Application/Database option, you can locate the PRC files in the Platforms\PalmOS\TargetImage directory under your AppForge installation and upload them to the emulator. Now, before POSE will function properly, you must reset it (similar to having to restart Windows after an installation). Once you reset the emulator, you can then install your application and databases on it. This is only required if you choose the Install option rather than using the HotSync menu option.

Before You Start Programming

In this section, I'll give you a small list of the things you need to start programming, and some specific tips I learned as I became familiar with AppForge.

The Palm SDK

Although you do not need anything except AppForge, a copy of Visual Basic (you can use any edition of Visual Basic 6, including Visual Basic Working Model, which is included on the CD), and either a real Palm OS device or the Palm OS Emulator (POSE) to get started, I would suggest that you obtain a copy of the Palm OS SDK, including the latest documentation (available from Palm Web site). You can also download their Conduit Developers Kit 4.01 for COM, which supports any COM-compliant language, including Visual Basic. This means that you can now develop custom conduits[4] using Visual Basic.

 NOTE *Neither the Learning Edition or the Working Model of Visual Basic allow you to compile a Windows EXE file. This is not a problem, as AppForge installs itself as an add-in with its own AppForge menu. From the AppForge menu, you can select the Compile option, which will compile your VB code as a Palm OS–compatible application file (PRC).*

The SDK contains three important items:

- *Example code:* You can peruse this code (although it's all in C/C++) to get a feel for how POSE works.

- *Documentation:* Think of the documentation as a dictionary in which you can look up all the possible system functions available for your code. The SDK documentation is not very interesting to read, unless you find reading a dictionary exciting.

- *Palm OS Emulator:* The emulator, shown in Figure 3-1, essentially functions as a virtual Palm on your desktop. POSE allows you to debug and run the programs you develop on your computer, instead of performing a HotSync every time you make a new build. You definitely need the emulator, unless you enjoy resetting your Palm device several times while writing your software. (See Chapter 2 for more information on using the POSE.)

---

[4] A conduit is a means of communication between a Palm OS device and a Desktop PC. For a more detailed explanation of conduits, see Chapter 9.

Figure 3-1. The Palm OS Emulator

The 1000-Foot Overview

Before you write any code, let's take a moment to review some simple basics.
Since you are probably new to the AppForge compiler and the Palm OS, you
should consider that not everything you want to do can necessarily be done the
way you did them in VB. Let me give you an example:

In AppForge, there is currently no support for dynamic arrays. This means
that if you want to have a dynamic array, it cannot be done in the traditional
sense (that is, using Dim, ReDim. . .Preserve). However, you can easily solve this
problem. The trick is quite simple. Using an AppForge AFListBox control (or
a grid if you need multiple elements), which is hidden on a form, you place the
values you want to serve as an array in the listbox (see Listing 3-2).

Listing 3-2. Code to Simulate a Dynamic Array

```
Private Sub ArrayAdd(ByVal cElement As String)
'-=-=-=-=-=-=-=-=-=-=-=-=-=-=-=-=-=-=-=-=-=-=-=-=-=-=-=-=-=-=
'
'   Sub        :   ArrayAdd(cElement)
'   Params     :   cElement - Element to Add
'   Returns    :   None
'
'   Author     :   Vivid Software Inc. - Jon Kilburn
'                  http://www.VividSoftware.com
'
```

```
'   Client     :   Apress
'   Purpose    :   Add Array Element to hidden Listbox
'
'-=-=-=-=-=-=-=-=-=-=-=-=-=-=-=-=-=-=-=-=-=-=-=-=-=-=-=-=-=-=-=


    ' Array Insert
    Me.lstArray.AddItem cElement

End Sub


Private Sub ArrayDel(ByVal nPos As Integer)
'-=-=-=-=-=-=-=-=-=-=-=-=-=-=-=-=-=-=-=-=-=-=-=-=-=-=-=-=-=-=-=
'
'   Sub        :   ArrayDel(nPos)
'   Params     :   nPos - Element to Delete
'   Returns    :   None
'
'   Author     :   Vivid Software Inc. - Jon Kilburn
'                  http://www.VividSoftware.com
'
'   Client     :   Apress
'   Purpose    :   Add Array Element to hidden Listbox
'
'-=-=-=-=-=-=-=-=-=-=-=-=-=-=-=-=-=-=-=-=-=-=-=-=-=-=-=-=-=-=-=


    ' Array Delete
    Me.lstArray.RemoveItem nPos

End Sub
```

So what's my point? Simply this: just change your thinking slightly, and you can accomplish almost anything in AppForge for the Palm OS that you can do in Windows. The code just won't look exactly the same.

Basically there are three steps to building an AppForge Palm application:

1. Create the application in Visual Basic and compile it using AppForge to a PRC file.

2. Install Booster onto the Palm device.

3. Upload your AppForge application.

There will be some additional steps, such as creating a device package or converting Access files to Palm Database files and the like, but overall this is the way it works. Now let's get to it.

Getting Started

Once you have completed the installation of the AppForge compiler (by running the Install program), you will notice that when you start Visual Basic, you may now select a new type of application, an AppForge application (see Figure 3-2).

Figure 3-2. The AppForge project

You have two ways to create an AppForge project. The first way is by selecting Start | Programs | AppForge and then clicking the Start AppForge option. This will open the AppForge Project Manager window, which prompts you to edit an existing project or to create a new one (see Figure 3-3). The other way is to open Visual Basic and choose to create a new project. You then select AppForge Project from the New Project window. Once you have opened the new project, a single form is added to the project. The form properties are set according to the size of the Palm window. Changing the form size will result in an AppForge compiler error.

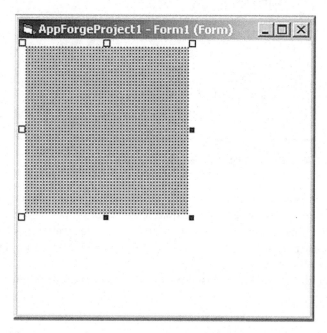

Figure 3-3. The AppForge form

Once you have started to create a new AppForge project, if you are using the Professional Edition of AppForge, you will be prompted to choose the type of AppForge project (see Figure 3-4).

Figure 3-4. The AppForge Select Target Platform dialog box

It is important to note that although you may still see the standard list of events and properties, not all of the displayed events or properties are supported by AppForge. This is not because AppForge has not made an effort to do so, but rather because the Palm OS is different from Windows. A classic example of this is the MsgBox() function.

The standard Visual Basic MsgBox function consists of the following parameters:

```
MsgBox(Prompt, [Buttons], [Title], [Helpfile], [Context])
```

The AppForge compiler supports the MsgBox() function, but the parameters are different. The AppForge version of the MsgBox() function has the following form:

```
MsgBox(Prompt, [Buttons])
```

Notice that there is no support for the Title, Helpfile, or Context parameters. Neither the Helpfile or Context parameter is supported, and the Title value is determined by the severity of the message box displayed, and is set to Error, Warning, Information, or Confirm. However, the Visual Basic IntelliSense feature will *not* display only those parameters that AppForge supports. This is true of all the AppForge functions, which do not have all the same corresponding parameters that exist in their Windows counterparts.

If a severity level is not specified via the Buttons parameter, the message box defaults to Information, unlike with Visual Basic, in which the message box defaults to no icon. The AppForge MsgBox does not support the following constants:

```
VbApplicationModal
VbSystemModal
vbMsgBoxSetForeground
```

The reason for the lack of support is that all of these values are meaningless under Palm OS. Along those same lines, none of the vbDefaultButtonX parameters are supported—after all, there are no default buttons on a handheld device since there is no Enter key (unless you're using an attached Palm keyboard). There are several differences like this one that run throughout the AppForge compiler. As I mentioned earlier, you should study the "Supported Visual Basic Functions" document of the online AppForge User's Guide so that you can familiarize yourself with AppForge's flavor of the Visual Basic functions.

 NOTE *In AppForge, only one form can be shown at a time. Therefore, before showing a new form, the old form must be hidden first. (Otherwise, an "overlapping" form error will occur.)*

Generally, you should use the Hide method when a form is no longer needed (setting the Visible property to false and then showing the form by setting Visible = True can cause weird behaviors on the actual Palm device). This prevents the overlapping error and allows for access to values on the hidden form. If no forms are shown, the screen will be blank. Be aware that you should try to keep from going too deep when hiding forms, as most Palm devices have less than 256KB (yes, that's kilobytes) of memory for the application to work with. Although I have successfully managed to go as many as five forms deep (using a Symbol 1500 with 8MB of RAM), the practical limit is probably around three forms. I say this because the limit can vary based on the number of controls you have on a form.

NOTE *Hiding an application that has only one form and no modules will also exit the application.*

Also, another trick I've used is to create an Owner property in the called form. By setting an Owner property you can create a "stack" which allows you to return to the previous form. Why do I do that instead of just using the form name? Two reasons:

First of all, since there is no support for vbModal when a form is shown, you cannot keep it visible or halt your code until the called form is unloaded. Usually you would perform a search lookup like so:

```
Sub cmdLookup_Click()
        frmLookup.Show vbModal
End Sub
```

In an application I developed, the same lookup form could be called from a couple of different places (that is, from different forms). So I had to figure out how to get around this problem—I solved it by creating an Owner variable in the frmLookup form.

```
Public Owner As Form
```

There is a caveat to doing this. You can only reference the functions and values of a Form object. You cannot call any specific Public subs or functions you may have designed for your form, unless you declare the Owner with the explicit name of your form. This has to do with the AppForge compiler resolving data types at compile time to prevent errors at runtime.

Next, when I called the frmLookup form, I hid the current form, set the owner of the frmLookup form, and then showed the whole thing:

```
Sub cmdLookup_Click()
        ' Hide this form
        Me.Hide
```

```
        ' Set the Owner form
        Set frmLookup.Owner = Me

        ' Show the Lookup form
        frmLookup.Show
End Sub
```

Next, in the cmdClose_Click event of the frmLookup, I simply showed the Owner form:

```
Sub cmdClose_Click()
        ' Hide this form
        Me.Hide

        ' Show the Owner
        Me.Owner.Show

        ' Unload this form
        Unload Me
End Sub
```

The second reason: This allows me to have a global return function, which can be called by all forms and requires less code.

The AppForge Ingots

Now let's move on to building some forms. In your toolbox, you will now find a new list of controls (see Figure 3-5). These controls are called *Ingots*. Ingots are AppForge ActiveX components that are similar to standard Visual Basic controls. They provide the feel and functionality of Visual Basic controls and are programmed using properties, events, and methods. The only difference is that they work in Windows, Windows CE, and Palm OS. Please note, these controls currently do not have the full range and functionality of Visual Basic controls.

Figure 3-5. AppForge Ingots added to the Visual Basic Toolbox

 NOTE *The Ingots shown here are provided with AppForge Professional Edition.*

There are currently 24 Ingots available for the AppForge compiler. Not all of these Ingots are available with each version (as I note later); however, by the time you complete the sections of this book on AppForge, you should have a good grasp of how to use each of these Ingots.

- AFButton

- AFCheckBox

- AFClientSocket

- AFComboBox

- AFFilmstrip

- AFGraphic

- AFGraphicButton

- AFGrid

- AFHScrollbar

- AFINetHTTP

- AFLabel

- AFListBox

- AFMovie

- AFRadioButton

- AFScanner

- AFSerial

- AFShape

- AFSignatureCapture

- AFSlider

- AFTextBox

- AFTimer

- AFTone

- AFVScrollbar

- Form

The AppForge Converters

AppForge provides a suite of converters and viewers that convert standard media files to AppForge-specific files. There are currently five converters and their associated viewers available for the AppForge compiler:

- Font

- Graphic

- Movie

- Project (this converter migrates prior AppForge Projects to 2.0)

- Database

Not all of these converters (like their Ingot counterparts) ship with each version of AppForge. All AppForge software editions include a graphic converter and viewer, project converter, and a database file converter.

AppForge Professional Edition provides additional converters and viewers for fonts and movies. Table 2-1 summarizes the file types supported by the AppForge file converters and viewers.

Table 3-1. File Types Supported by AppForge Converters and Viewers

MEDIA	DESCRIPTION	OUTPUT FILE TYPE
Database	Microsoft Access databases (*.mdb)	Palm Database file (*.pdb)
Graphics	Standard Windows bitmap (*.bmp)	AppForge graphic (*.rgx)
Font*	True Type Font (*.ttf)	AppForge font (*.cmf)
Movie*	Windows AVI File (*.avi)	AppForge movie (*.rvm)

* Denotes those converters included only in the Personal and Professional Editions

I will review the converters more in depth in the next chapter when I demonstrate how to build a more complicated AppForge application than the one presented later in this chapter.

The AppForge Shipping Versions

Currently there are two shipping versions of AppForge, AppForge Professional Edition and AppForge Personal Edition. AppForge Professional Edition is available for Palm OS, Pocket PC, or both.

NOTE *Times change, and so do companies, versions, and shipping editions. The current shipping information is based on what AppForge has listed as their available editions on both their Web site and those of their preferred vendors (such as Handango and VBXtras).*

The AppForge Personal Edition

The Personal Edition is the low-cost, entry-level development version. This is an ideal starting point for the hobbyist programmer or the programmer who is working on learning Palm programming at his or her own pace. It allows you to begin programming and developing applications for the Palm OS without having to spend a whole lot of money. This edition has some limitations, but overall is a good value, and if you decide to upgrade, AppForge will give you 100 percent credit towards the Professional Edition.

The AppForge Personal Edition offers the following:

- Access to several commonly used Palm Functions such as the Date Picker

- Most AppForge Ingots (see http://www.appforge.com/prod/featurelist.html for a complete listing)

- The ability to communicate through the serial and infrared ports

- A low introductory cost

- Purchase price is applied when upgrading to AppForge Professional Edition

The AppForge Professional Edition

The AppForge Professional Edition is the heavy hitter. This high-level development platform is geared for the serious developer who may wish to create applications using the advanced features (such as scanner integration and wireless Internet support) of the Palm device. The AppForge Professional Edition supports all the features in the Personal Edition, and adds the following power-user enhancements:

- *Palm OS Extensibility Library:* This library allows developers to augment AppForge features with code written in C/C++.

- *Wireless Internet support:* The AppForge Wireless Internet Ingot makes it easy to add the Internet to your application. A stock quote sample is included with the Professional Edition to help you get started writing Internet-enabled Palm applications.

- *AppForge AFScanner Ingot:* The AFScanner Ingot can be used to provide barcode scanning for inventory control, point-of-sale operations, and identification, and for reading virtually anything that has a barcode. The AFScanner Ingot supports Symbol Technologies' SPT-1500/1700 Symbol with Palm OS 3.5 (you must upgrade the OS from version 3.1), and the CSM-150 Barcode Scanner for the Handspring Visor.

- *The Universal Conduit:* The UC is a program that allows databases to be synchronized between AppForge-created applications[5] and ODBC data sources without writing code—that is, it creates a conduit without any code (for more information on the Universal Conduit, see Chapter 9).

- *The Font Converter/Viewer:* The Font Converter will convert any TrueType font to an AppForge font file for use on Palm OS devices (this is an exclusive feature of AppForge made possible by Booster).

- *The Movie Converter/Viewer:* The Movie Converter will convert standard Windows AVI files for use with the Movie Ingot. Please note that at the time of this writing, there are some limitations as to the size of AVI files that can be converted and stored on the Palm devices.

- *The Signature Capture Ingot:* The Signature Capture Ingot adds signature input, storage, and display capabilities to your AppForge applications.

- *AFScrollBar and AFSlider Ingots:* The AFScrollbar and AFSlider Ingots provide a mechanism to produce a range indicator. They have a minimum and maximum setting.

- *AFClientSocket Ingot:* The AFClientSocket Ingot allows TCP/IP communication on network-enabled handheld devices.

---

[5] The UC does not always work with applications that have been developed in other languages. This is due to the fact that AppForge writes schema information into the header of Palm Database files, which may not be available if the PDB file has been created using another tool.

NOTE *Upgrading the Symbol 1500/1700 to the 3.5 OS is described in detail at both the AppForge Web site (in the Developer Sector Knowledge Base) and the Symbol Web site.*

Working with Menus

In Windows, it's a common practice to use a menu for assigning and grouping actions. Not surprisingly, AppForge 2.0 supports menus. Menus provide a way to access multiple commands without occupying too much screen real estate. Each menu should contain one or more menu items, to which a command should be associated. You can visually group items using a separator bar, just like in Windows. Menus themselves are contained within a menu bar, and there can only be one menu bar per form. To create a new menu, select either the Menu Editor option from the Tools menu or click the icon on the standard toolbar.

Follow these steps to create a menu test program:

1. Start by creating a new Visual Basic AppForge project.

2. Name the application MenuTest.

3. Create the main form by renaming the default Form1 form as frmMenu.

4. Select the Tools | Menu Editor option.

5. Add a Main Menu Item named Test, set the Name property to mnuMain, and set the index property to 0 (see Figure 3-6).

6. Click the Next Button. This adds a new blank menu.

7. Press the Indent Button (the right arrow key).

8. Name the subitem Item1. Set the name property to mnuItem and the index to 1.

9. Now save the project.

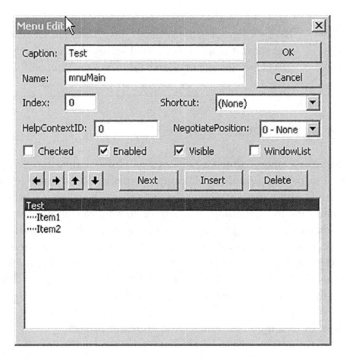

Figure 3-6. Using the Visual Basic menu editor

From the AppForge menu, select Compile and Validate. This will compile the project and validate all the referenced objects. When you choose to compile an AppForge project for the first time, you will be prompted to enter a CreatorID (see Figure 3-7).

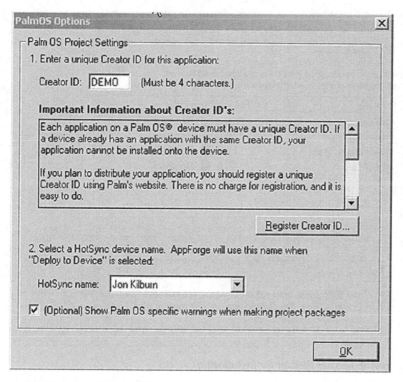

Figure 3-7. Entering a CreatorID

Before you can run any AppForge program, you must first install the AppForge virtual machine, or Booster, on the target device. Once the compile process has been completed, you can now create the Booster download. Booster comprises a number of separate runtime files. These files are combined on the Palm device to make up the final Booster based on what features you have included in your AppForge application.

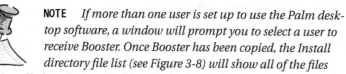

NOTE *If more than one user is set up to use the Palm desktop software, a window will prompt you to select a user to receive Booster. Once Booster has been copied, the Install directory file list (see Figure 3-8) will show all of the files to be installed on the specified handheld device during the next HotSync operation.*

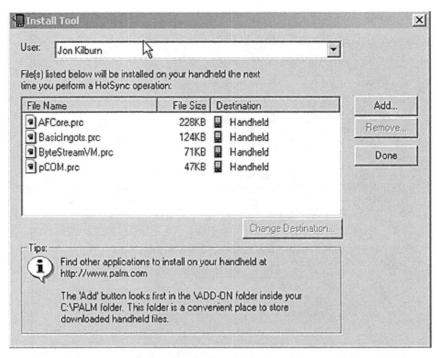

Figure 3-8. Booster files set for installation

To create the Booster package, access the AppForge menu and select the Install Booster To Device option. From the Booster options submenu, select the Palm OS platform. This will copy the required Booster files to the installation directory for installation during your next HotSync.

Once Booster has been installed on the target device, you can then install your MenuTest application. You have a couple of ways to do this. Starting from the AppForge menu, you can choose Deploy to Palm OS | Deploy to Device. Next, select the Palm OS option, or select the Save Project Package option, which will generate the Palm application in the folder of your choosing. Figure 3-9 shows the final menu working in the POSE.

Figure 3-9. The final menu running under POSE

Building Your First AppForge Application

Now that you've seen the basic components of AppForge, let's move on to creating a simple application and syncing the application to a Palm device. For this first program, let's build a simple application to calculate the daily production rate for piecework assembly. I got this idea from a program I wrote for one of my clients, which tracks assembled inventory. Since my client uses robots for product assembly, this program really wouldn't do the client much good, but it would be very useful to help a line supervisor estimate the average assembly time and average daily production for a given product.

Creating a VB AppForge Project

This simple application will take the number of pieces that are assembled in a minute and calculate the assembled production estimates for one hour and for a standard eight-hour day. Start building this application by creating a new Visual Basic AppForge project. Follow these steps:

1. Name the application ProductCalc.

2. Create the main calculation form by renaming the default Form1 form to frmCalc.

3. Clear the form's Caption property. If the form caption is set, AppForge will automatically create a Palm title bar for your form.

4. Now save the project. You have to save the project before AppForge will allow you to add any controls.

5. Next, select the AFLabel control from the Visual Basic Toolbox and drop the label onto the AppForge form.

6. Change the name of the AFLabel to "label".

7. Change the background color of the AFLabel to black and the foreground color to white.

8. Set the Alignment of the label to 2-Center, and change the FontName property to AFPalm Bold 12.

9. Set the caption of the label to Production Calculator.

10. Next, size the label to the width of the form and set the Height property to 16. AppForge uses pixels for its unit of measurement.

11. Add a label and set the caption to Assembled Pieces. Make this label's Height property 16, and change the font to AFPalm Bold 12. Now center the label.

12. Change the background to black and the foreground to white like the previous label. Next, change the name of the label to "label", and when Visual Basic prompts you to create a control array, select Yes. The label will automatically be renamed Label(1). Position this label slightly above the middle of the form.

13. Now add three more labels with the captions Per Minute:, Per Hour:, and Per Shift:.

14. Select an AFTextBox control from the Visual Basic Toolbox and place it to the right of the Per Minute: label.

15. Although it looks like you have three textboxes, you actually do not. Select the AFLabel control again and place two labels to the right of the Per Hour: and the Per Shift: labels. In the Properties window, change the Border Style property to be 1- Fixed Single. Next, change the Alignment property to 1- Right Justified. Lastly, change the Caption property to have a value 0. Now these two labels look like AFTextBox controls.

16. Drop a couple of AFButton controls on the form and name them cmdCalc and cmdClose. Change their captions to Calculate and Close.

17. Finally, make the form look a little more spiffy by adding a few AFShape controls. Set the AFShape controls' Border Width property to 1 so it appears to be a line instead of a rectangle. Now place three of these lines around the controls connected to the Assembled Pieces label to make a box. Figure 3-10 shows what your final form should look like.

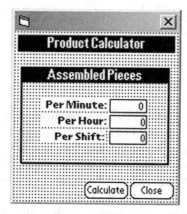

Figure 3-10. The completed Product Calculator form

Writing the Code

Now comes the fun part, adding the code. First, you'll write the code to exit the program. When exiting the Production Calculator program, you should confirm that the user does indeed wish to exit. Do this using the AppForge equivalent of the MsgBox function (see Listing 3-3).

Listing 3-3. Exit Code for Production Calculator

```
Private Sub cmdClose_Click()
'-=-=-=-=-=-=-=-=-=-=-=-=-=-=-=-=-=-=-=-=-=-=-=-=-=-=-=-=-=-=-=
'
'    Sub        :    cmdClose_Click()
'    Params     :    None
'    Returns    :    None
'
'    Author     :    Vivid Software Inc. - Jon Kilburn
'                      http://www.VividSoftware.com
'
'    Client     :    Apress
'    Purpose    :    Confirm Exit
'
'-=-=-=-=-=-=-=-=-=-=-=-=-=-=-=-=-=-=-=-=-=-=-=-=-=-=-=-=-=-=-=

    If MsgBox("Exit Production Calculator?", vbQuestion + vbYesNo) = vbYes Then
        ' Quit the Program
        End
    End If
End Sub
```

Now let's build the code to perform the piecework calculation. Assume that there are no breaks taken in each hour so you can calculate against a true sixty minutes. The shift workers get one full hour for lunch; however, they work eight hours in a shift (so they are scheduled in nine-hour increments). To calculate the pieces per hour, multiply the contents of txtPieces by a value of 60. You then take the resulting value and multiply it by 8, which will yield the number of estimated pieces per shift (see Listing 3-4). Write the resulting values into the Caption property of the two labels, LabelHour and LabelShift.

Listing 3-4. Calculation Code

```
Private Sub cmdCalc_Click()
'-=-=-=-=-=-=-=-=-=-=-=-=-=-=-=-=-=-=-=-=-=-=-=-=-=-=-=-=-=-=-=
'
'    Sub        :    cmdCalc_Click()
'    Params     :    None
'    Returns    :    None
'
```

```
'    Author      :   Vivid Software Inc. - Jon Kilburn
'                    http://www.VividSoftware.com
'
'    Client      :   Apress
'    Purpose     :   Calculate the number of pieces per hour,
'                    and per shift.
'
'-=-=-=-=-=-=-=-=-=-=-=-=-=-=-=-=-=-=-=-=-=-=-=-=-=-=-=-=-=
    Dim nHour   As Long
    Dim nShift  As Long

    ' Set Trap
    On Error GoTo Trap

    ' Calculate
    If Me.txtPieces.Text = vbNullString Then
        ' Must have a valid value
        MsgBox "Please enter the number of pieces.", vbExclamation
        Exit Sub
    Else
        ' Calculate Number of Pieces assembled per hour
        nHour = CInt(Me.txtPieces.Text) * 60

        ' Per Shift (8 Hours per shift)
        nShift = nHour * 8

        ' Fill in the labels
        Me.LabelHour.Caption = Trim(CStr(nHour))
        Me.LabelShift.Caption = Trim(CStr(nShift))
    End If

Exit_Rtn:
    Exit Sub

Trap:
    MsgBox "Sytem Error!" & vbCrLf & _
        Err.Description, vbExclamation

    GoTo Exit_Rtn

End Sub
```

Running Your Application

Once you have completed the code, you can now run the resulting AppForge application from inside the Visual Basic and Windows environment by selecting the Run menu option. This will launch a form that will look and act like a Palm form.

CAUTION: *Just because the application runs in the Windows environment without errors does not imply that it will function properly when uploaded to the Palm device. You should always upload your compiled project to a Palm OS device—at the very least the POSE—for testing.*

Now that you have tested the basic application functionality under the Windows environment, you should compile the Production Calculator using the AppForge compiler. Select the AppForge menu option and choose the Compile Project option. This will launch the AppForge compiler. When compiling a project, AppForge analyzes the code for errors and possible conflicts that may prevent the compiled program from functioning properly once it has been uploaded to the Palm OS device. When the compile operation is successful, the progress window will disappear to indicate the operation is complete.

With the application fully compiled, you must now begin the process of installing and testing the finished application.

Once you have performed the HotSync operation, the Booster.prc application will appear in your Palm device's main applications area (see Figure 3-11).

NOTE *For the POSE, you can also right-click and choose the Install Application/Database menu option. If you install Booster using this method, you must then select the Reset option.*

Figure 3-11. Booster in the Palm main applications area

Now that you have installed Booster on the target device, you have two options for uploading the compiled application. Although you have compiled the application, you have not created a device package (this is the step where the actual .PRC file is created). If you select the AppForge menu option Upload Project, then AppForge will create a PRC file and also copy the file into the Palm Install directory (in the same manner as it does for Booster). Upon your next HotSync, your application will be copied onto the target device. If you choose the Create Device Package option, AppForge will create the PRC file, but not place it in the Palm Install directory.

Finally, once you have selected the Deploy To Palm OS menu option (or used the Palm Install tool to select the ProductCalc.prc file) and specified you want to HotSync the file to the target device, the new program, Production Calculator, will now appear in your program group. Figure 3-12 shows the final compiled and uploaded application running.

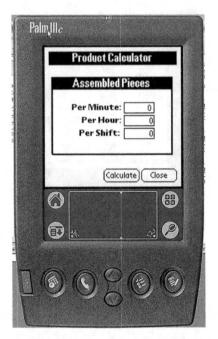

Figure 3-12. The Production Calculator running in the POSE

The Project Properties

The final item I would like to discuss is project preferences. From the AppForge menu, select AppForge Settings. This will bring up the AppForge Settings dialog box (see Figure 3-13). From this dialog box, you can control all aspects of the AppForge project.

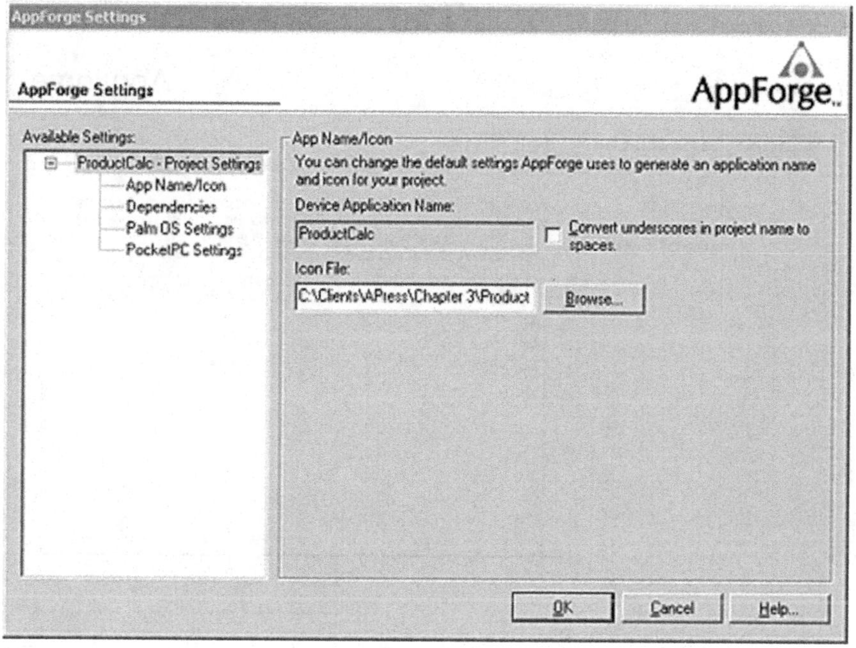

Figure 3-13. The AppForge Settings dialog box

The first item in the tree view is the App Name/Icon setting. Here you will see the name of the application (as it will appear on the Palm), and you can also assign an application icon.

The second item in the tree view is Dependencies. When you highlight this item, the main panel to the right will change to display the dependencies of your project (see Figure 3-14).

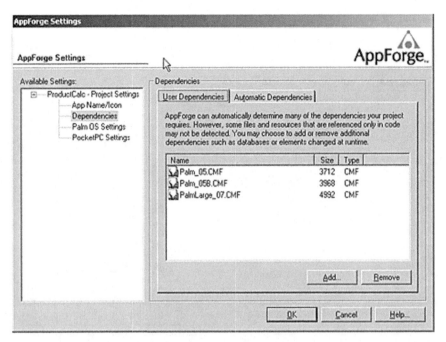

Figure 3-14. The AppForge Dependencies section of the AppForge Properties window

The next two items are the Palm OS and Pocket PC Settings. The Palm OS settings option simply contains the Creator ID information I mentioned earlier when saving a project.

Conclusion

In this chapter, I've given you a brief overview of how the AppForge compiler works and how to use it to build a simple application. I've also discussed the basic principles behind how to compile, install, and test your final application in the Palm environment.

Building the GolfPro Application Using AppForge

Most Palm solutions are composed of two pieces, the handheld application portion and the desktop conduit portion. In this next section, I'm going to focus on building the handheld application portion of the Palm application. (Conduits are covered in Chapter 9.)

As a practical exercise, I will take you step by step through creating an application for keeping track of your golf game at a given golf course. Although I don't play golf much (and I'm certainly not very good at it), I do like to see how much I can improve my game and at which courses I'm shooting the best score—thus the focus of the example application. This simple application will require a few tables, some graphics and a couple of simple lookups as well as reading and writing to Palm Database files.

The GolfPro Application Project Outline

First let's review the basic functionality of what you want to accomplish with what I am calling the Portable GolfPro application. If you don't play the game of golf, or if you do but it doesn't show from your scores (this is the category I fall into), I'll briefly explain the rules of the game, which are quite simple.

Often a game of golf is played at a golf club, or at a public golf course. These courses generally have a name and 18 holes. (Although I've heard that there are some courses that have only 9 holes, I've never seen one. And for those of you wondering, *yes*, it would improve my game.) Each hole is then assigned a par. A *par* is the number of shots required to sink the golf ball into the cup on the green. If you can achieve the feat of getting the ball into the cup in the required number of shots, you have achieved par on that hole.

It is from the par on each hole that the figure for *par for the course* is calculated. To determine this number, you add up the number of strokes required to play each course, and that is how you calculate your level of play. If you can complete the course using the same number of strokes as indicated on the score-card, you have *broken even*. The goal is to save as many strokes as possible and to complete the course at even or perhaps (in the make-believe world where I can actually play this frustrating game) under par.

Okay, so now you know the rules if you hadn't already. Generally speaking, there are a few aspects to the game that you want to include in this application.

- *The courses:* Before you can play a golf game, you have to determine which golf course you will be playing on. Clubs often contain more than one golf course, but, for the purposes of this example, each course is independent of an actual golf club.

- *The course scorecard:* The course scorecard contains the par setting (or number of strokes allowed to put the ball in the hole before applying a penalty of a lost stroke). When you play a hole of golf, you are allowed *x* number of strokes to complete the hole. If you complete the hole before using the allotted number of strokes, you are *under par*. If you sink the ball in the required number of strokes, you have *made par*. And if you sink the ball in two strokes fewer than required, you have made an *eagle*. Finally, if you sink a ball in only one shot, you have made a *hole in one*.

- *Course scoring:* This is the individual scorecard you carry for each course as you play it. When you play a hole, you enter the number of strokes you made to get the ball in the hole. This is also called a *scorecard*, but it refers to each individual's game.

- *Course notes:* When you play a course, you might wish to make notes about a particularly tough hole, say, about a bad dog leg (sharp bend) on the fourth hole. You may want to record that the best way to play this par 4 hole is to get to the green in two strokes, and which particular club you recommend for your tee shot.

On to Palm Database Files

Databases on a Palm device are similar to files on a desktop computer, except that the Palm OS databases reside inside the RAM of the device instead of on a permanent storage media such as a hard drive. Using functions in AppForge you can create, open, update, and delete database files and records easily.

Databases organize related records; every record belongs to one and only one database. A database may be a collection of all address book entries, all date-book entries, and so on. A Palm OS application can create, delete, open, and close databases as necessary, just as a traditional file system can create, delete, open, and close a traditional file.

The Portable GolfPro program will need a simple database. Now I know you are possibly going to read this and later e-mail me a better database design, but I'm not trying to create a great database design. Understand this: Palm Database (PDB) files are essentially the same as good old fashion DBF files. You may remember them—DBase made them popular in the '80s and early '90s, before SQL really became mainstream for the PC.

Well, here's what you have to keep in mind. These files need to be small and efficient, not always in the best third normal form design, because you will have to open each table, maintain a handle and seek your results. What do I mean by this? Hang on, and I'll show you a little later.

First, let's get some of the basics about PDB files out of the way. Palm Database files are flat files, not relational files. This means as the programmer, you are responsible for keeping track of relationships and cleaning up after yourself. Now, quite a few PDB* functions exist within AppForge, and there are several ways to create PDB files. Lucky for you, I'm lazy. I like Access for creating my database files, and thankfully so did somebody at AppForge, because they gave us a Palm Database Converter application.

Structure of a Palm Database File

Although you will probably not need to open a PDB file at the binary level and understand the structure of the file much beyond the basics, it is still a good idea to know a few things about how a PDB file is structured.

A database header consists of some basic database information and a list of records in the database. Each record entry in the header has the local ID of the record, 8 attribute bits, and a 3-byte unique ID for the record, for a total of 78 bytes:

FIELD	BYTES
DB Name	32
Flags	2
Version	2
Creation Time	4
Modification Time	4
Backup Time	4
Modification Number	4
App Info Offset	4
Sort Info Offset	4
Type (Database ID)	4

FIELD	BYTES
Creator (Application ID)	4
Unique ID Seed	4
Next Record List ID	4
Number of Records	2

This is followed by a table of record entries, which consists of 8 bytes. The first 4 bytes make up the offset of the record (n) from the beginning of the file, the next byte makes up the record attributes and the last 3 bytes contain the record unique ID (I'll discuss these more at length in the latter part of the chapter).

Creating Database Tables

Just as you can convert a graphics or font file, you can also convert a table inside of an Access database. This makes modeling a database quick and easy. Simply create the Access database and add four tables.

The first table should be the Courses table. This table will contain each course and the par value for each hole.

The second table will be the scorecard table. The scorecard table will be related to the Courses table by the field CourseID.

The third table will be the Players table. The Players table will be related to the Courses table by the PlayerID. The idea here is that you can now track a player's score on a golf course based on any given date. Later if you wished, you could then chart a player's improvement (or in the case of my golf game, deterioration).

The fourth and final table is the CourseNotes table. This table is related to a course by the CourseID. You will also add the hole as an integer (that is, 1 through 18) to help you read any notes on a course you may have made.

Below are the table layouts for each of the files needed by the Portable GolfPro system (Figure 4-1). To follow along with the example in this chapter, create all the tables inside an Access 2000 database and save the MDB as Golf.

Course Notes	
NotesID	Autonumber
CourseID	Long
Hole	Integer
Notes	Text

ScoreCard	
ScoreID	Autonumber
CourseID	Long
PlayerID	Long
GameDate	Date
Hole1	Integer
Hole2	Integer
Hole3	Integer
Hole4	Integer
Hole5	Integer
Hole6	Integer
Hole7	Integer
Hole8	Integer
Hole9	Integer
Hole10	Integer
Hole11	Integer
Hole12	Integer
Hole13	Integer
Hole14	Integer
Hole15	Integer
Hole16	Integer
Hole17	Integer
Hole18	Integer
FinalScore	Integer

Courses Table	
CourseID	Autonumber
Course_Name	Text
Hole1Par	Integer
Hole2Par	Integer
Hole3Par	Integer
Hole4Par	Integer
Hole5Par	Integer
Hole6Par	Integer
Hole7Par	Integer
Hole8Par	Integer
Hole9Par	Integer
Hole10Par	Integer
Hole11Par	Integer
Hole12Par	Integer
Hole13Par	Integer
Hole14Par	Integer
Hole15Par	Integer
Hole16Par	Integer
Hole17Par	Integer
Hole18Par	Integer

Player	
PlayerID	Autonumber
FirstName	Text
LastName	Text
Handicap	Integer

Figure 4-1. The tables in the Golf Access Database

NOTE *In AppForge, only certain data types are supported. For example, the ReplicationID data type is not supported. Nor do all data types convert to like types. Memos, for example, do not convert to Memo fields but rather to strings.*

Converting Access Tables into Palm Database Files

Okay, so now you're ready to convert these Access tables into Palm Database files. AppForge ships a great little utility called the AppForge Database Converter. Open the AppForge Database Converter and select the Golf MDB file you have created.

Since the AppForge Database Converter only converts one table at a time, you must select which table in the database to convert. In order to differentiate databases, two unique identifiers are assigned to each database. The CreatorID and Type are both user-defined values that help to identify a database.

The CreatorID is a unique identifier for a Palm OS application. If two applications on one Palm OS device have the same CreatorID, one of the applications will simply not show up.

This is why Palm asks for the CreatorID for every distributed application to be registered with the Palm official list. CreatorIDs that are all lowercase are reserved exclusively for Palm; otherwise, the four characters may consist of any ASCII characters from 33 to 127.

 NOTE *The address for looking up and registering CreatorIDs is* http://www.palmos.com/dev/tech/palmos/creatorid/.

The CreatorID for a database and the application it belongs to should always be the same. This ensures that the database will be deleted if the application is deleted. In most cases the type should be set to DATA. If one application has multiple databases, the CreatorID and the Type should be the same for all of the databases. Palm only uses the name of the table to distinguish between the various PDBs for an application.

There is one nice little twist here. When you create a Palm Database file using the converter, it will also (if you wish) write a module to open, read, and close the PDB file for you. Although the code looks like typical generated code, it works and saves you a ton of time (Figure 4-2).

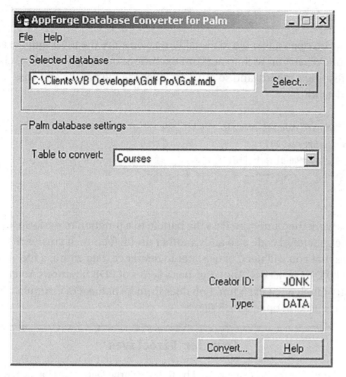

Figure 4-2. The AppForge Database Converter

 NOTE   *Although initially I used the modules created by the AppForge Database Converter, I later discovered that I needed to shrink the application size. To do so, I removed every unused function I could find. This included many of the Read and Write routines in these modules. The reason for this is that many of the functions consist of only one line of code. The thing to remember is one line takes up less space than three.*

Once the source code has been generated, you can simply add it to your VB project. If you make changes to the database structure, simply reconvert the database and make sure to regenerate the source code module.

Read the source code that is generated, and you will immediately see an important pattern. Working with a PDB file is just like working with a file opened with the Open Statement in Visual Basic:

```
Open (Insert file name) For Input as #Handle
```

When you open a text file in Visual Basic, you store the file handle to a memory variable. When you wish to perform operations on that file (such as checking for EOF, reading a record, and so on), you must use the handle and pass it to the requested action.

```
Do While Not EOF(Handle)
    buffer = Space(120)
    Line Input #Handle, buffer
    cOutString = cOutString & vbCrlf & buffer
Loop
```

PDBs work the same way. Pass the handle to a function to perform an operation. The generated code also adds another useful feature. It creates the record structures that you will need to use later to reference data within a file.

For all PDB file access, AppForge has a series of PDB functions. You can discern pretty much what each function does from its name. For example, PDBOpen is used to open a PDB file.

Compiler Directives

If you glanced at the code generated by the AppForge Database Converter, then you probably saw something you may not have seen before. You noticed the use of the pound sign surrounding a condition.

What does this mean? Well, it's quite simple. The use of the pound sign is referred to as a *compiler directive*. What this does is apply a condition to the state of the application at compile time. The APPFORGE constant is used by the AppForge compiler to distinguish code that should only be compiled for the Palm OS device, not for Windows. This technique can be used in general for any Palm OS– or Windows-specific code.

```
#If APPFORGE Then
    <Put Palm OS specific code here>
#Else
    <Put Windows specific code here>
#End If
```

Events and values surrounded by directives are conditionally compiled. So by using the APPFORGE directive, the compiler can make a decision on how to open a requested PDB file.

Accessing a Record

The way you access a record in AppForge is to read the contents of a PDB record into a memory structure. It is from this memory structure that you will read the data or make changes. Once you have completed your work with the memory structure, you can either discard it or update the PDB record with the new data. Listing 4-1 displays the contents of modCoursesDB, which is the generated source for the Courses database file.

Listing 4-1. The Generated Source Code for the Courses Table

```
'-------------------------------
'       AppForge PDB Converter auto-generated code module
'
'       Source Database: C:\Apress\Chapter 3\GolfPro\Golf.mdb
'       Source Table    : Courses
'
'       Num Records     : 2
'
'       PDB Table Name : Courses
'            CreatorID : JONK
'            TypeID     : DATA
'
'       Converted Time : 6/4/2001 4:52:33 PM
'
'-------------------------------

Option Explicit

' Use these constants for the CreatorID and TypeID
Public Const Courses_CreatorID As Long = &H4A4F4E4B
Public Const Courses_TypeID As Long = &H44415441

' Use this global to store the database handle
Public dbCourses As Long

' Use this enumeration to get access to the converted database Fields
Public Enum tCoursesDatabaseFields
    CourseID_Field = 0
    Course_Name_Field = 1
    Hole1Par_Field = 2
    Hole2Par_Field = 3
    Hole3Par_Field = 4
```

```
                Hole4Par_Field = 5
                Hole5Par_Field = 6
                Hole6Par_Field = 7
                Hole7Par_Field = 8
                Hole8Par_Field = 9
                Hole9Par_Field = 10
                Hole10Par_Field = 11
                Hole11Par_Field = 12
                Hole12Par_Field = 13
                Hole13Par_Field = 14
                Hole14Par_Field = 15
                Hole15Par_Field = 16
                Hole16Par_Field = 17
                Hole17Par_Field = 18
                Hole18Par_Field = 19
        End Enum


        Public Type tCoursesRecord
                CourseID As Long            'Primary ID Key
                Course_Name As String       'name of the course
                Hole1Par As Integer
                Hole2Par As Integer
                Hole3Par As Integer
                Hole4Par As Integer
                Hole5Par As Integer
                Hole6Par As Integer
                Hole7Par As Integer
                Hole8Par As Integer
                Hole9Par As Integer
                Hole10Par As Integer
                Hole11Par As Integer
                Hole12Par As Integer
                Hole13Par As Integer
                Hole14Par As Integer
                Hole15Par As Integer
                Hole16Par As Integer
                Hole17Par As Integer
                Hole18Par As Integer
        End Type


        Public Function OpenCoursesDatabase() As Boolean
```

```
    ' Open the database
    #If APPFORGE Then
        dbCourses = PDBOpen(Byfilename, "Courses", 0, 0, 0, 0, afModeReadWrite)
    #Else
        dbCourses = PDBOpen(Byfilename, App.Path & "\Courses", 0, 0, 0, 0,
afModeReadWrite)
    #End If

    If dbCourses <> 0 Then
        'We successfully opened the database
        OpenCoursesDatabase = True
    Else
        'We failed to open the database
        OpenCoursesDatabase = False
    End If

End Function

Public Sub CloseCoursesDatabase()
    ' Close the database
    PDBClose dbCourses
    dbCourses = 0
End Sub

Public Function ReadCoursesRecord(MyRecord As tCoursesRecord) As Boolean

    ReadCoursesRecord = PDBReadRecord(dbCourses, VarPtr(MyRecord))

End Function

Public Function WriteCoursesRecord(MyRecord As tCoursesRecord) As Boolean

    WriteCoursesRecord = PDBWriteRecord(dbCourses, VarPtr(MyRecord))

End Function
```

Let's review a few of the items of interest within this file. First, you will notice that a Long integer value has been assigned for both the CreatorID and the Type. These values are used for opening files by type or by creator. (As of this writing, I have not used them for anything within my Visual Basic applications.) The next important piece of information is that AppForge generates a Global handle for this file. The handle is generally named with a value of "db" plus the name of the converted table. In this case, dbCourses is used.

Understand the PDBOpen Method

There are two important points to note about the path argument of the PDBOpen method:

1. The path argument for the PDBOpen method is different when running in Palm OS than it is when running in Windows. Conditional compilation is used to ensure the proper path is assigned for each. (If you are unfamiliar with compiler directives, see the sidebar "Compiler Directives" later in this chapter or revisit your Visual Basic documentation.)

2. When running on a Palm device, the database name is case sensitive. Make sure that the name is entered in the correct case. Please note that you *cannot* change the PDB filename. The original name is stored in the first 32 bytes of the file, so if you change a file from MyFile.PDB to MyNewFile.PDB when you attempt to open the file with the PDBOpen function, the operation will fail without generating any error code.

Working with a PDB File in an AppForge Application

Now let's talk about the code required to open a Palm Database file and work with it inside an AppForge application. You will notice in the modCoursesDB Visual Basic module that there are several functions for reading and writing the data. The read function is ReadCourseRecord and the write function is WriteCourseRecord. In both cases the function VarPtr is employed. The VarPtr function is used to send the memory address of the data buffer; the results of a read are subsequently placed into the buffer, and in the case of a write, the values are referenced from the buffer.

NOTE *Some of you probably know this already, but VarPtr is a Visual Basic function. AppForge just implemented the function. Microsoft does not document VarPtr, so the only "official" place to learn about this function is Hard Core Visual Basic, which is included with the MSDN library. It is important to point out that the database schema must match the UDT[1] passed to Write/Read Record. The PDB library functions have no way to determine the format of the passed data. Instead, the PDB Write/Read Record functions insert data by offset. Arrays cannot be used in a user-defined type passed to these functions because Visual Basic uses safearrays. For a helpful explanation of VarPtr and several other Visual Basics Pointer functions, check out the knowledge base article #Q199824 on Microsoft's Web site.*

User-Defined Types

User-defined data types (referred to as UDTs in Visual Basic, *structures* in languages such as C and C++, and *records* in general scenarios) are groups of related data items declared as one type of information. User-defined data types are very useful when you want to group several related pieces of information in a structured way, as shown in this example:

```
Public Type tCar
        CarMake      As String
        CarModel     As String
        CarYear      As String
        EngineSize   As Integer
        Torque       As Integer
        WheelBase    As Integer
End Type
```

As you can see, this is a very simple layout, and it looks much like a database structure in Access or even a class structure. This is the easiest way to think of a UDT—as a record structure.

---

[1] UDT stands for user-defined type. See the sidebar "User-Defined Types" for more information.

Here is the example code for opening and browsing the Courses database (see Listing 4-2).

Listing 4-2. Code to Open the Courses Palm Database File

```
Private Sub Form_Load()
'-=-=-=-=-=-=-=-=-=-=-=-=-=-=-=-=-=-=-=-=-=-=-=-=-=-=-=-=-=-=
'
'    Sub        :    Form_Load
'    Params     :    None
'    Returns    :    None
'
'    Author     :    Vivid Software Inc. - Jon Kilburn
'                    http://www.VividSoftware.com
'
'    Client     :    Apress
'    Purpose    :    Load all the golf courses into this form from
'                    the Courses Database.
'
'-=-=-=-=-=-=-=-=-=-=-=-=-=-=-=-=-=-=-=-=-=-=-=-=-=-=-=-=-=-=
    Dim Result      As Boolean
    Dim iLoop       As Integer
    Dim RecCourses  As tCoursesRecord

    ' Set Error Trap
    On Error GoTo Trap


    ' Open the database file
    Result = OpenCoursesDatabase

    ' Check for open failure
    If Not Result Then
        ' Open failed, dump out
        MsgBox "Unable to Open Courses Database!", _
            vbExclamation
        End
    End If

    ' Reset Grid
    Me.grdCourses.Rows = 0
    Me.grdCourses.AddItem "ID" & vbTab & "Course Name"
```

```
    ' Configure the Columns
    Me.grdCourses.ColWidth(Col_ID) = 0
    Me.grdCourses.ColWidth(Col_Name) = 120

    ' Move to the first record
    Call PDBMoveFirst(dbCourses)

    ' Configure and Load the Grid
    Do While Not PDBEOF(dbCourses)

        ' Read the Record
        If Not ReadCoursesRecord(RecCourses) Then
            ' This record failed, skip it
        Else
            ' Load this item into the grid
            Me.grdCourses.AddItem RecCourses.ID & _
                vbTab & RecCourses.Course_Name
        End If

        ' Move to next record
        Call PDBMoveNext(dbCourses)
    Loop

    ' Set Grid Row Height
    For iLoop = 0 To Me.grdCourses.Rows - 1
        Me.grdCourses.RowHeight(iLoop) = 13
    Next iLoop

    ' Close the Course database
    CloseCoursesDatabase

Exit_Rtn:
    Exit Sub

Trap:

    ' Error Trap
    MsgBox "Error Code = " & Err.Number & _
            vbCrLf & Err.Description, vbExclamation

    ' Resume Next Not Supported...
    GoTo Exit_Rtn

End Sub
```

```
Private Sub Form_Activate()
'-=-=-=-=-=-=-=-=-=-=-=-=-=-=-=-=-=-=-=-=-=-=-=-=-=-=-=-=-=-=
'
'   Sub         :   Form_Activate
'   Params      :   None
'   Returns     :   None
'
'   Author      :   Vivid Software Inc. - Jon Kilburn
'                       http://www.VividSoftware.com
'
'   Client      :   Apress
'   Purpose     :   Show the form.
'
'-=-=-=-=-=-=-=-=-=-=-=-=-=-=-=-=-=-=-=-=-=-=-=-=-=-=-=-=-=-=


    ' Highlight the first row
    If Me.grdCourses.Rows > 1 And _
        Me.grdCourses.Row < 1 Then

        Me.grdCourses.Row = 1
    End If
End Sub
```

The Portable GolfPro Project

Following the steps for creating a new AppForge application, which I explained in
Chapter 3, let's create a new AppForge application and name it GolfPro. On your
first form (form 1), you'll create the standard splash screen. This will give you
practice in creating a form, placing some text, using a timer, and even placing
a picture on the form. After you name the project, change the name of Form1 to
frmSplash. On the splash form, select the AppForge label Ingot and place the
label on the form; change the name to Label and set its caption property to
Portable GolfPro 1.0.

When you drop the control onto the form, Visual Basic will inform you that you
must save the project before you can add any controls to this form. As I mentioned

earlier, this is different from standard VB, which allows you to create projects and forms without having to save them. So save the project, and then drop an AppForge Timer control on the form. Set its visible property to False and the interval to 2000 (2 seconds).

Now add the code to the timer event. In this case, since you have only one form, you will end the application when the timer is fired (see Listing 4-3).

Listing 4-3. The AFTimer Event Code

```
Private Sub TimerSplash_Timer()
'-=-=-=-=-=-=-=-=-=-=-=-=-=-=-=-=-=-=-=-=-=-=-=-=-=-=-=-=-=-=
'
'   Sub        :   TimerSplash_Timer()
'   Params     :   None
'   Returns    :   None
'
'   Author     :   Vivid Software Inc. - Jon Kilburn
'                      http://www.VividSoftware.com
'
'   Client     :   Visual Basic Developer
'   Purpose    :   Unload the Splash Form
'
'-=-=-=-=-=-=-=-=-=-=-=-=-=-=-=-=-=-=-=-=-=-=-=-=-=-=-=-=-=-=


    End

End Sub
```

Next, place an AppForge Graphic control on the form. This is where you begin to work with some of the tools that AppForge has besides the compiler. If you are using version 1.2.1 of AppForge, a graphics file must be converted to a Palm-compatible graphic before you can use it in your form. To do this, you must run the AppForge Graphics Converter program (see Figure 4-3).

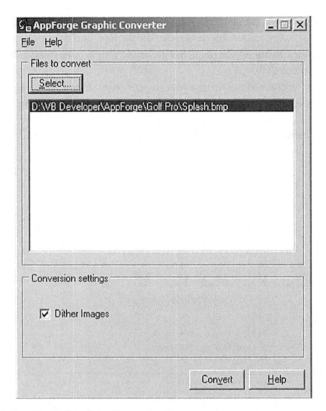

Figure 4-3. AppForge Graphics Converter Program

The converted graphic files are automatically saved to the same directory as the original bitmap files. The file extension for all AppForge graphic files is .rgx. To be recognized on the target device, AppForge graphic filenames must be no more than eight characters long (not counting the extension).

For those of you using AppForge 2.0 and higher, you can simply skip this step, as AppForge 2.0 supports .bmp and .jpg formats.

Now that you have a graphics file for your splash screen, you can select that file and load it into your Graphics control. When you click the Picture property of the Graphics control, a form will appear prompting you for the filename of the graphic to add to the project. Select Splash.bmp, and it will appear on your splash form. On the down side, you need to know about a few quirks when using graphics files. Once a file has been loaded (or converted), when you open the file and add it to the project, you cannot stretch or size the graphic within the AppForge Graphic control.

Finally, here is the kicker: you can run AppForge applications inside the Visual Basic IDE using the program Run feature. In fact, you can even compile the application down to a Windows executable. Although this is really cool, it has a small drawback: testing under Windows can mislead you in terms of performance, and what works in Windows may not work on the Palm. So I suggest you do a little testing in both environments.

Figure 4-4 shows the resulting form running in the Visual Basic IDE.

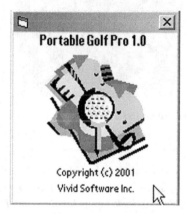

Figure 4-4. The splash screen for the Portable GolfPro application

Once the Timer event is fired by the AFTimer control, you will now call your frmMain form, which contains the previous code for loading the golf courses.

In the next sections of code, listed earlier, the record pointer was moved to the first record. (Although you would think this should happen by default, it does not.) Next you simply start walking the file, record by record. You can see that each record is loaded into a structure (also generated by the AppForge Converter program), and then values are loaded into the AFGrid Control. The final result is a grid of courses waiting to be played (see Figure 4-5).

Figure 4-5. Browsing the Courses list

NOTE   *I used labels to lock down the headers. Since AppForge's AFGrid control does not currently support a metaphor for locking the header rows, it is easier to use labels.*

Getting Your GolfPro Program to Run

Now there are several things that have to take place to make the GolfPro program work. First, you must set up the course you want to play on. As explained earlier, a course has a given number of strokes, which are assigned to all 18 holes. If the course is completed in this number of strokes, a player is considered to have played an even game (this comes up later).

So each course has a total number of strokes required for each hole, which is why you have created the Courses table. So let's consider what the Course database holds. It holds the name of the golf course, and the number of strokes allotted to each hole for par. That means each record requires an ID, course name, and the strokes (or par) for each hole (see Figure 4-6).

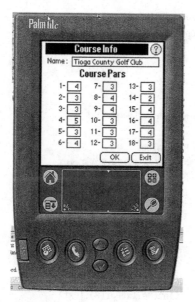

Figure 4-6. The Course Information screen

So now let's take a look at the code to save a new record and modify an existing record. As I've noted in the example code, there are dozens of ways to create a unique record ID. The code in Listing 4-4 is designed to show how to use the PDB* functions, not show you a technique you already know.

Listing 4-4. The Code to Save a Course Record

```
Private Sub cmdOK_Click()
'-=-=-=-=-=-=-=-=-=-=-=-=-=-=-=-=-=-=-=-=-=-=-=-=-=-=-=-=-=-=-=-=-=-=
'
'   Sub         :   cmdOK_Click()
'   Params      :   None
'   Returns     :   None
'
'   Author      :   Vivid Software Inc. - Jon Kilburn
'                       http://www.VividSoftware.com
'
'   Client      :   Apress
'   Purpose     :   Save Data and Exit
'
'-=-=-=-=-=-=-=-=-=-=-=-=-=-=-=-=-=-=-=-=-=-=-=-=-=-=-=-=-=-=-=-=-=-=
```

```
Dim RecCourse As tCoursesRecord
Dim CourseID  As Long

On Error GoTo Trap

' Save Field Values
RecCourse.Course_Name = Me.txtName.Text

' Load in the Hole Par Values
RecCourse.Hole1Par = CInt(Me.txtPar(0).Text)
RecCourse.Hole2Par = CInt(Me.txtPar(1).Text)
RecCourse.Hole3Par = CInt(Me.txtPar(2).Text)
RecCourse.Hole4Par = CInt(Me.txtPar(3).Text)
RecCourse.Hole5Par = CInt(Me.txtPar(4).Text)
RecCourse.Hole6Par = CInt(Me.txtPar(5).Text)
RecCourse.Hole7Par = CInt(Me.txtPar(6).Text)
RecCourse.Hole8Par = CInt(Me.txtPar(7).Text)
RecCourse.Hole9Par = CInt(Me.txtPar(8).Text)
RecCourse.Hole10Par = CInt(Me.txtPar(9).Text)
RecCourse.Hole11Par = CInt(Me.txtPar(10).Text)
RecCourse.Hole12Par = CInt(Me.txtPar(11).Text)
RecCourse.Hole13Par = CInt(Me.txtPar(12).Text)
RecCourse.Hole14Par = CInt(Me.txtPar(13).Text)
RecCourse.Hole15Par = CInt(Me.txtPar(14).Text)
RecCourse.Hole16Par = CInt(Me.txtPar(15).Text)
RecCourse.Hole17Par = CInt(Me.txtPar(16).Text)
RecCourse.Hole18Par = CInt(Me.txtPar(17).Text)

' Add new or simply update
If Not ModifyMode Then
    ' New Record
    ' Insert a record
    PDBCreateRecordBySchema dbCourses
Else
    ' Set Edit Mode
    Call PDBEditRecord(dbCourses)
End If

' Now Write the Record
Call WriteCoursesRecord(RecCourse)
```

```
' Update the Information
PDBUpdateRecord dbCourses

' Before we go, update the
' row on the main select course form
If ModifyMode Then
    ' Update Current row
    frmMain.grdCourses.TextMatrix( _
        frmMain.grdCourses.Row, _
        Course_Col_Name) = RecCourse.Course_Name
Else

    '-=-=-=-=-=-=-=-=-=-=-=-=-=-=-=-=-=-=-
    ' NOTE: There are several other ways to
    ' Get Unique IDs and to write them only
    ' once.  However, this is just an example
    ' and not intended to be used beyond that.
    ' For a complete explanation see the
    ' Chapter on Building Conduits.
    '-=-=-=-=-=-=-=-=-=-=-=-=-=-=-=-=-=-=-

    ' Get the New Unique ID
    CourseID = PDBRecordUniqueID(dbCourses)

    ' Set ID Field equal to CourseID
    RecCourse.ID = CourseID

    ' Edit the record
    Call PDBEditRecord(dbCourses)

    ' Now Write the Record
    Call WriteCoursesRecord(RecCourse)

    ' Update the Information
    PDBUpdateRecord dbCourses

    ' Add New Row
    frmMain.grdCourses.AddItem ( _
        CourseID & vbTab & _
        RecCourse.Course_Name)
```

```
            ' Set the Row Height
            frmMain.grdCourses.RowHeight( _
                frmMain.grdCourses.Rows - 1) = afRow_Height
        End If

        ' Done
        Unload Me

        ' Show the Main form
        frmMain.Show

Exit_Rtn:
        Exit Sub

Trap:

        ' Error Trap
        MsgBox "Error Code = " & Err.Number & _
                vbCrLf & Err.Description, vbExclamation

        ' Resume Next Not Supported. . .
        GoTo Exit_Rtn

End Sub
```

Adding Course Notes

When you have finished adding a course and assigning the scorecard, you can then look at adding the course notes. Course notes are notes that an individual player may make about a particular hole or area of the golf course.

A typical example of a course note would be to describe the way a ball might break on a green or even the speed of a green. Adding a course note is simple: you pass the course name and ID on to the Notes browse, and from there you can pass these values to the Notes edit form (see Figure 4-7).

Figure 4-7. Browsing the Notes Database

In the Notes browse, you must check the current Course ID against the Course ID in the Course Notes database to make sure that they match, since you really only want to see notes that pertain to the selected golf course. In the Form_Load of the frmNotesBrowse, you will apply a sort field and then filter against the records to make sure you load only the notes that belong to the selected course (see Listing 4-5).

Listing 4-5. Filter in the Form_Load Event

```
' Set the Sort to be by Course ID
Call PDBSetSortFields(dbCourseNotes, _
    tCourseNotesDatabaseFields.CourseID_Field)

' Find the first note that matches the
' current course selected
Call PDBFindRecordByField(dbCourseNotes, _
    tCourseNotesDatabaseFields.CourseID_Field, _
    CourseID)

' Configure and Load the Grid
Do While Not PDBEOF(dbCourseNotes)
```

```
' Read the Record
If Not ReadCourseNotesRecord(RecNotes) Then
' This record failed, give error
 MsgBox PDBGetLastError(dbCourseNotes), "Error"
Else
    If RecNotes.CourseID = Me.CourseID Then
    ' Load this item into the grid
    Me.grdNotes.AddItem CStr(RecNotes.NotesID) & _
        vbTab & RecNotes.Hole & vbTab & _
        RecNotes.Notes
    Else
    Exit Do
    End If
End If

' Move to next record
Call PDBMoveNext(dbCourseNotes)
Loop
```

The next step to working with the course notes is to determine what action to take when a user selects one of the buttons. The first action you'll tackle is the Add option. Adding a new course note is handled by setting a few flags in the frmCourseNotes form, which will identify whether or not this is an Add action or a Modify action. To do this, you need to add two public variables to the frmCourseNotes form: ModifyID (the Note ID being modified) and ModifyMode (which determines whether you are in Add or Edit mode).

As you can see in Listing 4-6, the values are set in the cmdAdd and cmdModify click events of the frmNotesBrowse form.

Listing 4-6. Code to Handle Add and Modify Clicks

```
Private Sub cmdAdd_Click()
'-=-=-=-=-=-=-=-=-=-=-=-=-=-=-=-=-=-=-=-=-=-=-=-=-=-=-=-=-=-=-=-=
'
'   Sub         :   cmdAdd_Click()
'   Params      :   None
'   Returns     :   None
'
'   Author      :   Vivid Software Inc. - Jon Kilburn
'                       http://www.VividSoftware.com
'
'   Client      :   Apress
'   Purpose     :   Add a new player
'
'-=-=-=-=-=-=-=-=-=-=-=-=-=-=-=-=-=-=-=-=-=-=-=-=-=-=-=-=-=-=-=-=
```

```
    Me.Hide
    frmCourseNote.LabelCourse.Caption = Me.CourseName
    frmCourseNote.Show

End Sub
Private Sub cmdMod_Click()
'-=-=-=-=-=-=-=-=-=-=-=-=-=-=-=-=-=-=-=-=-=-=-=-=-=-=-=-=-=
'
'    Sub         :   cmdMod_Click()
'    Params      :   None
'    Returns     :   None
'
'    Author      :   Vivid Software Inc. - Jon Kilburn
'                    http://www.VividSoftware.com
'
'    Client      :   Apress
'    Purpose     :   Add a new player
'
'-=-=-=-=-=-=-=-=-=-=-=-=-=-=-=-=-=-=-=-=-=-=-=-=-=-=-=-=-=

    On Error GoTo Trap

    ' Hide this form
    Me.Hide

    ' Set player modify id
    frmCourseNote.ModifyID = CLng(Me.grdNotes.TextMatrix( _
        Me.grdNotes.Row, Col_NotesID))

    ' Set Modify Mode switch
    frmCourseNote.ModifyMode = True

    ' Set course name
    frmCourseNote.LabelCourse.Caption = Me.CourseName

    ' Show the form
    frmCourseNote.Show

Exit_Rtn:
    Exit Sub

Trap:
```

```
' Handle Object was Unloaded
If Err.Number = 364 Then
    ' We will get an error 364 if the
    ' form fails to open the database
    GoTo Exit_Rtn
End If


End Sub
```

The final result is a form that loads with or without information based on the flags that were set in the frmNotesBrowse form (see Figure 4-8).

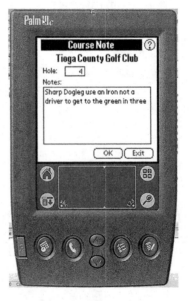

Figure 4-8. Editing course notes

Saving the Record

The final piece of the puzzle comes with saving the record. To save a record, you will need to do several things based on the Modify settings. The first decision you must make in the Save routine is to determine if you are adding a new record or modifying an existing one.

The function used for adding a new record is PDBCreateRecordBySchema, and for modifying a record you would use PDBEditRecord. Both functions accept the handle to the file as a parameter.

After you add or lock the record, you can write the changes using the generated Write routine. The final step is to update the database by using the PDBUpdate function. This function will flush the buffers and write the resulting data in the PDB file (see Listing 4-7).

Listing 4-7. Code to Update the Course Notes Database

```
Private Sub cmdOK_Click()
'-=-=-=-=-=-=-=-=-=-=-=-=-=-=-=-=-=-=-=-=-=-=-=-=-=-=-=-=-=
'
'    Sub        :   cmdOK_Click()
'    Params     :   None
'    Returns    :   None
'
'    Author     :   Vivid Software Inc. - Jon Kilburn
'                       http://www.VividSoftware.com
'
'    Client     :   Apress
'    Purpose    :   Save Data and Exit
'
'-=-=-=-=-=-=-=-=-=-=-=-=-=-=-=-=-=-=-=-=-=-=-=-=-=-=-=-=-=
    Dim RecNotes As tCourseNotesRecord
    Dim NotesID  As Long

    On Error GoTo Trap

    ' Save Field Values
    RecNotes.Hole = CInt(Me.txtHole.Text)
    RecNotes.Notes = Me.txtNotes.Text
    RecNotes.CourseID = frmNotesBrowse.CourseID

    ' Add new or simply update
    If Not ModifyMode Then
        ' New Record

        ' Insert a record
        PDBCreateRecordBySchema dbCourseNotes
```

```
        Else

            ' Set Edit Mode

            Call PDBEditRecord(dbCourseNotes)

        End If

        ' Now Write the Record
        Call WriteCourseNotesRecord(RecNotes)

        ' Update the Information
        PDBUpdateRecord dbCourseNotes

        ' Before we go, update the
        ' row on the main select course form
        If ModifyMode Then
            ' Update Current row
            Call frmNotesBrowse.RefreshRow(frmPlayerBrowse.grdPlayers.Row)
        Else

            ' Get the New Unique ID
            ModifyID = PDBRecordUniqueID(dbCourseNotes)

            ' Set ID Field equal to NotesID
            RecNotes.NotesID = ModifyID

            ' Edit the record
            Call PDBEditRecord(dbCourseNotes)

            ' Now Write the Record
            Call WriteCourseNotesRecord(RecNotes)

            ' Update the Information
            PDBUpdateRecord dbCourseNotes

            ' Add New Row
            frmNotesBrowse.grdNotes.AddItem ( _
                ModifyID & vbTab & _
```

```
            RecNotes.Hole & vbTab & _
            RecNotes.Notes)


      ' Set the Row Height
      frmNotesBrowse.grdNotes.RowHeight( _
          frmNotesBrowse.grdNotes.Rows - 1) = afRow_Height
    End If


    ' Done
    Unload Me


    ' Show the Player Browse form
    frmNotesBrowse.Show

Exit_Rtn:
    Exit Sub


Trap:

    ' Error Trap
    MsgBox "Error Code = " & Err.Number & _
            vbCrLf & Err.Description, vbExclamation


    ' Resume Next Not Supported...
    GoTo Exit_Rtn


End Sub
```

Working with Players

Whenever a golfer actually plays the game of golf, he or she generally carries
a handicap (unless he or she is a pro golfer). A *handicap* is a method for improving a player's score. The concept is that, by giving the player a handicap, you can
level the playing field. This means that, if I have a handicap of 12, when I have
finished playing a course, I can subtract 12 strokes from my golf game and
I should be close to even. The higher the handicap, the more a player needs to
improve his or her game. (Yes, I have a *very* high handicap. Now let's get back

to the example application, shall we?) Every player that the GolfPro system has can have a handicap. If a player has no handicap, then just leave the value 0.

Once the user has selected a course to play on, then the user must add or select an existing player. Working with players is handled in much the same manner as working with course notes. You pass the Course ID to the frmPlayersBrowse form, but do not actually use the value until the user adds a scorecard (see Figure 4-9).

Figure 4-9. Browsing players

The only real difference between working with players and working with course notes (besides the file structures) is that for this section I opted to include a graphic in the frmPlayers form (see Figure 4-10). Although having a graphic on the form does not actually do much in the way of improving the ease of use of the GolfPro program, it does help to take up some of the extra space and give the form a more completed look.

Figure 4-10. Combining an image with a form

Calculating the Score

Finally, let's take a look at how to calculate your score while playing a course. Generally this is achieved by comparing the number of strokes you have against the number of strokes required to maintain par and then subtracting your handicap. There are several pieces to this puzzle that you need to figure out:

- Loading the values for the course into an array so you can calculate the current score for each hole against the par

- Calculating scoring on the fly

- Dealing with a player's handicap

- Dealing with an incomplete scorecard (in other words, calculating the par as you play) and a 0 value, since 0 is referred to as even

Okay, now let's handle each item at a time. First, deal with the value for each hole. You'll read each hole's par into an array (aPar) element so you can later calculate your score against it. Normally you use the record structure UDT to store values retrieved from a record, but you can also retrieve a single field's value using PDBGetField(). This function is slower (quite a bit slower, actually) than reading the whole record into a structure, but it gives you the flexibility to read a record's value by field position. This means you could use a loop to load them (see Listing 4-8).

Listing 4-8. Code to Calculate the Course Par

```
' Calculate Par
For iLoop = 0 To 17
    Call PDBGetField(dbCourses, _
        tCoursesDatabaseFields.Hole1Par_Field + iLoop, _
        aPar(iLoop))
    nPar = nPar + aPar(iLoop)
Next iLoop
```

However, given that the process of loading a player's scorecard would be slowed even more by loading the card this way (in my tests on the emulator, I noticed a five-second difference), the card values will instead be loaded by referencing them directly. First, the values are loaded into a file wide array, since you will need them later to calculate a player's score, and then sum them up to calculate the course par value. This does add some code overhead in terms of the number of lines, but the program will execute much faster as a result (see Listing 4-9).

Listing 4-9. Loading the Score Card into an Array for Processing

```
Call ReadCoursesRecord(RecCourse)

' Calculate Par
' NOTE: You CANNOT do this in a loop as Structure
' elements are not "String" names.
aPar(0) = RecCourse.Hole1Par
aPar(1) = RecCourse.Hole2Par
aPar(2) = RecCourse.Hole3Par
aPar(3) = RecCourse.Hole4Par
aPar(4) = RecCourse.Hole5Par
aPar(5) = RecCourse.Hole6Par
aPar(6) = RecCourse.Hole7Par
aPar(7) = RecCourse.Hole8Par
aPar(8) = RecCourse.Hole9Par
aPar(9) = RecCourse.Hole10Par
aPar(10) = RecCourse.Hole11Par
aPar(11) = RecCourse.Hole12Par
aPar(12) = RecCourse.Hole13Par
aPar(13) = RecCourse.Hole14Par
```

```
aPar(14) = RecCourse.Hole15Par
aPar(15) = RecCourse.Hole16Par
aPar(16) = RecCourse.Hole17Par
aPar(17) = RecCourse.Hole18Par

' Calculate Par
For iLoop = 0 To 17
    nPar = nPar + aPar(iLoop)
Next iLoop
```

Now let's tackle the on-the-fly scoring. Pay close attention here: the AppForge TextBox Ingots do not support the same GotFocus, LostFocus, and Validate events as their Windows counterparts. In fact, only the Change and Click events are supported. The good news is that the Change event will work just fine for you to trigger the scoring routine (see Listing 4-10).

Listing 4-10. Change Event Code to Calculate the Score

```
Private Sub txtPar_Change(Index As Integer)
'-=-=-=-=-=-=-=-=-=-=-=-=-=-=-=-=-=-=-=-=-=-=-=-=-=-=-=-=
'
'    Sub        :    txtPar_Change(Index)
'    Params     :    Index - Which field generated the event
'    Returns    :    None
'
'    Author     :    Vivid Software Inc. - Jon Kilburn
'                    http://www.VividSoftware.com
'
'    Client     :    Apress
'    Purpose    :    Force a Score Calculation
'
'-=-=-=-=-=-=-=-=-=-=-=-=-=-=-=-=-=-=-=-=-=-=-=-=-=-=-=-=

    ' Calculate Score
    Call CalcScore

End Sub
```

Of course, there is one hiccup here. Whenever you load an AFTextBox control with a value, you will trigger the Change event. So in the prior example, not only was the score calculated on the form load, but the score was also calculated 18 more times for each Change event fired. Now that chews up some processing power.

Creating Your Own GotFocus and LostFocus Events

Okay, basically AppForge only supports two events in the AFTextBox control—Change and Click. But what you really want is a GotFocus/LostFocus event.

You could try Click, except that this event fires only when a TextBox control is selected, so it's not really useful for validation. The other is the Change event. Change is fired for everything, including the keyboard events. However, generally speaking, most Palm users don't have the portable keyboard hooked up, so this shouldn't be a problem.

When a change event occurs you can jump to a function, which does your validation. You can do this by placing the controls into a control array, thereby simulating LostFocus and GotFocus by keeping track of the last control index (see Listing 4-11).

Listing 4-11. Code Example Which Simulates GotFocus and LostFocus Events

```
' File wide
Dim LastControlIndex As Integer

Private Sub Form_Load
    ' Set the LastControlIndex to -1
    ' so we can determine what to do
    ' with it in the Change Event Handler
    LastControlIndex = -1
End Sub

' Use the Change event to act like
' GotFocus and LostFocus
Private Sub txtTest_Change(Index As Integer)

    ' Only worry about firing the events
    ' If we are not in Windows
    #If APPFORGE Then
        ' Check for "GotFocus"
        If LastControlIndex < 0 Then
            ' Fire GotFocus
            LastControlIndex = Index
            Call txtTestGotFocus(Index)
        Else
            If LastControlIndex <> Index Then
                ' Fire "LostFocus" Event
                Call txtTestLostFocus(LastControlIndex)
```

```
                ' Set to Current Index
                LastControlIndex = Index

                ' Fire the "GotFocus" Event
                Call txtTestGotFocus(Index)
            End If
        End If
    #End If

End Sub

Private Sub txtGotFocus(Index As Integer)
    . . . Do something . . .
End Sub

Private Sub txtLostFocus(Index As Integer)
    . . . Do something . . .
End Sub
```

Finally, you need to add to the Click event of other controls (such as buttons) code to call the LostFocus and reset the LastControlIndex (see Listing 4-12).

Listing 4-12. Code to Simulate a LostFocus Event

```
#If APPFORGE Then
    If Not LastControlIndex < 0 Then
        ' Call LostFocus
        Call txtTestLostFocus(LastControlIndex)

        ' Reset Last Control Index
        LastControlIndex = -1
    End If
#End If
```

So, how do you get around this Change event problem? Use a file wide variable, which you will call ProcessEvents, and set it to False in the Form_Load event. When the user actually clicks into one of the edits in the Click event of the AFTextBox control, you set the ProcessEvents value to True. In the AFTextBox Change event, you also modify the code to check the value of ProcessEvents before running the calculation routine (see Listing 4-13).

Listing 4-13. Handling the Calculation and Events

```vb
Private Sub txtPar_Click(Index As Integer)
'-=-=-=-=-=-=-=-=-=-=-=-=-=-=-=-=-=-=-=-=-=-=-=-=-=-=-=-=-=-=-=
'
'   Sub        :   txtPar_Click(Index)
'   Params     :   Index - Which field generated the event
'   Returns    :   None
'
'   Author     :   Vivid Software Inc. - Jon Kilburn
'                  http://www.VividSoftware.com
'
'   Client     :   Apress
'   Purpose    :   Begin processing events
'
'-=-=-=-=-=-=-=-=-=-=-=-=-=-=-=-=-=-=-=-=-=-=-=-=-=-=-=-=-=-=-=

    ' Switch to processing events
    ProcessEvents = True

End Sub
Private Sub txtPar_Change(Index As Integer)
'-=-=-=-=-=-=-=-=-=-=-=-=-=-=-=-=-=-=-=-=-=-=-=-=-=-=-=-=-=-=-=
'
'   Sub        :   txtPar_Change(Index)
'   Params     :   Index - Which field generated the event
'   Returns    :   None
'
'   Author     :   Vivid Software Inc. - Jon Kilburn
'                  http://www.VividSoftware.com
'
'   Client     :   Apress
'   Purpose    :   Force a Score Calculation
'
'-=-=-=-=-=-=-=-=-=-=-=-=-=-=-=-=-=-=-=-=-=-=-=-=-=-=-=-=-=-=-=

    If ProcessEvents Then
        Call CalcScore
    End If

End Sub
```

Finally, within the CalcScore routine, you need to deal with three items. The first item is determining which hole the player is on and the current score as it applies to this hole. Second is dealing with 0 as even, and the final item is to adjust for the player's handicap.

You can accomplish the first task by simply checking the Text property of each of the txtPar(index) controls. The first empty one that you encounter indicates the next hole to be played, so you just sum the current values for par and the current strokes, and presto, you have the running score. Second, you simply check the result of strokes against par, and if they are 0, you display the word even. Finally, after you calculate the player's current score, you subtract his or her handicap from the total, which yields the player's adjusted score (see Listing 4-14).

Listing 4-14. Code to Calculate a Golf Score

```
Private Sub CalcScore()
'-=-=-=-=-=-=-=-=-=-=-=-=-=-=-=-=-=-=-=-=-=-=-=-=-=-=-=-=-=
'
'    Sub        :    CalcScore()
'    Params     :    None
'    Returns    :    None
'
'    Author     :    Vivid Software Inc. - Jon Kilburn
'                    http://www.VividSoftware.com
'
'    Client     :    Apress
'    Purpose    :    Calculate Par for this Course and the
'                    current score on a card.
'
'-=-=-=-=-=-=-=-=-=-=-=-=-=-=-=-=-=-=-=-=-=-=-=-=-=-=-=-=-=
    Dim iLoop   As Integer
    Dim nScore  As Integer
    Dim nCurPar As Integer
    Dim cSign   As String

    For iLoop = 0 To 17
        If Me.txtPar(iLoop).Text = "" Then
            ' Current Hole, so stop here
            Exit For
        End If

        ' Calculate Current Par
        nCurPar = nCurPar + aPar(iLoop)
```

```
                ' Calculate current strokes
                nScore = nScore + CInt(Me.txtPar(iLoop).Text)
        Next iLoop

        ' Determine Par
        nCurPar = nScore - nCurPar

        ' Subtract the Player's Handicap from
        ' the total score giving an adjusted score
        nCurPar = nCurPar - Handicap

        If nCurPar = 0 Then
            Me.LabelScore.Caption = "Score : Even"
        Else
            If nCurPar > 0 Then
                cSign = "+"
            Else
                ' Make number Positive
                nCurPar = nCurPar * (-1)

                ' Set Sign
                cSign = "-"
            End If

            Me.LabelScore.Caption = "Score : " & _
                cSign & Trim(CStr(nCurPar))
        End If
End Sub
```

Compiling

Now that you have the application developed, you want to compile it. As you may have noticed when you first installed AppForge, a new menu option was added to the main VB menu. Under the AppForge menu option, you will find several choices, including the following:

- Compile and Validate

- Deploy to Palm OS

- Deploy to Device

- Save Project Package

- Install Booster on Device

Get used to using the Compile option. Until you become familiar with the differences between VB and AppForge, you will find yourself changing quite a few lines of valid VB code to make them compile with AppForge.

When you compile a project with AppForge, you may notice that it throws a number of warnings for such things as controls overlapping (please note this is only under version 1.x, as version 2.0 added ZOrder support). Don't worry—these warnings, such as the one shown in Figure 4-11, do not affect your program. You will, however, discover that a lot of things that you used to do one way under Windows you'll have to rethink under the Palm OS.

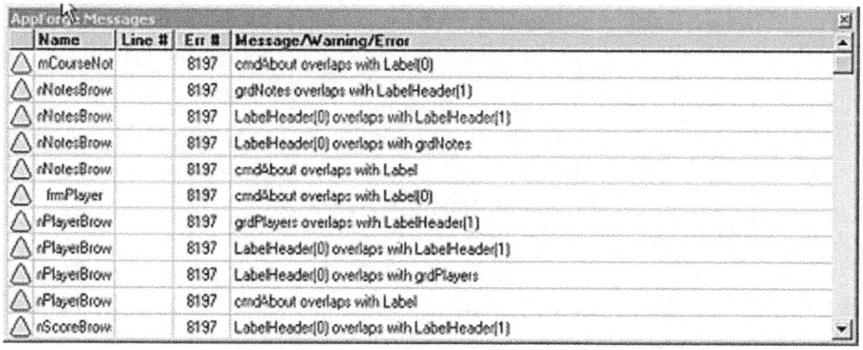

Name	Line #	Err #	Message/Warning/Error
mCourseNot		8197	cmdAbout overlaps with Label(0)
rNotesBrow.		8197	grdNotes overlaps with LabelHeader(1)
rNotesBrow.		8197	LabelHeader(0) overlaps with LabelHeader(1)
rNotesBrow.		8197	LabelHeader(0) overlaps with grdNotes
rNotesBrow.		8197	cmdAbout overlaps with Label
frmPlayer		8197	cmdAbout overlaps with Label(0)
rPlayerBrow		8197	grdPlayers overlaps with LabelHeader(1)
rPlayerBrow		8197	LabelHeader(0) overlaps with LabelHeader(1)
rPlayerBrow		8197	LabelHeader(0) overlaps with grdPlayers
rPlayerBrow		8197	cmdAbout overlaps with Label
rScoreBrow.		8197	LabelHeader(0) overlaps with LabelHeader(1)

Figure 4-11. AppForge warning messages

Once you have the project compiled, you must install the new program on a target device. Before you can install the GolfPro application, you must first upload Booster to the device. Once Booster has been properly installed, you can upload your program. To install Booster on your Palm device, select the AppForge menu option Install Booster on Device.

This is where things can get hairy. In the previous version of AppForge, Booster was a single file. In version 2.0, Booster has been broken up into several programs (seven in all). The idea of separate programs was to decrease the required size of the runtime. So now you have to specify the Install Booster To Device option to determine which packages are deployed in the Booster core. As you add components to your application, you will find these Booster extensions added to your program upload.

Once you have selected the Install Booster To Device option, the files will be copied to your Palm Install directory, and a window will open displaying which

Booster files will be installed on your Palm Device with the next HotSync (see Figure 4-12).

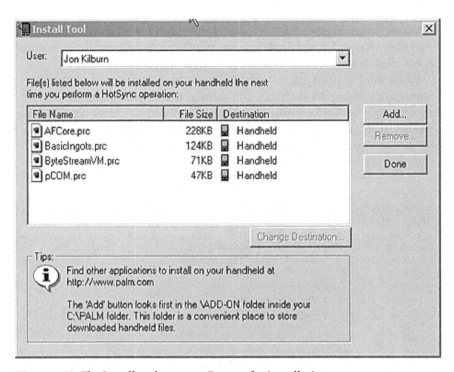

Figure 4-12. The Install tool prepares Booster for installation.

After completing your compilation of the GolfPro program and the installation of Booster on your Palm device, you are now ready to upload the compiled GolfPro program to your Palm device. You can do this in one of two ways. The first way is the simplest and works the best if you have a cradle attached to your PC. From the AppForge menu, select the Deploy to Palm OS menu option.

This option will do the same thing that the Install Booster To Device option does, and by that I mean it will copy your compiled program to the Palm Install directory, along with any supplemental Booster files that may be required, and the next time you HotSync, the file will be copied onto your Palm Device.

NOTE *Compiling an AppForge project does not create the PRC file required to install your application on a Palm OS device. You must select the Deploy to Palm OS option or the Save Project Package option to create the PRC file for your application. Each time an AppForge project is compiled, three files are created. The AFX file contains a compiled version of your source code, the RSP file contains a table of strings used by your application, and the RPP file contains properties for all controls used in your application.*

One final note: to upload your PDB files, you should use the Palm desktop's Install tool. This allows you to select multiple files and then HotSync them directly to the device in one shot.

NOTE *When you create your PDBs, make sure they have the same CreatorID as the application; otherwise, they cannot be beamed along with the application, and will not be deleted if the application is deleted from the Palm device.*

Moving to Pocket PC

AppForge offers a unique approach to programming for the Mobile device arena. AppForge Professional Edition allows users to create both Palm applications and applications that run under Pocket PC. There are some differences, but the majority of your code can be cross-compiled.

Advanced AppForge Functions

Although I did spend a pretty good amount of time discussing how to build an AppForge application, I'm not going to get too in-depth on the advanced functions provided by AppForge. I will, however, touch briefly on the more advanced features of the compiler so you will have a good idea what else there is to it.

- *Extended Functions Library:* The AppForge Extended Functions Library provides several useful functions that allow you to get or change many of the Palm OS settings. While your AppForge project is open in Microsoft

Visual Basic, click the Project menu option and select References. Scroll to AppForge Palm OS Extended Functions and click the checkbox beside it. This will add the AppForge Extended Library functions to your application.

NOTE *You must include the Extended Functions Library as a reference in your application to use any of the AppForge Extended functions. Be aware that adding the Extended Function Library will increase the size of your project file on the handheld device.*

The AppForge Extended functions allow you to interact with different parts of the Palm OS directly, such as getting the writing preferences to the Palm preferences internal database, determining the remaining battery power, or turning off the sleep function of the Palm device so that it always stays on.

- *AppForge Numeric Library:* The AppForge Numeric Library generates pseudo-random numbers. It consists of only two functions, RandomLong and SeedRandomLong. RandomLong will return a Random Long integer value, and SeedRandomLong allows you to set the seed value of RandomLong.

- *AppForge System Library:* The AppForge System Library consists of only four functions. These include functions for determining device key presses and releasing the key afterwards, determining the username on the device, and retrieving system time in milliseconds.

- *Palm OS Extensibility Library:* The AppForge Palm OS Extensibility Library provides methods to switch control over to another PRC. This is accomplished using either CallApp or LaunchApp. CallApp will call another application as a subroutine, whereas LaunchApp will exit the current application and turn over control to the newly launched application.

NOTE *The Palm OS Extensibility Library is only available in the AppForge Professional Edition.*

Conclusion

Well, it's been a wild ride, and it's far from over; after all, I have only scratched the surface of what AppForge is capable of. AppForge is a great product, one that opens the door to a whole new world of opportunity for the Visual Basic developer.

If there's a chink in the armor of AppForge, it is the size of Booster. Standard Palm devices with 2MB of memory will be hard-pressed to squeeze Booster's beefy 335KB onto their system and still have room for other information. However, the (x) models of the Palm series come with 8MB of memory, and the other devices using the Palm OS (Symbol, Sony CLIÉ, and so on) come with variations of more than 2MB as well, so this isn't really a delimiting factor, but more of an observation.

Technical support is excellent, and there are already some great forums and discussion groups devoted to AppForge. AppForge shows tremendous potential, and with its last release it is looking even more promising.

Overall the product is solid and provides excellent functionality. As handheld devices become even more popular, the ability to program for them will become a very sought-after commodity, and thanks to AppForge, the VB programmer can be there waiting.

Introduction to
NS Basic

PROGRAMMING FOR THE Palm isn't the easiest thing to do because it is a lot like programming in DOS again. You have all the same elements, flat type files, memory constraints, and storage issues, with the added twist of a new flavor of OS. The good news is that, thanks to a handful of VB and Delphi-like programming environments that have sprung up recently, programming for the Palm is getting easier. In this chapter, you get a chance to scratch the surface of the NS Basic for Palm compiler.

NS Basic Fundamentals

The NS (Nice and Smart) Basic Corporation first came out with a development environment for the Apple Newton in 1994, and they've since released NS Basic for Windows CE and also NS Basic for the Palm OS. NS Basic 2.0 is sure to establish a strong presence as a powerful alternative development environment. Written 100 percent in Visual Basic, this development environment and compiler are a testament to the programming power offered by Visual Basic. This product is available directly from NS Basic Corporation's Web site (check out http://www.nsbasic.com for single user and enterprise licensing), or you can get it from one of the product's distributors.

NS Basic/Palm is a complete development environment for Palm OS (see Figure 5-1) that provides a full, modern implementation of Basic. NS Basic has taken great pains to ensure that its flavor of Basic is very similar to Visual Basic, by including proper subroutines and user-defined data types, and excluding line numbers. Programs can be tested using the Palm OS Emulator (POSE), or on the device itself. NS Basic/Palm produces standard Palm device program files (with the extension .prc) as executables.

CROSS REFERENCE *See Chapter 2 for a discussion of POSE.*

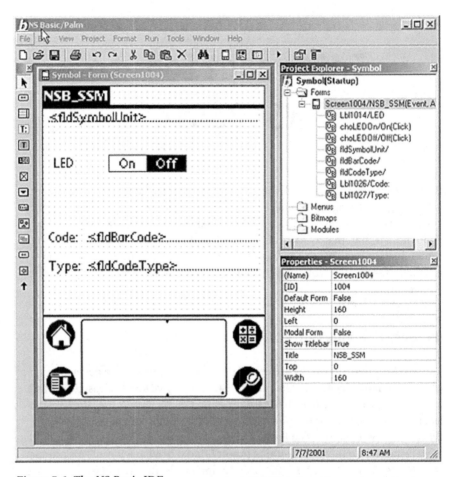

Figure 5-1. The NS Basic IDE

NS Basic Pros and Cons

The following Palm development environments are available in addition to NS Basic:

- CodeWarrior (C/C++)
- Java (KVM)
- CASL (sort for Compact Application Solution Language)
- Pocket Technologies' Pocket Studio (a Delphi-like language)
- GNU C Compiler

Although NS Basic includes the simplicity of the Basic programming language, and a visual development environment that is easy and familiar to use, it's not without its pros and cons.

NS Basic pros:

- Based on easy-to-use, standard, structured Basic
- Includes over a dozen screen objects
- Supports buttons, fields, pop-up forms, true menus, and more
- Includes built-in serial communications support
- Supports math and trigonometric functions
- Includes the capability to compile the runtime engine directly into the PRC or leave it external
- Produces standard Palm applications
- Allows you to create applications that exceed 64KB in size
- Encompasses a broad range of PDB database functions
- Ships with a printed, well-written manual and lots of good samples on the CD, with another dozen good user-contributed samples available online
- Serves as the main focus of an active newsgroup (at nsbasic-palm-subscribe@yahoogroups.com), from which you can get advice and product news

NS Basic cons:

- Excludes IntelliSense features.
- Does not come with a debugger.
- Does not display bitmap images in the IDE. You must view them by downloading them to the POSE.
- Excludes a control for drawing a line. (Drawing lines requires using a function.)
- Doesn't have an online searchable knowledge base. (FAQs and tech notes are available online, however.)
- Doesn't save the settings. The IDE always loads a blank project, and you can't resize the forms, close windows, or otherwise tweak the IDE and have it reopen with your saved changes.
- Doesn't let you save forms as separate files to be added to a project. In order to paste a form between projects, you must open a copy of NS Basic that contains the project with the form you wish to copy and another copy of NS Basic as a target. You must then highlight the form name in the Project Explorer, click Copy, select the target version of NS Basic, highlight the Project Explorer, right-click, and then select Paste. Could it be any more difficult?

- Doesn't go automatically into edit mode when you click a property and then start typing, as it would in VB. (This is only on properties such as Caption where text input is allowed.)
- Doesn't let you select multiple controls by dragging the mouse around a grouping. Instead, you must shift-click on each control. When you have more than a few controls, this is annoying.
- Limits PDB sorting to the key column only.

Although it may sound silly, one of the nicest things (at least in my opinion) about NS Basic was that the software arrived in a box[1] and was accompanied by a printed manual. All too often these days the software comes as a download with all documentation as PDF files or even only Help files.

The manual is very well written and nicely laid out. It leads the programmer through basic Palm programming concepts, and the use of the IDE and the various parts of building your first Palm programming project. All the visual components are well described before launching into the Basic language itself. The final sections deal with Palm database programming.

NS Basic supports a large subset of the Visual Basic programming language. You will find that most of the more common Visual Basic functions are available and work identically to their desktop PC counterparts. There are a few annoying differences—for example, to end a program, instead of the familiar End command you must use Stop. You will find a few of these minor annoyances along the way, but for the most part the language provides a very similar Visual Basic look and feel, which takes very little time to get used to.

You will find that for the most part, NS Basic attempts to mirror Visual Basic where possible. Some of the biggest disadvantages I noticed was the lack of Visual Basic IntelliSense and a debugger. Although this is not critical (after all, some of us have programmed ASP all these years without a debugger), I have become quite spoiled with VB's IntelliSense features and found that for the first couple of programs I built I had to leave the Help file open for the duration so I could look up the functions I was using. NS Basic is a compiler but requires a runtime support library. The NS Basic runtime library (NSBRuntime.Prc) can be installed separately, or compiled into your program, generating a "fat" application. NS Basic also has a shared library of math functions that can be installed on your Palm device. There are a number of these now, with more on the way. Think of a shared library as being like a Windows DLL that provides additional functionality for special purposes. You load and unload these libraries as needed.

---

[1] Although my copy arrived in a box, it should be noted that whether or not you receive a box depends on where you buy your copy.

Although you do not need anything except NS Basic and either a real Palm or the POSE to get started, you should obtain a copy of the SDK, including the latest documentation (available from Palm Web site). The SDK contains these three important items:

- *Example code:* You can peruse this code (although it's all in C/C++) to get a feel for Palm programming "under the hood."

- *Documentation:* Think of the documentation as a dictionary in which you can look up all the possible system functions available for your code. The SDK documentation is not very interesting to read, unless you find reading a dictionary exciting.

- *Palm OS Emulator:* The emulator essentially functions as a virtual Palm on your desktop. POSE allows you to debug and run the programs you develop on your computer, instead of performing a HotSync every time you make a new build. You definitely need the emulator, unless you enjoy resetting your Palm device several times while writing your software (see Figure 5-2).

Figure 5-2. The Palm OS Emulator (POSE)

 NOTE   *NS Basic includes a copy of POSE.*

CROSS REFERENCE *For a more detailed explanation of conduits, see Chapter 9.*

You can also download the Conduit Developers Kit (CDK) 4.02 for COM, which supports any COM-compliant language, including Visual Basic. This means that you can now develop custom conduits using Visual Basic. A *conduit* is a means of communication between a Palm OS device and a desktop PC. NS Basic does not ship with a conduit development tool. So in order to develop a conduit to pass information between the PC and your NS Basic application, you will need the CDK. Although you have several other choices for conduit development, the CDK is free from Palm.

Getting Started

Once you have run the installation program and completed the installation of the NS Basic compiler, you will notice that when you start the compile process, it looks and acts almost exactly like Visual Basic: prompting you at startup to select a new application, or to open an existing application or the recent projects (see Figure 5-3).

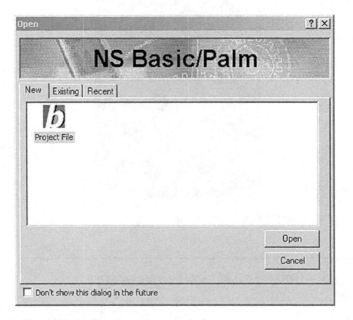

Figure 5-3. The select application startup window

There are some distinct differences between these options, but for the moment concentrate on creating a new application and begin familiarizing yourself with the NS Basic IDE.

After starting a new project you will be presented with the NS Basic IDE (configured based on your preferences). The IDE looks and functions very much like that of Visual Basic, in that it has a Project Explorer, Properties window, and a toolbox pallet. These windows cannot, however, be undocked and repositioned as they can be within VB. They can be closed or opened. The toolbar and status bar may also be hidden if you so desire.

> **NOTE**   *You will notice that NS Basic names its objects with an object name followed by a number (ranging from 1003 up). The reason for this is that these numbers are what the Palm OS uses to refer to these objects internally. NS Basic is tightly integrated with the Palm OS, so things are referred to in the same way. These numbers can be used in many of the API calls as well (SysTrapFunc allows you to call a Palm OS API function by number).*

Project Explorer

The Project Explorer (see Figure 5-4) contains these four sections:

- Forms

- Menus

- Bitmaps

- Modules

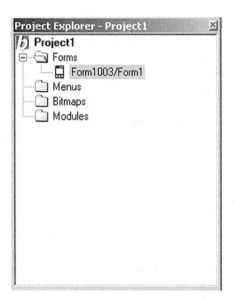

Figure 5-4. The Project Explorer

Just like in Visual Basic, each of these sections are relative to their corresponding object. For example, under Forms you will find a list of all the forms contained in your NS Basic Palm application, under Menus you will find the menus, and so on. The only twist here is the Bitmap section.

Bitmaps are different from the normal project objects in that they can be edited externally by using another program. The NS Basic IDE does not physically include a bitmap image in the project. You can now use any external graphics editor to include an image file, such as BMPs, GIFs, and JPEGs. NS Basic will convert the bitmap file to the required Palm OS file type before uploading it to the Palm device (see Figure 5-5).

Figure 5-5. A bitmap displayed using the POSE

Properties Window

The Properties window contains the properties for the currently selected object, control, or form. For example, if you open NS Basic, select the New project option (making sure in the new project that you have the Properties window set to visible), and click the blank form window, you should see properties similar to those in Figure 5-6.

 NOTE *Bitmap images are not displayed. This control is simply a placeholder. To correctly determine size (if you don't have your graphics program that was used to create the graphic handy), you have to compile and sync to the POSE.*

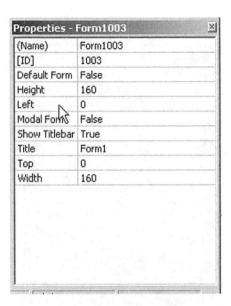

Figure 5-6. The Properties window in the NS Basic IDE

Toolbox Pallet

On the left-hand side of the NS Basic IDE, you will see a toolbox pallet. Just as in Visual Basic, this toolbox contains all of the controls (or screen objects, which we will discuss shortly) that can be added to a Palm form (see Figure 5-7). There are certain controls that do not exist. For example, you have no control for drawing a line; to do so you must use the DrawLine function.

Figure 5-7. The Toolbox window of the NS Basic IDE

Form Layout Window

The Form Layout window (called the Palm Screen in NS Basic terminology) looks like a physical Palm device screen (see Figure 5-8). This window has a screen section and a silkscreen section. The silkscreen section is inactive, and does not allow for controls to be placed in this region. The screen layout section is where you place the controls for each form you are creating. If you click the border, you can change the Palm screen to be the size it will appear on the Palm device.

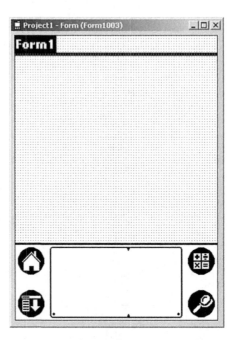

Figure 5-8. The Form Layout window in the NS Basic IDE

NOTE   *Although changing the screen size can be cool, after a while (and a few errant clicks later) it can get annoying. NS Basic should add the ability to disable this feature, but unfortunately it doesn't.*

The standard Palm OS device supports a screen resolution of 160×160. A location on the screen is described using x and y coordinates (0 through 159 respectively). One nice feature is that NS Basic supports a title bar. Unlike some of the other programming tools for the Palm, you do not have to draw the title for each form.

Controlling the IDE

Controlling the IDE is quite simple. Access the Options dialog box from the main menus (Tools I Options) in order to tweak the user interface (UI) to your heart's content. This dialog box contains the General, Editor, Palm Screen, and Compile Download form tabs.

General Tab

The General tab contains the global project path and the path to the POSE. The compiler uses this information for default storage and for opening the POSE. This tab also contains a list for changing the startup behavior of NS Basic (see Figure 5-9).

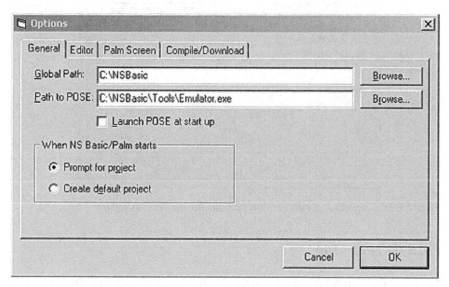

Figure 5-9. The General tab on the Options dialog box for the NS Basic IDE

Editor Tab

The Editor tab contains a single button, Editor Preferences. When you click the button, another window opens to reveal the editor configuration options (see Figure 5-10). The Editor configurations dialog box in NS Basic would be a welcome addition to the Visual Basic IDE. The NS Basic Editor allows for some features not found in the Visual Basic editor, such as column selection.

Figure 5-10. The editor configuration options for the NS Basic IDE

Palm Screen Tab

The next tab, Palm Screen, simply allows the user to configure the Palm simu-lated display window. Here you can change such options as the font, snap to grid, and the grid pixel density (see Figure 5-11).

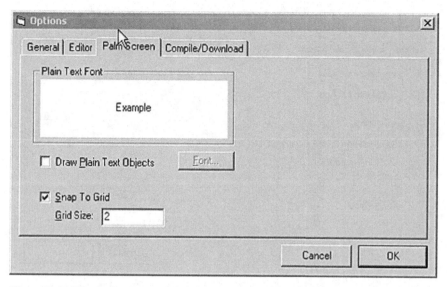

Figure 5-11. The Palm Screen tab on the Options dialog box for the NS Basic IDE

Compile/Download Tab

The final tab, Compile/Download, contains several configuration options. In the first series of checkboxes, you have options for saving the project before compiling, compiling to a "fat" application, and changing to high resolution for HandEra devices. The next section contains settings for controlling the behavior of the NS Basic IDE after the compile process has been completed. These options include sending the compiled program directly to the POSE (if you select this option you can flag it to run immediately upon completion of the compiler), HotSyncing directly to your Palm device, or doing nothing (see Figure 5-12).

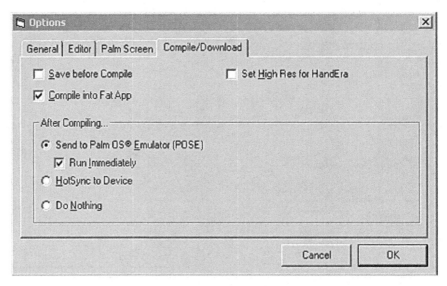

Figure 5-12. The Compile/Download tab on the Options dialog box for the NS Basic IDE

NOTE   *Recall that compiling to a fat application involves binding the NS Basic runtime to the finished PRC.*

Now you are ready to begin writing some code. NS Basic allows you to write code that is fired on startup and on the termination of a program. You can find these options under Projects on the main menu. An example of using the startup code would be loading application preferences, and then upon termination of the program, using the project termination code to write any changed preferences (see Figure 5-13).

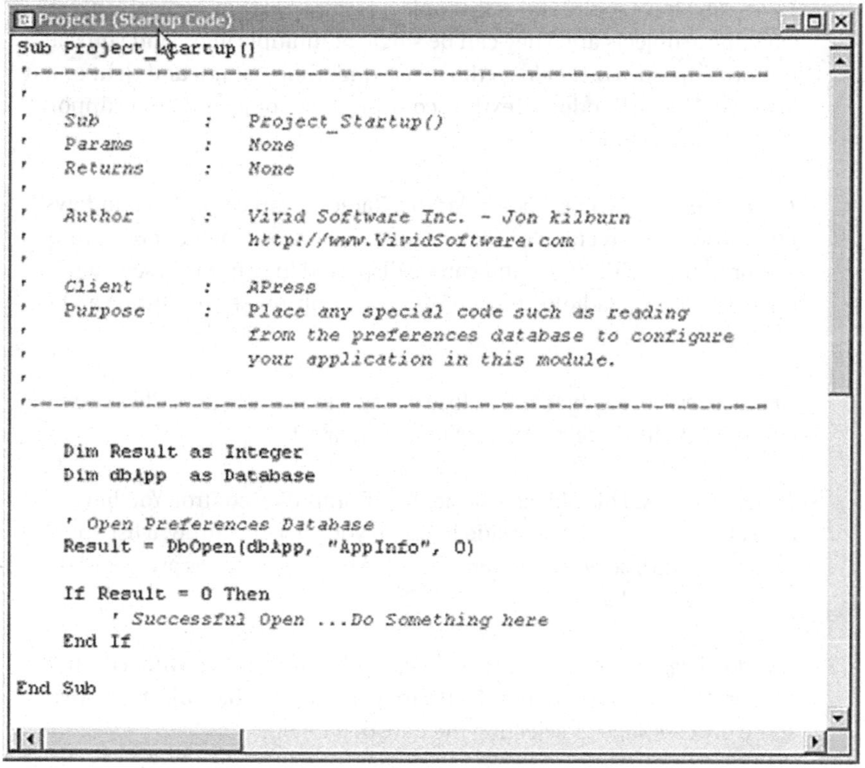

```
Project1 (Startup Code)                                        _ □ ×
Sub Project_Startup()                                            ▲
' _-_-_-_-_-_-_-_-_-_-_-_-_-_-_-_-_-_-_-_-_-_-_-_-_-_-_-_-_-_-_-
'
'    Sub        :    Project_Startup()
'    Params     :    None
'    Returns    :    None
'
'    Author     :    Vivid Software Inc. - Jon kilburn
'                    http://www.VividSoftware.com
'
'    Client     :    APress
'    Purpose    :    Place any special code such as reading
'                    from the preferences database to configure
'                    your application in this module.
'
' _-_-_-_-_-_-_-_-_-_-_-_-_-_-_-_-_-_-_-_-_-_-_-_-_-_-_-_-_-_-_-

     Dim Result as Integer
     Dim dbApp  as Database

     ' Open Preferences Database
     Result = DbOpen(dbApp, "AppInfo", 0)

     If Result = 0 Then
          ' Successful Open ...Do Something here
     End If

End Sub
                                                                ▼
 ◄                                                              ►
```

Figure 5-13. The code window in the NS Basic IDE

Understanding the Screen Objects

Currently, Palm supports the following 13 screen objects, which are akin to
ActiveX controls in Standard Visual Basic:

- *Buttons:* These are oval-shaped objects, which have a label and function
  very much like their Windows counterparts. When a button is clicked,
  some associated action is fired.

- *Lists:* These objects are cousins of the Windows ListBox control. Items are
  presented in separate rows. If more items are in the list than can be displayed on the screen, a scrollbar appears allowing the user to scroll the
  entire list.

- *Labels:* These objects contain text and function like Windows labels.

- *Fields:* All I have to say about this object is think TextBox control. That's what these objects are. They can be single or multiple lines, and you can set the properties of a field so the text is underlined or not and right or left justified. Unlike Windows TextBox controls, these objects do not support tab or return characters.

- *PushButtons:* This object is similar to a RadioButton control in Windows, but is drawn as a rectangle. A PushButton is always a member of a group of two or more PushButtons and can be displayed in two states, selected or unselected. Like RadioButtons in Windows, only one PushButton can be highlighted at a time.

- *Checkboxes:* These objects are close cousins to the Windows CheckBox controls and indicate a setting of either on or off.

- *Popup Triggers:* This object is basically a ComboBox control. You have a text field with an arrow beside it. When you click the arrow, a list appears. When you have selected an item from the list, this list goes away and the new item is displayed.

- *Selector Triggers:* These objects at first appear to be a label with a dotted border. The dotted border indicates that clicking on this object will invoke some process such as selecting the date or a time.

- *Bitmaps:* A graphic display object used for picture displays in a variety of color depths.

- *Gadgets:* These objects are a bit more complicated to explain. Gadgets have no visual properties, and once dropped on the screen are represented by nothing more than a simple rectangle. Any graphical display information must be handled by you as the programmer.

- *Repeating Buttons:* Unlike a standard Button object, which fires an event only once when tapped, this object continues to fire events while the user holds the stylus down on it.

- *Scrollbars:* These objects function like their Windows brethren, providing a means to control directional movement.

- *Graffiti Shift Indicator:* Any form with editable text fields should also contain the Graffiti Shift Indicator. The indicator allows the user to select a Graffiti shift state such as punctuation, symbol, uppercase shift, and uppercase lock.

The NS Basic objects are based on the underlying Palm OS objects. You build NS Basic programs using the same building blocks as the built-in apps. This makes NS Basic programs small and efficient, with a real Palm look and feel. Another advantage is that in doing so NS Basic has attempted to ensure its compatibility with future OS versions.

Working with Menus

In Windows it's a common practice to use a menu for assigning and grouping actions. Not surprisingly a variation of menus is supported by NS Basic. It is interesting to note that a menu is really a screen object, yet does not appear within the toolbox as an option; instead it can be found on the Standard toolbar or under the Tools menu option.

Creating a Menu

Menus provide a way to access multiple commands without occupying too much screen real estate. Each menu should contain one or more menu items, to which a command should be associated. You can visually group items using a separator bar, just like in Windows. Menus themselves are contained within a menu bar, and there can only be one menu bar per form. Follow these steps to create a new menu:

1. Select either the Menu Editor option from the Tools menu or click the icon on the standard toolbar. Or, click the menu icon on the lower-left of the Palm screen. If no menus currently exist, you will be prompted to enter the name of a new menu.

2. Once you enter the name of the new menu, the Menu Editor window will open (see Figure 5-14). When you have created the menu element, press the Next button to insert more menu bar elements. You may choose to insert a submenu under each top menu bar option by using the Insert Dropdown button.

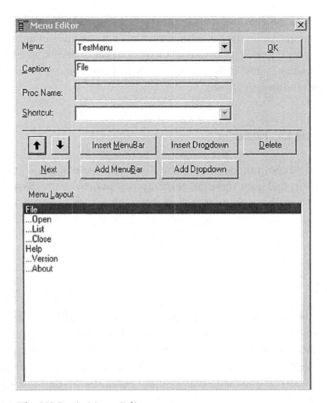

Figure 5-14. The NS Basic Menu Editor

3. When you have finished building the menu, click the OK button to save it. This menu will now appear in the Project Explorer window under the Menus listing. Once the menu has been saved, you can view it by selecting it in the Project Explorer (see Figure 5-15).

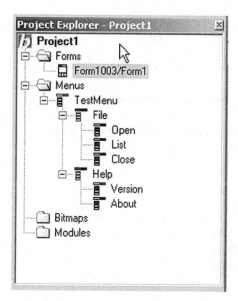

Figure 5-15. The menu opened in the Project Explorer

Attaching a Menu to a Form

Although creating the menu is easy, there is no way from within the IDE to attach the menu directly to a form. This is a Palm OS issue, not an NS Basic problem. Palm's reasoning is that in doing so it allows the possibility of multiple menus for one form, or the reuse of menus across other forms. Instead, to attach a menu to a form, you must use the MenuDraw function (see Listing 5-1).

Listing 5-1. MenuSample Code from the Form to Draw the Menu

```
Sub Form1003_Event()
'-=-=-=-=-=-=-=-=-=-=-=-=-=-=-=-=-=-=-=-=-=-=-=-=-=-=-=-=-=-=-=-=-=
'
'    Sub        :    Form1003_Event()
'    Params     :    None
'    Returns    :    None
'
'    Author     :    Vivid Software Inc. - Jon Kilburn
'                    http://www.VividSoftware.com
'
```

```
'   Client      :   Apress
'   Purpose     :   Draw the Sample Menu
'
'-=-=-=-=-=-=-=-=-=-=-=-=-=-=-=-=-=-=-=-=-=-=-=-=-=-=-=-=-=

    ' Check Event Type for Key or Buttons
    ' Events Only
    If Not GetEventType()= nsbKeyOrButton Then
        Exit Sub
    End If

    ' Deal with Key Values
    If Asc(GetKey()) = MenuKeyOnSilkScreen Then
        ' Draw the Sample Menu
        MenuDraw "TestMenu"
        SetEventHandled
    End If
End Sub
```

Opening a Code Window

In the process of attaching a menu, you will also discover one of the little quirks of the NS Basic IDE. Most VB programmers know that by double-clicking a form or control, the VB IDE will open a code window; they can also select View | Code or click the View Code Icon at the top of the Project Explorer to do the same thing. This behavior is not mimicked exactly in NS Basic. Instead (depending on the object), there are several ways to get to the code window. One way is to double-click the control in the Project Explorer, or you can right-click and from the supplied menu (it is different based on the select object) choose the code to edit.

The FormXXXX_Event subroutine shown in Listing 5-1 is very powerful. In fact, almost every Palm event is passed to this routine. The exceptions are any events handled otherwise by NS Basic and most internal OS events. Any events generated by external routines such as shared libraries or non-Palm devices will be passed through.

All screen taps get passed through, which is why you check to see what kind of event it is. Events that you don't handle completely will then be handled by the OS. To stop the OS from taking action as well, you use the SetEventHandled function. For example, the Calculator button sends an event to the Form Events code. If you choose to intercept it and issue a SetEventHandled function, you could prevent the calculator from coming up.

Using Constants

Next, consider the use of constants. Many of you probably noticed the MenuKeyOnSilkScreen value. This value is actually a constant. Although VB programmers have grown accustomed to the familiar Const within their code, the use of the Const declaration does not exist in NS Basic. Instead, you use the Global declaration. You should place these either in the Project Startup or in a module. Listing 5-2 uses the Project Startup where the value is declared and set as well.

Listing 5-2. Code to Set the Constant Values in Project Startup

```
Global MenuKeyOnSilkScreen as Integer   ' Menu Key On SilkScreen Area
Sub Project_Startup()
'-=-=-=-=-=-=-=-=-=-=-=-=-=-=-=-=-=-=-=-=-=-=-=-=-=-=-=-=-=
'
'   Sub         :   Project_Startup()
'   Params      :   None
'   Returns     :   None
'
'   Author      :   Vivid Software Inc. - Jon Kilburn
'                   http://www.VividSoftware.com
'
'   Client      :   Apress
'   Purpose     :   Set Variable
'
'-=-=-=-=-=-=-=-=-=-=-=-=-=-=-=-=-=-=-=-=-=-=-=-=-=-=-=-=-=


    ' Set the Value of MenuOnSilkScreen
    MenuKeyOnSilkScreen = 5

End Sub
```

What's interesting about this is that a Global is a variable type, which means that you've created a variable, rather than just supplying a marker for the preprocessor.

Constants (in the VB, Delphi, or C type compiler) are replaced by the preprocessor. The preprocessor is a process that runs through all your code, finds any declared constants, and replaces them with the actual constant value (it also removes comments, formats, and does a few other things as well). For an example, see Listing 5-3.

Listing 5-3. Code for Constants

```
' Array Offset Constant
Const eFirstName = 0
Const eLastName = 1
Const eSSN = 2

' Declare Array
Dim aUser(2) As String

Public Sub ReadValues()
'-=-=-=-=-=-=-=-=-=-=-=-=-=-=-=-=-=-=-=-=-=-=-=-=-=-=-=-=-=-=-=
'
'   Sub        :    ReadValues()
'   Params     :    None
'   Returns    :    None
'
'   Author     :    Vivid Software Inc. - Jon Kilburn
'                   http://www.VividSoftware.com
'
'   Client     :    Apress
'   Purpose    :    Save the Contents of an Array
'
'-=-=-=-=-=-=-=-=-=-=-=-=-=-=-=-=-=-=-=-=-=-=-=-=-=-=-=-=-=-=-=

        If aUser(eFirstName) = "Jon" And aUser(eLastName) = "Kilburn" Then
                ' Do Something
                MsgBox "AAAARRGH!"
        End If
End Sub
```

Although simple enough, if you've ever seen the results of code after it has been run through a preprocessor, it would look like this:

```
Dim aUser(2) As String
Public Sub ReadValues()
    If aUser(0) = "Jon" And aUser(1) = "Kilburn" Then
        MsgBox "AAAARRGH!"
    End If
End Sub
```

Well, okay, it would probably not be as well formatted and most likely everything would be on the same line, but you get the point. However, whereas Public variables use memory in Windows and VB, Global variables under NS Basic and the Palm OS are a bit different. The way Palm memory works, it's necessary to keep all constants, literals, and variables in the symbol table. There's just no room for them in the dynamic heap (which can be as little as 40KB). So, the use of a Global variable instead of a constant does not affect your dynamic heap memory consumption.

Attaching Code to a Menu Item Click Event

The next step is attaching code to a menu item click event. Open the Menu folder in the Project Explorer and expand it. Locate the menu bar option that you wish to attach code to. If you double-click the menu item, it will open a code window. Place your menu code in this window (see Listing 5-4).

Listing 5-4. Menu Event Code Linked to a Menu Item

```
Sub Menu1010_click()
'-=-=-=-=-=-=-=-=-=-=-=-=-=-=-=-=-=-=-=-=-=-=-=-=-=-=-=-=-=
'
'    Sub         :    Menu1010_Click()
'    Params      :    None
'    Returns     :    None
'
'    Author      :    Vivid Software Inc. - Jon Kilburn
'                     http://www.VividSoftware.com
'
'    Client      :    Apress
'    Purpose     :    Code to Deal with the Open Menu Click
'
'-=-=-=-=-=-=-=-=-=-=-=-=-=-=-=-=-=-=-=-=-=-=-=-=-=-=-=-=-=


    ' Display a Message box
    MsgBox "Open A File."


End Sub
```

Once you have entered all the event code you can, click the Compile button and, depending on how you have configured your POSE and compiler settings, the POSE should start with the Menu Sample application (see Figure 5-16).

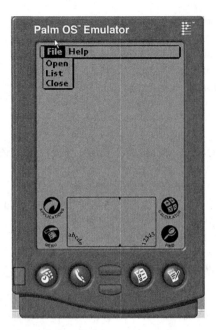

Figure 5-16. The Menu Sample application

Writing the Exit Code

The final piece of the puzzle is to write the exit code. This step contradicts the Palm Programming Guidelines, but is being done here to expose you to handling menu events and using a few more of NS Basic functions. To do this you need to use a slightly different approach. Since NS Basic's MsgBox function accepts only one parameter (which is the string to be displayed), you cannot confirm the user's desire to exit your menu program using this function. (This conforms to the Palm OS standards, not to VB's use of the MsgBox function.) Instead, NS Basic has provided you with another function, Alert(). The Alert function accepts several parameters: the title, a message string, type of alert box, and a variable number of buttons. The type of alert box can be one of the following:

- 0 = Displays an information type of alert box

- 1 = Displays a confirmation type of alert box

- 2 = Displays a warning type of alert box

- 3 = Displays an error type of alert box

To make the standard type of confirm exit message box, you simply attach the check to the File | Close menu item click. The Alert function returns the value of the button that was clicked so that you simply need to check for the button that corresponds to your confirmation of "yes" (see Listing 5-5).

Listing 5-5. The Confirm Exit Code in the Menu Close Click Event

```
Sub Menu1009_click()
'-=-=-=-=-=-=-=-=-=-=-=-=-=-=-=-=-=-=-=-=-=-=-=-=-=-=-=-=-=-=
'
'   Sub        :   Menu1009_Click()
'   Params     :   None
'   Returns    :   None
'
'   Author     :   Vivid Software Inc. - Jon Kilburn
'                      http://www.VividSoftware.com
'
'   Client     :   Apress
'   Purpose    :   Code to End the Program
'
'-=-=-=-=-=-=-=-=-=-=-=-=-=-=-=-=-=-=-=-=-=-=-=-=-=-=-=-=-=-=
    Dim nResult as Integer  ' Store the Return Result

    ' Display a Message box
    nResult = Alert("Confirm Exit", "Exit this menu sample?", 1, "Yes", "No")

    ' Determine Result
    If nResult = 0
        ' End Program
        Stop
    End If

End Sub
```

Working with Screen Objects

Now that you have experimented with menus and learned a bit about the NS Basic compiler, it's time to write your first program. You'll build a simple application to calculate the daily production rate for piecework assembly. It will take the number of pieces that are assembled in a minute and then calculate the assembled production estimates for one hour and for a standard eight-hour work day. Begin by creating a new project in NS Basic as follows:

1. Name the application ProductCalc.

2. Create the main calculation form by renaming the default Form1 form to frmMain.

3. Change the title of the Form to Production Calculator.

4. Select a Label control and drop it on the form layout. Change the Font ID to 7 – Large Bold.

5. Now add three more labels, and change their Label properties so that they read Per Minute, Per Hour, and Per Shift.

6. Next insert a field. For the Per Minute label name, make the associated field txtMinute. Change the Numeric property to True. This will prevent any character entry.

7. Drop two more labels on the form. Name these LabelHour (across from the Per Hour label) and LabelShift (across from the Per Shift label). Finally, make sure that the .Label property contains a string large enough to hold the calculated values. For example "   0". A point that should be made here is that the total number of characters that are in the label at compile time will be the number of characters that can be placed in the label.

8. Add two buttons and place them in the bottom-right corner of the screen. Change one of the button label properties to Close[2] and the other to Calculate. Set the width of both buttons to 46.

Now you are ready to add the calculation code (see Listing 5-6). You know there are sixty minutes in an hour and eight hours in a shift. So to calculate the pieces per hour, multiply the contents of txtMinute by a value of 60. Take the resulting value and multiply it by eight, which will yield the number of estimated pieces per shift. Finally, write the resulting values into the Label property of the two labels, LabelHour and LabelShift.

---

[2] Again I'm violating Palm OS UI standards.

Listing 5-6. The Code to Calculate the Number of Pieces

```
Sub object1017()
'-=-=-=-=-=-=-=-=-=-=-=-=-=-=-=-=-=-=-=-=-=-=-=-=-=-=-=-=-=-=-=
'
'    Sub        :    object1017()
'    Params     :    None
'    Returns    :    None
'
'    Author     :    Vivid Software Inc. - Jon Kilburn
'                    http://www.VividSoftware.com
'
'    Client     :    Apress
'    Purpose    :    Calculate the number of pieces per hour,
'                    and per shift.
'
'-=-=-=-=-=-=-=-=-=-=-=-=-=-=-=-=-=-=-=-=-=-=-=-=-=-=-=-=-=-=-=
    Dim nHour   as Integer
    Dim nShift  as Integer


    ' Calculate
    If txtMinute.Text = "" Then
        ' Must have a valid value
        MsgBox "Please enter the number of pieces."
        Exit Sub
    Else
        ' Calculate per hour (60 minutes in an hour)
        nHour = Val(txtMinute.Text) * 60

        ' Per Shift (8 Hours per shift)
        nShift = (nHour * 8)

        ' Fill in the labels
        LabelHour.Label = Str(nHour)
        LabelShift.Label = Str(nShift)
    End If

    ' Redraw the Screen
    Redraw
End Sub
```

Once you have completed the code, you can now run the resulting NS Basic application. Select Run | Compile ProductCalc. The project will be compiled and then uploaded to the POSE (see Figure 5-17).

Figure 5-17. The NS Basic Production Calculator application

Conclusion

This chapter gave you a brief overview of how the NS Basic compiler works and how to use it to build menus and even an application. It also discussed the basic principals behind how to compile, install, and test your NS Basic application in the Palm environment.

CHAPTER 6

Building the GolfPro Application Using NS Basic

MOST PALM SOLUTIONS ARE composed of two pieces, the handheld application portion and the desktop conduit portion. In this next section, I am going to focus on building the handheld application portion of the Palm application. (Conduits are covered in Chapter 9.)

As a practical exercise, I will take you step by step through creating an application for keeping track of your golf game at a given golf course. Although I don't play golf much (and I'm certainly not very good at it), I do like to see how much I can improve my game and at which courses I'm shooting the best score—thus the focus of the example application. This simple application will require a few tables, some graphics, and a couple of simple lookups as well as reading and writing operations to Palm database files.

The Project Outline

First let's review the basic functionality of what you want to accomplish with what I am calling the Portable GolfPro application. If you don't play the game of golf, or if you do but it doesn't show from your scores (this is the category I fall into), I'll briefly explain the rules of the game, which are quite simple.

Often a game of golf is played at a golf club, or at a public golf course. These courses generally have a name and 18 holes. (Although I've heard that there are some courses that have only 9 holes, I've never seen one. And for those of you wondering, *yes*, it would improve my game.) Each hole is then assigned a par. A *par* is the number of shots required to sink the golf ball into the cup on the green. If you can achieve the feat of getting the ball into the cup in the required number of shots, you have achieved par on that hole.

It is from the par on each hole that the figure for *par for the course* is calculated. To determine this number, you add up the number of strokes required to play each course, and that is how you calculate your level of play. If you can finish the course in the same number of strokes as the scorecard indicates, then you have *broken even.* The goal is to save as many strokes as possible to complete the course at even par or perhaps (in the make-believe world where I can actually play this frustrating game) under par.

Okay, so now you know the rules if you hadn't already. Generally speaking, there are a few aspects to the game that you want to include in this application:

- *The courses:* Before you can play a golf game, you have to determine which golf course you will be playing on. Clubs often contain more than one golf course, but for the purposes of this example, each course is independent of an actual golf club.

- *The course scorecard:* The course scorecard contains the par setting (or number of strokes allowed to put the ball in the hole before applying a penalty of a lost stroke). When you play a hole of golf, you are allowed *x* number of strokes to complete the hole. If you complete the hole before using the allotted number of strokes, you are *under par.* If you sink the ball in the required number of strokes, you have *made par.* And if you sink the ball two strokes less than required, you have made *an eagle.* Finally, if you sink a ball in only one shot, you have made a *hole in one.*

- *Course scoring:* This is the individual scorecard you carry for each course as you play it. When you play a hole, you enter the number of strokes required to get the ball in the hole. This is also called a scorecard, but it refers to each individual's game.

- *Course notes:* When you play a course, you might wish to make notes about a particularly tough hole, say, about a bad dog leg (sharp bend) on the fourth hole. You may want to record that the best way to play this Par 4 hole is to get to the green in two strokes, and which particular club you recommend for your tee shot.

On to Palm Database Files

Databases on a Palm device are similar to files on a desktop computer, except that the Palm OS databases reside inside the RAM of the device instead of on a permanent storage media such as a hard drive. Using functions in NS Basic you can create, open, update, and delete database files and records easily.

Databases organize related records; every record belongs to one and only one database. A database may be a collection of all address book entries, all datebook entries, and so on. A Palm OS application can create, delete, open, and close databases as necessary, just as a traditional file system can create, delete, open, and close a traditional file.

The Portable GolfPro program will need a simple database. Now I know you are possibly going to read this and later e-mail me a better database design, but I'm not trying to create a great database design. Understand this: Palm database (PDB) files are essentially the same as good old fashion DBF files. You may remember them—DBase made them popular in the '80s and early '90s, before SQL really became mainstream for the PC.

Well, here's what you have to keep in mind. These files need to be small and efficient, not always in the best third normal form design, because you will have to open each table, maintain a handle, and seek your results. What do I mean by this? Hang on, and I'll show you a little later.

First, let's get some of the basics about PDB files out of the way. Palm database files are akin to flat files, not relational files. This means as the programmer, you are responsible for keeping track of relationships and cleaning up after yourself. Now, quite a few DB* functions exist within NS Basic, and there are several ways to create PDB files.

NOTE *Lucky for you I'm lazy. I like Access for creating my database files, and thankfully so did somebody on the NS Basic Yahoo forum because they posted an ActiveX COM DLL for creating Palm database files from the PC. The DLL comes with a help file and a readme file.*

Structure of a Palm Database File

Although you will probably not need to open a PDB file at the binary level and understand the structure of the file much beyond the basics, it is still a good idea to know a few things about how a PDB file is structured.

A database header consists of some basic database information and a list of records in the database. Each record entry in the header has the local ID of the record, 8 attribute bits, and a 3-byte unique ID for the record, for a total of 78 bytes:

FIELD	BYTES
DB Name	32
Flags	2
Version	2
Creation Time	4
Modification Time	4
Backup Time	4
Modification Number	4
App Info Offset	4
Sort Info Offset	4
Type (Database ID)	4
Creator (Application ID)	4
Unique ID Seed	4
Next Record List ID	4
Number of Records	2

This is followed by a table of record entries, which consists of 8 bytes. The first 4 bytes make up the offset of the record (n) from the beginning of the file, the next byte makes up the record attributes and the last 3 bytes contain the record unique ID (I'll discuss these more at length in the latter part of the chapter).

The first table you should create will be the Courses table. This table, which will contain each course and the par value for each hole, has to be created first because you need to use it before all the other related tables. You have several options for creating this table (including using a PDB file creation utility for the PC), but the easiest way is to do so through code using the DBCreate[1] function of NS Basic. The parameters for the DBCreate function, as demonstrated in the code that follows, are the database variable, the name of the database as a string, the memory card where the database file should reside (this is almost always 0), and finally the CreatorID (more on this shortly).

```
nResult = dbCreate(dbCourse, "Course", 0, "JONK")
```

---

[1] A complete, detailed description of using all the DB* functions appears in the NS Basic manual. There are also several example programs that ship with the product which demonstrate the DB* function capabilities.

However, before you can even create the table, your program must be able to determine that the file for the table does not exist. To test for the existence of a file, you simply have to attempt to open it. Under NS Basic, you have a specific data type known as Database.[2] Conceptually, this data type functions similarly to the OPEN statement in VB, which is used to open a handle to a file. Before any action can take place against a file, the function must be provided with the database "handle" so that it knows which table to apply actions to.

When you attempt to open a file that does not exist, you'll get back the result code 519.[3] Once you have detected the error, you can now create the database.

```
' Open Course Database
nResult = dbOpen(dbCourse, "Courses", 0)

' Check Result
If nResult <> 0 Then
    ' Check for File Not Found which indicates
    ' we need to create the database
    If nResult = 519 Then
        ' File does not exist so create it
        nResult = DBCreate(dbCourse, "Courses", 0, "JONK")
        ' Check result
        If nResult <> 0 Then
            GoTo Trap
        End If
    End If
End If
```

The second table will be the ScoreCard table. The ScoreCard table will be related to the Courses table by the field CourseID.

The third table will be the Player table. The Player table will be related to the Courses table by the PlayerID. The idea here is that you can now track a player's score on a golf course based on any given date. Later if you wished, you could then chart a player's improvement (or in the case of my golf game, deterioration).

The fourth and final table is the CourseNotes table. This table is related to a course by the CourseID. You will also add the hole as an integer (that is, 1–18) to help you read any notes on a course you may have made.

Below are the table layouts for each of the files needed by the Portable GolfPro system (Figure 6-1).

---

[2] NS Basic does not support all the same variable types as VB. Refer to the DIM statement in the Help file for a listing of the supported data types.
[3] For a complete list of the DB* functions return codes, refer to the DBOPEN function in the help file.

Course Notes	
NotesID	Autonumber
CourseID	Long
Hole	Integer
Notes	Text

ScoreCard	
ScoreID	Autonumber
CourseID	Long
PlayerID	Long
GameDate	Date
Hole1	Integer
Hole2	Integer
Hole3	Integer
Hole4	Integer
Hole5	Integer
Hole6	Integer
Hole7	Integer
Hole8	Integer
Hole9	Integer
Hole10	Integer
Hole11	Integer
Hole12	Integer
Hole13	Integer
Hole14	Integer
Hole15	Integer
Hole16	Integer
Hole17	Integer
Hole18	Integer
FinalScore	Integer

Courses Table	
CourseID	Autonumber
Course_Name	Text
Hole1Par	Integer
Hole2Par	Integer
Hole3Par	Integer
Hole4Par	Integer
Hole5Par	Integer
Hole6Par	Integer
Hole7Par	Integer
Hole8Par	Integer
Hole9Par	Integer
Hole10Par	Integer
Hole11Par	Integer
Hole12Par	Integer
Hole13Par	Integer
Hole14Par	Integer
Hole15Par	Integer
Hole16Par	Integer
Hole17Par	Integer
Hole18Par	Integer

Player	
PlayerID	Autonumber
FirstName	Text
LastName	Text
Handicap	Integer

Figure 6-1. The tables in the Portable GolfPro application

Earlier when I showed you the code to create a database using NS Basic, I mentioned the CreatorID. In order to differentiate databases, two unique identifiers are assigned to each database. The CreatorID and Type are both user-defined values that help to identify a database.

The CreatorID is a unique identifier for a Palm OS application. If two applications on one Palm OS device have the same CreatorID, one of the applications will simply not show up.

This is why Palm asks for the CreatorID for every distributed application to be registered with Palm's "official" list. CreatorIDs that are all lowercase are reserved exclusively for Palm; otherwise, the four characters may consist of any ASCII characters from 33 to 127.

NOTE *The address for looking up and registering CreatorIDs is* http://www.palmos.com/dev/tech/palmos/creatorid/.

The CreatorID for a database and the application it belongs to should always be the same. This ensures that the database will be deleted if the application is deleted. In most cases, the Database type should be set to DATA. If one application has multiple databases, the CreatorID and the Type should be the same for all of the databases. Palm only uses the name of the table to distinguish between the various PDBs for an application.

Working with a PDB file is just like working with a file opened with the Open Statement in Visual Basic:

```
Open (Insert file name) For Input as #Handle
```

When you open a text file in Visual Basic, you store the file handle in a memory variable. When you wish to perform operations on that file (such as checking for EOF, reading a record, and so on), we must use the handle and pass it to the requested action.

```
Do While Not EOF(Handle)
    buffer = Space(120)
    Line Input #Handle, buffer
    cOutString = cOutString & vbCrlf & buffer
Loop
```

PDBs work the same way. Use the database handle to pass it to a function or to perform an operation. NS Basic has a series of DB* functions for all PDB file access. You can discern pretty much what each function does from its name. For example, DBOpen is used to open a file, whereas DBClose is used to close a file, and so on.

Database Sorting

Although NS Basic provides a good set of functions for dealing with PDB files, one feature that is not present is the capability to sort the database on any column other than the first key column.

This is partly due to the fact that you can store whatever you want in your Palm OS database. As far as the OS is concerned, a record is just a series of bytes. NS Basic does not store record schema information. This brings us to the issue of how to perform a sort.

Although you can sort records using a standard sort routine or algorithm such as a bubble or shell sort (examples of which can be found on the NS Basic Yahoo Groups forum), there is also one other way you can use. In the days of DBF files, there existed a second file type, the index file.

Index files were created by taking the field, which represents the requested sort, and then creating a new database that contained only the key (in sorted order) and then a pointer (either a record number or physical offset) back to the original database. Consider the following example:

A customer table contains customer IDs (key), customer first names, and customer last names. When the PDB file was created, the first column was defined as the customer ID field. Into this field the primary key was stored. Now suppose you want to sort the database by a field other than the customer ID— for example, by the last name (which would be convenient for searching for customers by their last names). This now presents a problem, as NS Basic only recognizes the first field as the key field.

The solution is to create a second PDB file (let's call this file the customer index file), and into that file you would write the last name to the first field position (which now makes the last name field the key for the customer index table) and then the customer ID. This way the database is "sorted" by the last name, and the customer ID is also stored so that when a customer is found by his or her last name you could immediately go search for that customer in the master (customer) database using the correct customer ID.

There are two major drawbacks to this method:

- *Size:* You must now keep a second database of redundant information.
- *Complexity:* Now when you insert, delete, or modify a record, you must also take care to properly update the customer index table as well. Failure to do so will cause records to be out of sync with the master customer database.

Is there a better solution? There are several ways to increase the speed of the performance of sorted tables, and you could also devise a schema that could be stored in a PDB file's AppInfo block to improve performance.

There are two ways you can access a record in NS Basic. The first is to have a nonkeyed database. Although this is the simplest method of writing to a database, it is also the more difficult of the two to maintain. The way nonkeyed database records work is by seeking an offset position (a la dbPosition) and then reading or writing the contents using the dbPut or dbGet functions. When data is written using the dbPut method, the pointer is positioned at the end of the last piece of data. Likewise, when the data is read in using dbGet, the pointer is positioned at the end of the piece of data.

The second method is to use a keyed database. Writing to a keyed database is just a matter of providing a unique number or ID (referred to as a key) for each record. NS Basic keeps track of the key information inside the PDB file header, along with the information for offsets into the file where data is then stored. This means that if you want to find a value by the key field, all you have to do is search by that key. In a nonkeyed database, you would need to do a sequential search or first perform a sort routine and then search the sorted results. I have found that for most uses, the keyed database approach works best, and I will be demonstrating the use of it here.

That said, the easiest way to read and write data into your database is to read the contents of a PDB record into a memory structure. It is from this memory structure that you can read the data or make changes. Once you have completed your work with the memory structure, you can either discard it or update the PDB record with the new data. Listing 6-1 shows an example of creating the UDT for keeping track of the Course record. UDT definitions should be placed in the startup code or in a module within the NS Basic IDE.

Listing 6-1. Code for the UDT Definition of a Course PDB Record

```
'-=-=-=-=-=-=-=-=-=-=-=-=-=-=-=-=-=-=-=-=-=-=-=-=-=-=-=-=-=-=-=-=
'
'    Sub        :   Main()
'    Params     :   None
'    Returns    :   None
'
'    Author     :   Vivid Software Inc. - Jon Kilburn
'                       http://www.VividSoftware.com
'
'    Client     :   Apress
'    Purpose    :   Startup, declare types and globals
'
'-=-=-=-=-=-=-=-=-=-=-=-=-=-=-=-=-=-=-=-=-=-=-=-=-=-=-=-=-=-=-=-=
    Global dbCourse    as Database   ' Courses Database
    ' Course Record layout
    Type tCoursesRecord
CourseID      as Integer   ' Course Internal ID
Course_Name as String     ' Name of the CourseHole1Par    as Integer   ' Hole 1 Par
Hole2Par     as Integer   ' Hole 2 Par
Hole3Par     as Integer   ' Hole 3 ParHole4Par     as Integer   ' Hole 4
ParHole5Par       as Integer    ' Hole 5 Par
Hole6Par     as Integer   ' Hole 6 Par
        Hole7Par     as Integer   ' Hole 7 Par
        Hole8Par     as Integer   ' Hole 8 Par
        Hole9Par     as Integer   ' Hole 9 Par
```

```
        Hole10Par   as Integer   ' Hole 10 Par
        Hole11Par   as Integer   ' Hole 11 Par
        Hole12Par   as Integer   ' Hole 12 Par
        Hole13Par   as Integer   ' Hole 13 Par
        Hole14Par   as Integer   ' Hole 14 Par
        Hole15Par   as Integer   ' Hole 15 Par
        Hole16Par   as Integer   ' Hole 16 Par
        Hole17Par   as Integer   ' Hole 17 Par
        Hole18Par   as Integer   ' Hole 18 Par
    End Type
```

In NS Basic, almost all functions return a value. It is from this value that you can then deduce the result of the called function. Some returns are simply 0 or –1, others (such as the DB functions) return the actual error code result. See Table 6-1 for the list of error codes.

Table 6-1. DB Operation Error Codes

VALUE	DESCRIPTION
-1	EOF on DbGet
0	Operation Successful
1	Operation Failed
2	Key Not Found—Next Higher Key Returned
513	Memory Error
514	Index Out of Range
515	Invalid Param
516	Read Only
517	Database Open
518	Can't Open
519	Can't Find
520	Record in Wrong Card
521	Corrupt Database
522	Record Deleted
523	Record Archived
524	Not Record DB
525	Not Resource DB
526	ROM Based or Invalid Database Name
527	Record Busy
528	Resource Not Found

529	No Open Database
530	Invalid Category
531	Not Valid Record
532	Write Out of Bounds
533	Seek Failed
534	Already Open for Writes
535	Opened by Another Task
536	UniqueID Not Found
537	Already Exists
538	Invalid Database Name
539	Database Protected
540	Database Not Protected

Let's review a few of the items of interest within Listing 6-1. The first item of importance is that a Global handle is used for this file and the data type for this is Database. A good rule of thumb is to name database variables starting with a value db plus the name of the table. In this case, dbCourses is used.

Now let's talk about the code required to open a Palm database file and work with it inside an NS Basic application. There are five primary functions you want to use (other than dbOpen and dbClose): dbReset, dbFind, dbInsert, dbRead, and dbReadNext.

User-Defined Types

User-defined data types (referred to as UDTs in Visual Basic, *structures* in languages such as C and C++, and *records* in general scenarios) are groups of related data items declared as one type of information. User-defined data types are very useful when you want to group several related pieces of information in a structured way, as shown in this example:

```
Public Type tCar
    CarMake     As String
    CarModel    As String
    CarYear     As String
    EngineSize  As Integer
    Torque      As Integer
    WheelBase   As Integer
End Type
```

As you can see, this is a very simple layout, and it looks much like a database structure in Access, or even a class structure. And this is the easiest way to think of a UDT—as a record structure.

Here is the example of opening the Courses database and loading the records into a List control. Please note that there are several things that go on when loading this form. If you open the GolfPro project (see Figure 6-2), then you'll notice I use two lists. The first list is the large list of all the courses, whereas the second list is a List control that has its visible property set to false. Unlike VB ListBox and ComboBox controls, NS Basic does not provide an ItemData array property. So to make this work, you need to load the name of the course into the Course List control (lstCourse) and then place the course key (CourseID) into the list of CourseIDs (arrayCourse).

Figure 6-2. The layout of the Course form in the NS Basic IDE

There are three events that you can trap in a standard NS Basic form. The first is the Before event. This event is fired before the form is drawn and visible. In the Before event, you should avoid any operations that update the form's appearance, as they will not work because the controls have not been created yet. The exception to this rule is the List control. You may manipulate this control in the Before event without incident. So in the GolfPro application in the Before event of the Course Browse form, reset the lists as shown in Listing 6-2.

Listing 6-2. Course Browse Form Before Event Code

```
Sub Form1013_Before()
'-=-=-=-=-=-=-=-=-=-=-=-=-=-=-=-=-=-=-=-=-=-=-=-=-=-=-=-=-=
'
'    Sub        :    Form1013_Before()
'    Params     :    None
'    Returns    :    None
'
'    Author     :    Vivid Software Inc. - Jon Kilburn
'                      http://www.VividSoftware.com
'
'    Client     :    Apress
'    Purpose    :    Clears Listboxes
'
'-=-=-=-=-=-=-=-=-=-=-=-=-=-=-=-=-=-=-=-=-=-=-=-=-=-=-=-=-=


    ' Clear the ListBox
    lstCourse.Clear
    arrayCourse.Clear

End Sub
```

Now with the lists cleared, you can open the Course database file and begin loading the data into the lstCourse List control. You do this in the Form After event. In this event, you will open the database, position your pointer at the top of the file, read all the records into the UDT structure, and then populate the List control. Once you have completed loading the List control, you are finished with the database, so close the file and exit the After event (see Listing 6-3).

Listing 6-3. Code to Open the Courses Database File and Load the Lists

```
Sub Form1013_After()
'-=-=-=-=-=-=-=-=-=-=-=-=-=-=-=-=-=-=-=-=-=-=-=-=-=-=-=-=-=
'
'    Sub        :    Form1003_After()
'    Params     :    None
'    Returns    :    None
'
'    Author     :    Vivid Software Inc. - Jon Kilburn
'                      http://www.VividSoftware.com
'
```

```
'   Client      :   Apress
'   Purpose     :   Load Records Into ListBox
'
'-=-=-=-=-=-=-=-=-=-=-=-=-=-=-=-=-=-=-=-=-=-=-=-=-=-=-=-=-=-=-=-=
    Dim nRecCount as Integer        ' Record Count
    Dim cError    as String         ' Error Text
    Dim iOffset   as Integer        ' Offset Into Database
    Dim nResult   as Integer        ' Result of DBReset
    Dim rec       as tCoursesRecord ' Record Structure
    Dim cKey      as String         ' Record Key

    ' Draw Help Bitmap
    DrawBitmap 1015, 144, 0

    ' Open Course Database
    nResult = dbOpen(dbCourse, "Courses", 0)

    ' Check Result
    If nResult <> 0 Then
        ' Check for File Not Found which indicates
        ' we need to create the database
        If nResult = 519 Then
            ' File does not exist so create it
            nResult = DBCreate(dbCourse, "Courses", 0, "JONK")

            ' Check result
            If nResult <> 0 Then
                ' Failed to Create
                cError = ProcessDBOpen(nResult)

                ' Can't really go any further
                MsgBox(cError)
                Stop
            End If

            ' File is Now created, so open it
            nResult = dbOpen(dbCourse, "Courses", 0)

            ' Check result
            If nResult <> 0 Then
                GoTo Trap
            End If
        End If
    End If
```

```
' Return Number of Records
nRecCount = dbGetNoRecs(dbCourse)


' Reset to Start of File
nResult = dbReset(dbCourse)


If nResult > 0 Then
    ' Unable to Reposition
    GoTo Trap
End If


iOffset = 1


' Loop Through, Reading the Records
Do While iOffset <= nRecCount

    ' Read the Next Record
    nResult = dbReadNext(dbCourse, cKey, rec.CourseID, rec.Course_Name, _
        rec.Hole1Par, rec.Hole2Par, rec.Hole3Par, rec.Hole4Par, _
        rec.Hole5Par, rec.Hole6Par, rec.Hole7Par, rec.Hole8Par, _
        rec.Hole9Par, rec.Hole10Par, rec.Hole11Par, rec.Hole12Par, _
        rec.Hole13Par, rec.Hole14Par, rec.Hole15Par, rec.Hole16Par, _
        rec.Hole17Par, rec.Hole18Par)


    ' Process Result
    If nResult > 0 Then
        GoTo Trap
    End If


    ' Add the Items
    lstCourse.Add rec.Course_Name, NODISPLAY


    ' Add to "hidden" array
    arrayCourse.Add Str(rec.CourseID)


    ' Increment Offset
    iOffset = iOffset + 1
Loop


' Close Database
nResult = dbClose(dbCourse)
```

```
                    ' Check Result
                    If nResult > 0 Then
                        GoTo Trap
                    End If

                    ' Select the First Item
                    If lstCourse.NoItems > 0 Then
                        lstCourse.Selected = 1
                        arrayCourse.Selected = 1
                    End If

                    ' Exit Routine
                    Exit Sub

            ' No Support for On Error Goto But
            ' we can still use Line Labels to process
            ' error conditions cleanly
            Trap:
                    ' Check Result
                    If nResult <> 0 Then
                        ' Failed to Create
                        cError = ProcessDBOpen(nResult)

                        ' Can't really go any further
                        MsgBox(cError)
                    End If
            End Sub


            Function ProcessDBOpen(nResult as Integer) as String
            '-=-=-=-=-=-=-=-=-=-=-=-=-=-=-=-=-=-=-=-=-=-=-=-=-=-=-=-=-=
            '
            '   Function    :   ProcessDBOpen( nResult ) - STRING
            '
            '   Params      :   nResult - Value Returned From Failed Open
            '
            '   Author      :   Vivid Software Inc. - Jon Kilburn
            '                       http://www.VividSoftware.com
            '
            '   Client      :   Apress
            '   Purpose     :   Returns Error String for nResult
            '
            '   NOTE        :   This function is only processing those return
            '                       codes which are relevant to a DBopen function
            '
```

```
'                   call, and not those which pertain to other DB
'                   related operations.
'
'-=-=-=-=-=-=-=-=-=-=-=-=-=-=-=-=-=-=-=-=-=-=-=-=-=-=-=
    Dim cError as String

    ' Process Error Result
    Select Case nResult
        Case 513
            ' Memory Error!
            cError = "Memory Error Opening Database!"

        Case 516
            ' Database Read Only
            cError = "Database Is Read Only!"

        Case 517
            ' Database is Already Open
            cError = "Database Already Open!"

        Case 518
            ' Can't Open Database
            cError = "Unable To Open Score Card File"

        Case 520
            ' Database is in another Card
            cError = "Record In Wrong Card"

        Case 521
            ' Database is Corrupted
            cError = "Database is Corrupted!"

        Case 527
            ' Record is busy. . .operation hung?
            cError = "Record is Busy!"

        Case 528
            ' Resource Not Found
            cError = "Resource Not Found!"

        Case 534
            ' Already Open. . .
            cError = "Already Open For Writes!"
```

```
        Case 536
            ' Unique ID is Missing
            cError = "UniqueID Not Found"

        Case 537
            ' File Already Exists
            cError = "Already Exists"

        Case 538
            ' Invalid Database Name
            cError = "Invalid Database Name"

        Case Else
            ' All other errors
            cError = "Error Code = " + Trim(Str(nResult))
    End Select

    ' Return Result
    ProcessDBOpen = cError
End Function
```

The Portable GolfPro Project

Following the steps for creating a new NS Basic application, which I explained in the previous chapter, let's create a new NS Basic application and name it GolfPro. On your first form (Form1), you'll create the standard splash screen. This will give you practice creating a form, placing some text, using a timer, and even placing a picture on it. After you name the project, change the name of Form1 to frmSplash. On the splash form, select the NS Basic Properties window and change the Show Titlebar setting to False. Next, add a Label control, and then place the control on the form and set its Label property to Portable GolfPro 1.0.

Now add a few other controls, starting with a bitmap image. The Bitmap image control in NS Basic (as explained in the prior chapter) does not contain the actual bitmap and is really just a placeholder. So get the bitmap image you wish to insert into the project to serve as the splash screen. Usually the images used will be 1-bit black-and-white images. Some devices allow you to use 2-, 4-, and 8-bit color images, however.

To add a bitmap image (NS Basic also supports .jpg and .gif file types as well), you need to select Project I Add Bitmap from the main menu, or you can right-click in the Project Explorer and select Add > Bitmap (see Figure 6-3).

Figure 6-3. *The properties of a bitmap and adding the bitmap to the GolfPro project*

Once you have selected the bitmap, it will be assigned an ID. Switch back to the frmSplash form and click the Bitmap image control. Next, highlight the Resource ID property and set it to the ID of the bitmap you just added to the GolfPro Project (see Figure 6-4).

Properties - Bitmap1006	
(Name)	Bitmap1006
[ID]	1006
[Type]	Form Bitmap
Height	108
Left	18
Resource ID	1004
Top	16
Visible	True
Width	126

Figure 6-4. *Assigning the newly added bitmap to the Bitmap image control on the frmSplash form*

Now add the code for the timer, shown in Listing 6-4. In this case, since you only have one form, you will end the application when the timer is finished.

Listing 6-4. The Timer Code in the frmSplash Forms After Event

```
Sub Form1003_After()
    '-=-=-=-=-=-=-=-=-=-=-=-=-=-=-=-=-=-=-=-=-=-=-=-=-=-=-=-=-=-=-=
    '
    '    Sub        :    frmSplash_after()
    '    Params     :    None
    '    Returns    :    None
    '
    '    Author     :    Vivid Software Inc. - Jon Kilburn
    '                    http://www.VividSoftware.com
    '
    '    Client     :    Apress
    '    Purpose    :    Delay, then move on
    '
    '-=-=-=-=-=-=-=-=-=-=-=-=-=-=-=-=-=-=-=-=-=-=-=-=-=-=-=-=-=-=-=
    ' Timer of 2 seconds     Delay(2)

    MsgBox("Click To Close This Form.")
    End Sub
```

Figure 6-5 shows the resulting form running in the POSE.

Figure 6-5. The splash screen for the Portable GolfPro Application

Once the Delay function has waited two seconds, you will now call your frmCourseBrowse form, which contains the previous code for loading the golf courses. To call another form in NS Basic, you use the NextForm() function:

```
NextForm("frmCourseBrowse")
```

In the sections of code listed earlier, the record pointer was moved to the first record (though you would think this should happen by default, it does not), then you get the record count of all the records in the database. You will need this record count so that you can process all the records, as you must load them into the list one record at a time.

Next you simply start walking the file by using the DBReadNext function. This function will read the next record in the file into the supplied variable list. You can see that each record is loaded into the tCourseRecord structure defined earlier, and then the course name is loaded into the lstCourse List control. The final result is a grid of courses waiting to be played (Figure 6-6).

Figure 6-6. Browsing the Courses list

Now there are several things that have to take place to make the GolfPro program work. First you must set up the course on which you want to play. As explained earlier, a course has a given number of strokes, which are assigned to all 18 holes. If the course is completed in this number of strokes, a player is considered to have played an even game (this comes up later).

So each course has a total number of strokes required for each hole, which is why you have created the Courses table. So let's consider what the Course database holds. It holds the name of the golf course and the number of strokes allotted to each hole for par. That means each record requires an ID, course name, 18 holes, and the strokes (or par) for each hole (see Figure 6-7).

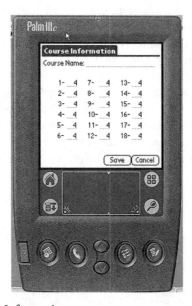

Figure 6-7. The Course Information screen

So now let's take a look at the code to save a new record and modify an existing record. As I've noted in the example code, there are dozens of different ways to create a unique record ID. The example in Listing 6-5 is designed to show how to use the DB* functions, not show you a technique you already know; however, I have included the SetNextSequence code in the listing for you to examine. For more information on creating sequence records, see Chapter 9.

Listing 6-5. The Code to Save a Course Record

```
Sub cmdSaveCourse_Click()
'-=-=-=-=-=-=-=-=-=-=-=-=-=-=-=-=-=-=-=-=-=-=-=-=-=-=-=-=-=-=-=-=
'
'   Sub         :   cmdSaveCourse_Click()
'   Params      :   None
'   Returns     :   None
'
```

```
'   Author      :   Vivid Software Inc. - Jon Kilburn
'                   http://www.VividSoftware.com
'
'   Client      :   Apress
'   Purpose     :   Save A Course Record
'
'-=-=-=-=-=-=-=-=-=-=-=-=-=-=-=-=-=-=-=-=-=-=-=-=-=-=-=-=-=-=
    Dim nResult    as Integer          ' Result of DB* Actions
    Dim cError     as String           ' Error Result String
    Dim rec        as tCoursesRecord   ' Record Structure
    Dim cKey       as String           ' Search Key

       ' Open Course Database
    nResult = dbOpen(dbCourse, "Courses", 0)

    ' Check Result
    If nResult <> 0 Then
        GoTo Trap
    End If

    ' First load the Record structure
    rec.CourseID    = nNextSeq
    rec.Course_Name = txtCourseName.Text
    rec.Hole1Par    = Val(txtHole1.Text)
    rec.Hole2Par    = Val(txtHole2.Text)
    rec.Hole3Par    = Val(txtHole3.Text)
    rec.Hole4Par    = Val(txtHole4.Text)
    rec.Hole5Par    = Val(txtHole5.Text)
    rec.Hole6Par    = Val(txtHole6.Text)
    rec.Hole7Par    = Val(txtHole7.Text)
    rec.Hole8Par    = Val(txtHole8.Text)
    rec.Hole9Par    = Val(txtHole9.Text)
    rec.Hole10Par   = Val(txtHole10.Text)
    rec.Hole11Par   = Val(txtHole11.Text)
    rec.Hole12Par   = Val(txtHole12.Text)
    rec.Hole13Par   = Val(txtHole13.Text)
    rec.Hole14Par   = Val(txtHole14.Text)
    rec.Hole15Par   = Val(txtHole15.Text)
    rec.Hole16Par   = Val(txtHole16.Text)
    rec.Hole17Par   = Val(txtHole17.Text)
    rec.Hole18Par   = Val(txtHole18.Text)
```

```
' Are we in Add Mode?
If (AddMode = True) Then
    ' Save out the data

    ' Now Insert the Record
    nResult = dbInsert(dbCourse, Str(nNextSeq), _
            rec.CourseID, rec.Course_Name, _
            rec.Hole1Par, _
            rec.Hole2Par, _
            rec.Hole3Par, _
            rec.Hole4Par, _
            rec.Hole5Par, _
            rec.Hole6Par, _
            rec.Hole7Par, _
            rec.Hole8Par, _
            rec.Hole9Par, _
            rec.Hole10Par, _
            rec.Hole11Par, _
            rec.Hole12Par, _
            rec.Hole13Par, _
            rec.Hole14Par, _
            rec.Hole15Par, _
            rec.Hole16Par, _
            rec.Hole17Par, _
            rec.Hole18Par)

    ' Check Result
    If nResult > 0 Then
        GoTo Trap
    End If

    ' Update Next Sequence
    nResult = SetNextSequence()

Else
    ' Find Modify Record
    cKey = Str(ModifyID)
    nResult = dbFind(dbCourse, cKey)

    If nResult > 0 Then
        GoTo Trap
    End If
```

```
    ' Update
    nResult = dbUpdate(dbCourse, cKey, _
            rec.CourseID, rec.Course_Name, _
            rec.Hole1Par, _
            rec.Hole2Par, _
            rec.Hole3Par, _
            rec.Hole4Par, _
            rec.Hole5Par, _
            rec.Hole6Par, _
            rec.Hole7Par, _
            rec.Hole8Par, _
            rec.Hole9Par, _
            rec.Hole10Par, _
            rec.Hole11Par, _
            rec.Hole12Par, _
            rec.Hole13Par, _
            rec.Hole14Par, _
            rec.Hole15Par, _
            rec.Hole16Par, _
            rec.Hole17Par, _
            rec.Hole18Par)


    ' Check result
    If nResult > 0 Then
        GoTo Trap
    End If
End If


' Close the Courses Table
nResult = dbClose(dbCourse)

' Return to Course Browse
NextForm("frmCourseBrowse")

' Exit Routine
Exit Sub


' No Support for On Error Goto But
' we can still use Line Labels to process
' error conditions cleanly
Trap:
    ' Check Result
    If nResult <> 0 Then
```

```
            ' Failed to Create
            cError = ProcessDBOpen(nResult)

            ' Can't really go any further
            MsgBox(cError)
      End If
End Sub


Function SetNextSequence() as Integer
'-=-=-=-=-=-=-=-=-=-=-=-=-=-=-=-=-=-=-=-=-=-=-=-=-=-=-=-=-=
'
'   Function    :    SetNextSequence() - Integer
'
'   Params      :    None
'   Returns     :    0 - Valid, Otherwise DB* Error Code
'
'   Author      :    Vivid Software Inc. - Jon Kilburn
'                        http://www.VividSoftware.com
'
'   Client      :    Apress
'   Purpose     :    Updates the Sequence Internal Table
'
'   NOTE        :    This function is based on the Oracle approach
'                        to having a single sequence table.
'
'-=-=-=-=-=-=-=-=-=-=-=-=-=-=-=-=-=-=-=-=-=-=-=-=-=-=-=-=-=
      Dim nResult as Integer    ' Result Flag
      Dim cError  as String     ' Error Return String

      ' Check for Seed Table
      nResult = DBOpen(dbSeed, "GPSeed", 0)

      ' Check result
      If nResult <> 0 Then
          ' Failed to Create
          cError = ProcessDBOpen(nResult)

          ' Can't really go any further
          MsgBox(cError)
          Stop
      End If
```

```
    ' Increase Next Sequence
    nNextSeq = nNextSeq + 1

    ' Update Sequence Number
    nResult = DBPosition(dbSeed, 1, 0)
    nResult = DBPut(dbSeed, nNextSeq)

    ' Close the Seed file
    nResult = dbClose(dbSeed)

    ' Set return
    SetNextSequence = nResult
End Function
```

Adding Course Notes

When you have finished adding courses and assigning scorecards, then you can look at adding the course notes. Course notes are notes that an individual player may make about a particular hole or area of the golf course.

A typical example of a Course Note would be to note the way a ball might break on a green or even the speed of a green. Adding a course note is simple: you pass the course name and CourseID to the Notes browse form and from there you can pass these values to the Notes edit form (see Figure 6-8).

Figure 6-8. Browsing the Notes database

In the Notes browse form, you must check the current CourseID against the CourseID in the Course Notes database to make sure that they match, since you really only want to see notes that pertain to the selected golf course. In the Form_After event of frmNotesBrowse, you will filter against the records to make sure you load only the notes that belong to the selected course (see Listing 6-6).

Listing 6-6. Filtering in the Form_After Event

```
Sub Form1083_After()
'-=-=-=-=-=-=-=-=-=-=-=-=-=-=-=-=-=-=-=-=-=-=-=-=-=-=-=-=
'
'   Sub         :   Form1083_After()
'   Params      :   None
'   Returns     :   None
'
'   Author      :   Vivid Software Inc. - Jon Kilburn
'                       http://www.VividSoftware.com
'
'   Client      :   Apress
'   Purpose     :   Load Records Into ListBox
'
'-=-=-=-=-=-=-=-=-=-=-=-=-=-=-=-=-=-=-=-=-=-=-=-=-=-=-=-=
        Dim nRecCount as Integer            ' Record Count
        Dim cError    as String             ' Error Text
        Dim iOffset   as Integer            ' Offset Into Database
        Dim nResult   as Integer            ' Result of DBReset
        Dim rec       as tCourseNotesRecord ' Record Structure
        Dim cKey      as String             ' Record Key

        ' Draw Help Bitmap
        DrawBitmap 1015, 144, 0

        ' Open Course Notes Database
        nResult = dbOpen(dbNotes, "CourseNotes", 0)

        ' Check Result
        If nResult <> 0 Then
            ' Check for File Not Found which indicates
            ' we need to create the database
            If nResult = 519 Then
                ' File does not exist so create it
                nResult = DBCreate(dbNotes, "CourseNotes", 0, "JONK")
```

```
        ' Check result
        If nResult <> 0 Then
            ' Failed to Create
            cError = ProcessDBOpen(nResult)

            ' Can't really go any further
            MsgBox(cError)
            Stop
        End If

        ' File is Now created, so open it
        nResult = dbOpen(dbNotes, "CourseNotes", 0)

        ' Check result
        If nResult <> 0 Then
            GoTo Trap
        End If
    End If
End If

' Return Number of Records
nRecCount = DbGetNoRecs(dbNotes)

' Reset to Start of File
nResult = DBReset(dbNotes)

If nResult > 0 Then
    ' Unable to Reposition
    GoTo Trap
End If

iOffset = 1

' Loop Through, Reading the Records
Do While iOffset <= nRecCount

    nResult = dbReadNext(dbNotes, cKey, rec.NotesID, _
                rec.CourseID, rec.Hole, rec.Notes)

    ' Only notes for this course
    If PlayerInfo.CourseID = rec.CourseID Then
```

```
                    ' Add the Items
                    lstHole.Add Pad(Str(rec.Hole), " ", 3, "R")
                    lstNotes.Add Mid(rec.Notes, 1, 25), NODISPLAY

                    ' Add this Key
                    arrayNotes.Add cKey
                End If

                ' Increment Offset
                iOffset = iOffset + 1
            Loop

            ' Close Database
            nResult = DBClose(dbNotes)

            If nResult > 0 Then
                GoTo Trap
            End If

            ' Select the First Item
            If lstNotes.NoItems > 0 Then
                lstHole.Selected = 1
                lstNotes.Selected = 1
            End If

            ' Exit Routine
            Exit Sub

    ' No Support for On Error Goto But
    ' we can still use Line Labels to process
    ' error conditions cleanly
    Trap:
        ' Check Result
        If nResult <> 0 Then
            ' Failed to Create
            cError = ProcessDBOpen(nResult)

            ' Can't really go any further
            MsgBox(cError)
        End If
    End Sub
```

There are a few things you have to do along the way. In order to work with the
Courses, Player, and ScoreCard tables, you will need a way to pass variables

between forms. You can create separate Global variables for this, or you can create one Global variable that is a UDT containing the pieces of information you want to pass around. Here I chose to demonstrate how you would do this using a UDT and a single Global variable. The Global variable and the Type definition are placed in the application startup code (see Listing 6-7).

Listing 6-7. Defining Application Variables as a Structure in the Startup Code

```
Sub Main()
'-=-=-=-=-=-=-=-=-=-=-=-=-=-=-=-=-=-=-=-=-=-=-=-=-=-=-=-=-=-=-=-=-=
'
'    Sub        :   Main()
'    Params     :   None
'    Returns    :   None
'
'    Author     :   Vivid Software Inc. - Jon Kilburn
'                   http://www.VividSoftware.com
'
'    Client     :   Apress
'    Purpose    :   Startup, declare types and globals
'
'-=-=-=-=-=-=-=-=-=-=-=-=-=-=-=-=-=-=-=-=-=-=-=-=-=-=-=-=-=-=-=-=-=
    ' Player Information Structure
    Type tPlayerInfo
        CourseID    as Integer   ' Course we're playing on
        CourseName  as String    ' Name of the course
        PlayerID    as Integer   ' Players ID (needed for record retrievals)
        Handicap    as Integer   ' Players Handicap
    End Type

    ' Define Player Info Block
    Global PlayerInfo  as tPlayerInfo
```

> **NOTE** *I define PlayerInfo after I declared the Type. This is because the NS Basic compiler will not recognize the PlayerInfo variable declaration as the Type tPlayerInfo until it has encountered the Type tPlayerInfo.*

The next step to working with the Course Notes is to determine what action to take when a user selects one of the buttons. The first action you'll tackle is the Add option. Adding a new course note is handled by setting a Global flag in the frmCourseNotes form cmdAddNotes_Click event, which will identify this as an Add action. To do this, you need to add two Global variables to the application startup code: ModifyID (the Note ID being modified) and AddMode (which determines whether you are in Add or Edit mode). Since NS Basic does not support the type Boolean, but does support the use of the keywords True and False, declare AddMode as an Integer data type and simply set it to True or False.

As you can see in Listing 6-8, the values are set in the cmdAddNotes and cmdEditNotes click events of the frmNotesBrowse form.

Listing 6-8. Code to Handle Add and Modify Clicks

```
Sub cmdAddNotes_Click()
'-=-=-=-=-=-=-=-=-=-=-=-=-=-=-=-=-=-=-=-=-=-=-=-=-=-=-=-=-=-=
'
'    Sub        :    cmdAddNotes_Click()
'    Params     :    None
'    Returns    :    None
'
'    Author     :    Vivid Software Inc. - Jon Kilburn
'                    http://www.VividSoftware.com
'
'    Client     :    Apress
'    Purpose    :    Set Add Mode and Call the Add Course
'                    Notes Form
'
'-=-=-=-=-=-=-=-=-=-=-=-=-=-=-=-=-=-=-=-=-=-=-=-=-=-=-=-=-=-=

    ' Add Mode Switch
    AddMode = True

    ' Load next form
    NextForm("frmCourseNotes")
End Sub

Sub cmdEditNotes_Click()
'-=-=-=-=-=-=-=-=-=-=-=-=-=-=-=-=-=-=-=-=-=-=-=-=-=-=-=-=-=-=
'
'    Sub        :    cmdEditNotes_Click()
'    Params     :    None
'    Returns    :    None
'
'    Author     :    Vivid Software Inc. - Jon Kilburn
'                    http://www.VividSoftware.com
'
```

```
'   Client       :    Apress
'   Purpose      :    Set Add Mode and Call the Add Course
'                     Notes Form
'
'-=-=-=-=-=-=-=-=-=-=-=-=-=-=-=-=-=-=-=-=-=-=-=-=-=-=-=-=-=
      ' Handle Empty Notes List w/ Edit Click
      If lstNotes.NoItems = 0 Then
          ' Out we Go
          MsgBox "You Must First Select a Note!"
          Exit Sub
      End If

      ' Flip Add Mode Switch
      AddMode = False

      ' Save the Record Modify ID
      ModifyID = Val(arrayNotes.Text(lstHole.Selected))

      ' Load next form
      NextForm("frmCourseNotes")
End Sub
```

The final result is a form that loads with or without information based on the flags that were set in the frmNotesBrowse form (see Figure 6-9).

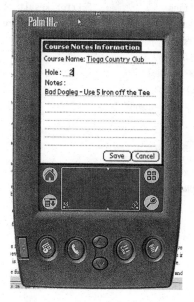

Figure 6-9. Editing course notes

The final piece of the puzzle comes with saving the record. To save a record, you will need to do several things based on the Modify settings. The first decision you must make in the Save routine is to determine if you are adding a new record or editing an existing one.

The function used for adding a new record is DBInsert, and for modifying a record you will use a combination of DBFind and DBUpdate. Both functions accept the database handle as a parameter (see Listing 6-9).

Listing 6-9. Code to Update the Course Notes Database

```
Sub cmdSaveNotes_Click()
'-=-=-=-=-=-=-=-=-=-=-=-=-=-=-=-=-=-=-=-=-=-=-=-=-=-=-=-=-=-=-=-=
'
'   Sub         :    cmdSaveNotes_Click()
'   Params      :    None
'   Returns     :    None
'
'   Author      :    Vivid Software Inc. - Jon Kilburn
'                        http://www.VividSoftware.com
'
'   Client      :    Apress
'   Purpose     :    Save A Course Record
'
'-=-=-=-=-=-=-=-=-=-=-=-=-=-=-=-=-=-=-=-=-=-=-=-=-=-=-=-=-=-=-=-=
    Dim nResult    as Integer            ' Result of DB* Actions
    Dim cError     as String             ' Error Result String
    Dim rec        as tCourseNotesRecord ' Record Structure
    Dim cKey       as String             ' Search Key

    ' Can't enter 0 for the hole
    If Val(txtHole.Text) <= 0 Then
        MsgBox "Invalid Hole Number!"
        Exit Sub
    End If

    ' Open Course Database
    nResult = dbOpen(dbNotes, "CourseNotes", 0)

    ' Check Result
    If nResult <> 0 Then
        GoTo Trap
    End If
```

```
' First load the Record structure
rec.NotesID      = nNextSeq
rec.CourseID     = PlayerInfo.CourseID
rec.Hole         = Val(txtHole.Text)
rec.Notes        = txtHoleNotes.Text

' Are we in Add Mode?
If (AddMode = True) Then
    ' Save out the data

    ' Now Insert the Record
    nResult = dbInsert(dbNotes, Str(nNextSeq), rec.NotesID, _
            rec.CourseID, rec.Hole, rec.Notes)

    ' Check Result
    If nResult > 0 Then
        GoTo Trap
    End If

    ' Update Next Sequence
    nResult = SetNextSequence()
Else
    ' Get Current Key
    cKey = Str(ModifyID)

    ' Find Record
    nResult = dbFind(dbNotes, cKey)

    ' Check Result of Find
    If nResult > 0 Then
        GoTo Trap
    End If

    ' Now Update the Record
    nResult = dbUpdate(dbNotes, cKey, rec.NotesID, _
            rec.CourseID, rec.Hole, rec.Notes)

    ' Check Result of Update
    If nResult > 0 Then
        GoTo Trap
    End If
End If
```

```
        ' Close the Courses Table
        nResult = dbClose(dbNotes)

        ' Return To Notes Browse
        NextForm("frmNotesBrowse")

        ' Exit Routine
        Exit Sub


' No Support for On Error Goto But
' we can still use Line Labels to process
' error conditions cleanly
Trap:
        ' Check Result
        If nResult <> 0 Then
            ' Failed to Create
            cError = ProcessDBOpen(nResult)

            ' Can't really go any further
            MsgBox(cError)
        End If
End Sub
```

Working with Players

Whenever a golfer actually plays the game of golf he or she generally carries a handicap (unless he or she is a pro golfer). A *handicap* is a method for improving a player's score. The concept is that by giving the player a handicap, you can level the playing field. This means that if I have a handicap of 12, when I have finished playing a course I can subtract 12 strokes from my golf game, and I should be close to even. The higher the handicap, the more a player needs to improve his or her game. (Yes, I have a *very* high handicap, now let's get back to the example application, shall we?) Every player that the GolfPro system has can have a handicap. If a player has no handicap, then just leave the value 0.

Once the user has selected a course to play on, then he or she must add or select an existing player. Working with players is handled in much the same manner as working with course notes. You pass the CourseID and the Course Name by placing them in the PlayerInfo UDT, but do not actually use the value until the user adds a scorecard (see Figure 6-10).

Figure 6-10. Browsing players

The only real difference between working with players and working with course notes (besides the file structures) is that for this section I opted to include a graphic in the frmPlayers form (see Figure 6-11).

Figure 6-11. Combining an image with a form

Although having a graphic on the form does not actually do much in the way of improving the ease of use of the GolfPro program, it does help to take up some of the extra space and give the form a more completed look. Please note that in order to bring the fields and labels to the foreground after painting the bitmap, you have to refresh each individual control (see Listing 6-10).

Listing 6-10. Code to Bring Controls Back to the Foreground after Painting a Bitmap

```
' Redraw Labels
LabelFirstName.Redraw
LabelLastName.Redraw
LabelHandicap.Redraw

' Redraw Text Boxes
txtFirstName.Redraw
txtLastName.Redraw
txtHandicap.Redraw

' Redraw Buttons
cmdSavePlayer.Redraw

' Set Focus to Name
txtFirstName.SetFocus
```

Calculating the Score

Finally, let's take a look at how to calculate your score while playing a course. Generally this is achieved by comparing the number of strokes you have against the number of strokes required to maintain par and then subtracting your handicap. There are several pieces to this puzzle that you need to figure out:

- Loading the values for the course into an array so you can calculate the current score for each hole against the par

- Calculating scoring on the fly

- Dealing with a player's handicap

- Dealing with an incomplete scorecard (in other words, calculating the par as you play) and a 0 value, since 0 is referred to as even

Okay, now let's handle each item one at a time. First, let's deal with the value for each hole. You'll read each hole's par into an array (aPar) element so later on you can calculate your score against it (see Listing 6-11).

Listing 6-11. Code to Load the ScoreCard Form and Set Up the aPar Array

```
Sub frmScoreCard_after()
'-=-=-=-=-=-=-=-=-=-=-=-=-=-=-=-=-=-=-=-=-=-=-=-=-=-=-=-=-=-=-=-=
'
'    Sub        :    frmScoreCard_after()
'    Params     :    None
'    Returns    :    None
'
'    Author     :    Vivid Software Inc. - Jon Kilburn
'                    http://www.VividSoftware.com
'
'    Client     :    Apress
'    Purpose    :    Default the Course Record (if in add mode) to
'                    a value of 4 for each hole
'
'-=-=-=-=-=-=-=-=-=-=-=-=-=-=-=-=-=-=-=-=-=-=-=-=-=-=-=-=-=-=-=-=
    Dim nResult    as Integer              ' Result of DBReset
    Dim rec        as tScoreCardRecord     ' Record Structure
    Dim recPar     as tCoursesRecord       ' Score Card Par
    Dim nPar       as Integer              ' Course Par
    Dim iLoop      as Integer              ' Loop Counter
    Dim cError     as String               ' Error Text
    Dim cKey       as String               ' Record Key
    Dim uDate      as Date                 ' Date

    ' Draw Help Bitmap
    DrawBitmap 1015, 144, 0

    ' Get the Date
    uDate = Today()

    ' Set the Selector
    txtDate.Text = DateMMDDYY(uDate)

    ' Fill in the fields
    txtDisplayCourseName.Text = Trim(PlayerInfo.CourseName)
```

```
' Are we in Add Mode?
If (AddMode = True) Then
    ' Yes so initialize the Pars
    txtScoreHole1.Text = "0"
    txtScoreHole2.Text = "0"
    txtScoreHole3.Text = "0"
    txtScoreHole4.Text = "0"
    txtScoreHole5.Text = "0"
    txtScoreHole6.Text = "0"
    txtScoreHole7.Text = "0"
    txtScoreHole8.Text = "0"
    txtScoreHole9.Text = "0"
    txtScoreHole10.Text = "0"
    txtScoreHole11.Text = "0"
    txtScoreHole12.Text = "0"
    txtScoreHole13.Text = "0"
    txtScoreHole14.Text = "0"
    txtScoreHole15.Text = "0"
    txtScoreHole16.Text = "0"
    txtScoreHole17.Text = "0"
    txtScoreHole18.Text = "0"
Else
    ' Modify Mode, so open the Course ScoreCard
    ' Table and Load the values for the Modify ID
    nResult = dbOpen(dbScoreCard, "ScoreCard", 0)

    ' Check Result
    If nResult <> 0 Then
        GoTo Trap
    End If

    ' Reset to Start of File
    nResult = dbReset(dbScoreCard)

    ' Find Modify Record
    cKey = Str(ModifyID)
    nResult = dbFind(dbScoreCard, cKey)

    ' Check Result
    If nResult > 0 Then
        GoTo Trap
    End If
```

```
' Found the Record, load the values
nResult = dbRead(dbScoreCard, cKey, _
                     rec.ScoreID, rec.CourseID, _
                     rec.PlayerID, rec.GameDate, _
                     rec.Hole1, rec.Hole2, _
                     rec.Hole3, rec.Hole4, _
                     rec.Hole5, rec.Hole6, _
                     rec.Hole7, rec.Hole8, _
                     rec.Hole9, rec.Hole10, _
                     rec.Hole11, rec.Hole12, _
                     rec.Hole13, rec.Hole14, _
                     rec.Hole15, rec.Hole16, _
                     rec.Hole17, rec.Hole18, _
                     rec.FinalScore)


' Check Result
If nResult > 0 Then
    GoTo Trap
End If


' Close Database
nResult = dbClose(dbScoreCard)

' Check Result
If nResult > 0 Then
    GoTo Trap
End If


' Read in the Score Card
txtScoreHole1.Text  = Trim(Str(rec.Hole1))
txtScoreHole2.Text  = Trim(Str(rec.Hole2))
txtScoreHole3.Text  = Trim(Str(rec.Hole3))
txtScoreHole4.Text  = Trim(Str(rec.Hole4))
txtScoreHole5.Text  = Trim(Str(rec.Hole5))
txtScoreHole6.Text  = Trim(Str(rec.Hole6))
txtScoreHole7.Text  = Trim(Str(rec.Hole7))
txtScoreHole8.Text  = Trim(Str(rec.Hole8))
txtScoreHole9.Text  = Trim(Str(rec.Hole9))
txtScoreHole10.Text = Trim(Str(rec.Hole10))
txtScoreHole11.Text = Trim(Str(rec.Hole11))
txtScoreHole12.Text = Trim(Str(rec.Hole12))
txtScoreHole13.Text = Trim(Str(rec.Hole13))
txtScoreHole14.Text = Trim(Str(rec.Hole14))
```

```
                        txtScoreHole15.Text = Trim(Str(rec.Hole15))
                        txtScoreHole16.Text = Trim(Str(rec.Hole16))
                        txtScoreHole17.Text = Trim(Str(rec.Hole17))
                        txtScoreHole18.Text = Trim(Str(rec.Hole18))


            End If


            ' Calculate Par
            nResult = dbOpen(dbCourse, "Courses", 0)


            ' Check Result
            If nResult > 0 Then
                GoTo Trap
            End If


            ' Reset to Start of File
            nResult = dbReset(dbCourse)


            ' Find Modify Record
            cKey = Str(PlayerInfo.CourseID)
            nResult = dbFind(dbCourse, cKey)


            ' Load the Pars
            If nResult = 0 Then
                ' Found the Record, load the values
                nResult = dbRead(dbCourse, cKey, _
                    recPar.CourseID, recPar.Course_Name, _
                    recPar.Hole1Par, recPar.Hole2Par, _
                    recPar.Hole3Par, recPar.Hole4Par, _
                    recPar.Hole5Par, recPar.Hole6Par, _
                    recPar.Hole7Par, recPar.Hole8Par, _
                    recPar.Hole9Par, recPar.Hole10Par, _
                    recPar.Hole11Par, recPar.Hole12Par, _
                    recPar.Hole13Par, recPar.Hole14Par, _
                    recPar.Hole15Par, recPar.Hole16Par, _
                    recPar.Hole17Par, recPar.Hole18Par)


                ' load the array
                aPar(0)  = recPar.Hole1Par
                aPar(1)  = recPar.Hole2Par
                aPar(2)  = recPar.Hole3Par
                aPar(3)  = recPar.Hole4Par
                aPar(4)  = recPar.Hole5Par
```

```
        aPar(5)  = recPar.Hole6Par
        aPar(6)  = recPar.Hole7Par
        aPar(7)  = recPar.Hole8Par
        aPar(8)  = recPar.Hole9Par
        aPar(9)  = recPar.Hole10Par
        aPar(10) = recPar.Hole11Par
        aPar(11) = recPar.Hole12Par
        aPar(12) = recPar.Hole13Par
        aPar(13) = recPar.Hole14Par
        aPar(14) = recPar.Hole15Par
        aPar(15) = recPar.Hole16Par
        aPar(16) = recPar.Hole17Par
        aPar(17) = recPar.Hole18Par


        ' Calculate Par
        For iLoop = 0 To 17
            nPar = nPar + aPar(iLoop)
        Next

        ' Set Course Par Text
        txtCoursePar.Text = Str(nPar)
    End If


    ' Calculate Par
    nResult = dbClose(dbCourse)

    ' Check Result
    If nResult > 0 Then
        GoTo Trap
    End If


    ' Display the Players handicap
    txtDisplayHandicap.Text = Str(PlayerInfo.Handicap)

    ' Set Focus to the Score Field
    txtScoreHole1.SetFocus

    ' Modifying and existing score card?
    If (AddMode = False) Then
        ' Yes so Calculate the score
        txtCalcScore.Text = Str(rec.FinalScore)
    End If
```

```
        ' Exit Routine
        Exit Sub


' No Support for On Error Goto But
' we can still use Line Labels to process
' error conditions cleanly
Trap:
        ' Check Result
        If nResult <> 0 Then
            ' Failed to Create
            cError = ProcessDBOpen(nResult)

            ' Can't really go any further
            MsgBox(cError)
        End If


End Sub
```

Now let's tackle the on-the-fly scoring. Pay close attention here. The NS Basic TextBox controls do not support control arrays, so you must now open all 18 textbox events and make a call to your score calculation routine (see Listing 6-12).

Listing 6-12. One of the Textbox Events Calling the CalcScore Routine

```
Sub object1246()
'-=-=-=-=-=-=-=-=-=-=-=-=-=-=-=-=-=-=-=-=-=-=-=-=-=-=-=-=-=-=-=
'
'    Sub        :    object1246()
'    Params     :    None
'    Returns    :    None
'
'    Author     :    Vivid Software Inc. - Jon Kilburn
'                    http://www.VividSoftware.com
'
'    Client     :    Apress
'    Purpose    :    Recalculate Score
'
'-=-=-=-=-=-=-=-=-=-=-=-=-=-=-=-=-=-=-=-=-=-=-=-=-=-=-=-=-=-=-=

        ' Exiting Field, Calculate New Score
        CalcScore()

End Sub
```

Finally, within the CalcScore routine, you need to deal with three items. The first item is determining which hole you're on and the current score as it applies to this hole. The second item is dealing with 0 as even, and the final item is to adjust for the player's handicap.

You can accomplish the first task by simply checking the Text property of each of the txtScoreHole*N* controls. The first score that you encounter with a value of 0 indicates the next hole to be played, so you just add the current values for par and the current strokes and presto, you have the running score. Second, you simply check the result of strokes against par, and if they are 0, you display the word "even." Finally, after you calculate the player's current score, you subtract the player's handicap from the total, which yields the adjusted score (see Listing 6-13).

Listing 6-13. Code to Calculate a Golf Score

```
Sub CalcScore()
'-=-=-=-=-=-=-=-=-=-=-=-=-=-=-=-=-=-=-=-=-=-=-=-=-=-=-=-=-=
'
'    Sub         :   CalcScore
'    Params      :   None
'
'    Author      :   Vivid Software Inc. - Jon Kilburn
'                    http://www.VividSoftware.com
'
'    Client      :   Apress
'    Purpose     :   Calculate the Golf Score
'
'-=-=-=-=-=-=-=-=-=-=-=-=-=-=-=-=-=-=-=-=-=-=-=-=-=-=-=-=-=
    Dim iLoop       as Integer   ' Loop Counter
    Dim nScore      as Integer   ' Current Score
    Dim nCurPar     as Integer   ' Current Par Total
    Dim nCurHole    as Integer   ' Currently Scoring this Hole
    Dim cSign       as String    ' Even, Under or Over

    ' Default to First Hole
    nCurHole = 1

    ' Determine Current Hole (Moving Forewards
    ' Until you encounter a hole with a value of 0
    If Val(txtScoreHole1.Text)  > 0 Then nCurHole = 1
    If Val(txtScoreHole2.Text)  > 0 Then nCurHole = 2
    If Val(txtScoreHole3.Text)  > 0 Then nCurHole = 3
    If Val(txtScoreHole4.Text)  > 0 Then nCurHole = 4
```

```
If Val(txtScoreHole5.Text)  > 0 Then nCurHole = 5
If Val(txtScoreHole6.Text)  > 0 Then nCurHole = 6
If Val(txtScoreHole7.Text)  > 0 Then nCurHole = 7
If Val(txtScoreHole8.Text)  > 0 Then nCurHole = 8
If Val(txtScoreHole9.Text)  > 0 Then nCurHole = 9
If Val(txtScoreHole10.Text) > 0 Then nCurHole = 10
If Val(txtScoreHole11.Text) > 0 Then nCurHole = 11
If Val(txtScoreHole12.Text) > 0 Then nCurHole = 12
If Val(txtScoreHole13.Text) > 0 Then nCurHole = 13
If Val(txtScoreHole14.Text) > 0 Then nCurHole = 14
If Val(txtScoreHole15.Text) > 0 Then nCurHole = 15
If Val(txtScoreHole16.Text) > 0 Then nCurHole = 16
If Val(txtScoreHole17.Text) > 0 Then nCurHole = 17
If Val(txtScoreHole18.Text) > 0 Then nCurHole = 18

' Calculate the Current Scoring Par(s)
For iLoop = 0 To (nCurHole - 1)
    ' Calculate Current Par
    nCurPar = nCurPar + aPar(iLoop)
Next

' Calculate current strokes
nScore = Val(txtScoreHole1.Text)
nScore = nScore + Val(txtScoreHole2.Text)
nScore = nScore + Val(txtScoreHole3.Text)
nScore = nScore + Val(txtScoreHole4.Text)
nScore = nScore + Val(txtScoreHole5.Text)
nScore = nScore + Val(txtScoreHole6.Text)
nScore = nScore + Val(txtScoreHole7.Text)
nScore = nScore + Val(txtScoreHole8.Text)
nScore = nScore + Val(txtScoreHole9.Text)
nScore = nScore + Val(txtScoreHole10.Text)
nScore = nScore + Val(txtScoreHole11.Text)
nScore = nScore + Val(txtScoreHole12.Text)
nScore = nScore + Val(txtScoreHole13.Text)
nScore = nScore + Val(txtScoreHole14.Text)
nScore = nScore + Val(txtScoreHole15.Text)
nScore = nScore + Val(txtScoreHole16.Text)
nScore = nScore + Val(txtScoreHole17.Text)
nScore = nScore + Val(txtScoreHole18.Text)

' Determine Par
nCurPar = nScore - nCurPar
```

```
' Subtract the Player's Handicap from
' the total score giving an adjusted score
nCurPar = nCurPar - PlayerInfo.Handicap

If nCurPar = 0 Then
    txtCalcScore.Text = "Even"
Else
    If nCurPar > 0 Then
        cSign = "+"
    Else
        ' Make number Positive
        nCurPar = nCurPar * (-1)

        ' Set Sign
        cSign = "-"
    End If

    ' Display a Score w/ Sign
    txtCalcScore.Text = cSign + Trim(Str(nCurPar))
End If

End Sub
```

Compiling

Now that you have the application developed, let's compile it. Get used to using the Compile option. Since NS Basic is designed to build applications to run on the Palm, the only way to test your application is to compile it and then test it using POSE. The good news is that NS Basic will install your application on POSE and even start it for you.

After completing your compilation of the GolfPro program, you are now ready to upload the compiled GolfPro program to your Palm device.

Conclusion

NS Basic is an excellent choice for building Palm-based applications. It offers a decent amount of functionality at a price that will not break your bank. After reading this chapter and working through the GolfPro sample application (the full source of which is provided on the CD), you should have a good grasp of NS Basic's functionality and how to use it to develop Palm-based applications.

Technical support is excellent, and there are already two great Yahoo Groups forums you can go to for help if you need it. NS Basic is evolving and continues to improve every day. It shows tremendous potential, and in its latest release has silenced the critics with a solid compiler and very user friendly IDE.

Overall the product is solid, fairly inexpensive, and provides excellent functionality. As more job opportunities for handheld development arise, the NS Basic programmer can be there to offer a more cost-effective solution than C-based development.

CHAPTER 7

Palm Programming
with CASL

WHEN I FIRST THOUGHT ABOUT getting into Palm programming, I read several books
that explained the concepts using C and C++. In many of these books, there was
always a sidebar mention of Compact Application Solution Language (CASL).
Although many of these books called CASL a Basic-like language, as you'll discover, CASL has a lure all its own. CASL was first released in 1996, making CASL
software one of the earliest supporters of the Palm OS. What makes this product
so special that it's mentioned in nearly every C programming book, yet for some
reason has no book dedicated to it? Read on and you'll see why it's such an awe-
some product.

CASL Soft

CASL IDE is a complete development environment for the Palm OS and the
Windows desktop OS, with a Windows CE OS version in beta (see Figure 7-1). It
provides a full, modern integrated development environment (IDE) and a complete debugger, and is fully customizable to make your programming experience
more pleasant. For those of you that have purchased the Pro version, there is also
the ability to compile your completed project into C seamlessly in the background; the free GNU C compiler is called by the CASL IDE to create a standalone
program with no runtime engine.

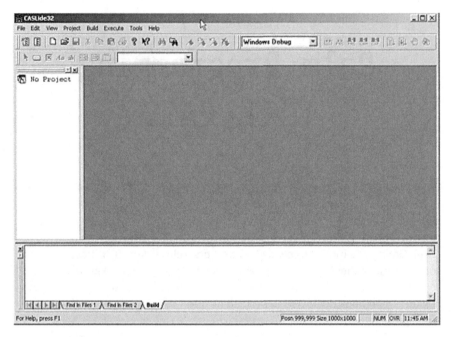

Figure 7-1. The CASL IDE

 TIP *By default, the CASL IDE doesn't allow multiple instances to be running at the same time. You can turn this functionality off by selecting Tools | IDE Settings. There you will find a checkbox option for allowing multiple CASL IDEs to run.*

CASL Pros and Cons

There are a number of Palm development environments available: CodeWarrior (C/C++), Java (KVM), NS Basic, AppForge, and the GNU C Compiler. What helps set CASL apart? Its great, user-friendly IDE and an enthusiastic support group. However, as with every compiler, there are always a few things I'd like to see different.

Some of the cons:

- This is not Visual Basic, so you have no IntelliSense features (although when entering the dot format for object properties, the IDE will automatically prompt you with a list of objects, and then with a list of properties for that object).

- There is no printed documentation, and getting started is not as easy as it should be. Although a "hello world" example is included, it's not nearly enough.
- Although a manual on the IDE and the language is provided, explanations of the different file types (package, project, form, and so on) were not easy to find.
- The code is not separated and grouped by control and control events automatically. You have to do that yourself (not a terrible task, just something you have to get used to).
- To view properties, you must double-click a control. Not a problem—it's just that most VB programmers have grown accustomed to seeing a Properties window.
- Doesn't have an online searchable knowledge base (FAQs, tech notes, user group support board, and the complete searchable archives of all user support posts are available online however).
- PDB sorting is limited to the key column only.

Some of the pros:

- It has an easy-to-use IDE and a solid development environment.
- You can size the forms to be larger than the screen environment.
- It comes with a well-organized language reference and a good guide to using the CASL IDE as printable Word documents.
- Color support is quite easy to implement. Just change the colors of the control within the IDE and presto!—color on the Palm.
- I can't say this enough—CASL is fast!
- You can lock controls in place preventing the accidental movement of an object.
- You can use expressions inside of controls for display purposes.
- You can find active support group on the CASL board.

Before you can really begin programming with CASL, you need to take care of one little tidbit. CASL supports creating applications for the Palm and the Windows environments. To ensure that you are developing for the proper target environment, you should keep the target platform combo box setting to the default Windows Release option. This allows the creation of executables that will run on your Windows platform, which is useful for quick testing. By selecting the Windows Debug option, you can test and debug by running your application on your desktop. The IDE has single step and variable watch options, similar to those you're used to with VB. Once you're satisfied with your application, you can do final testing on your Palm OS device by selecting Palm Release. This will set the target environment as a Palm OS device.

Although CASL ships with a number of help files, HTML documents, and several references in the form of Word documents, there is no really good guide or tutorial for getting started. This is not Visual Basic, and the IDE functions a bit more like the MS Visual C IDE, but this is an easy-to-use layout that requires very little to become proficient at navigating. What does require some time is acquainting yourself with where things are and how they work. Let's start by building a very simple project, and I'll explain each part of the IDE as you work with it.

CASL is a compiler, but requires a runtime support library (unless you use CASL Pro, and I'll talk more about that later). The CASL runtime library (CASLRt.Prc) is installed separately. CASL also has a shared library of math functions that can be installed on your Palm device. There are a number of these libraries now, with more on the way. Think of a shared library as being like a Windows DLL that provides additional functionality for special purposes. You load and unload these libraries as needed.

Virtual Machines

CASL is a compiler, but it compiles the target application into a code form known as p-code. P-code stands for pseudocode, and also requires a virtual machine to execute when compiled. This is similar to Java in that you need a runtime (or virtual machine) to execute your code. In older compilers such as Clipper (a DBase compiler), the runtime interpreter was actually compiled into the final EXE. You will also discover later on in this book that several of the compilers available for the Palm (but not necessarily reviewed or explained in this book) also use this technique.

So you ask, what is a virtual machine? Well let's review a bit about virtual machines. The term *virtual machine* has been used to mean either an operating system or any program that runs on a computer.

A running program is often referred to as a virtual machine—a machine that doesn't exist as a matter of physical reality. The idea of a virtual machine is itself one of the most elegant in the history of technology, and is a crucial step in the evolution of ideas about software. In order to come up with it, scientists and technologists had to recognize that a computer running a program isn't merely a washing machine doing some dirty laundry. On the contrary, a washing machine is a washing machine no matter what kind of clothes you put inside, but when you put a new program in a computer, presto, by virtue of the new program it is also a new virtual machine.[1]

---

[1] This discussion on virtual machines is based on the David Gelernter article, "Truth, Beauty, and the Virtual Machine," *Discover Magazine*, September 1997.

In the most recent computer usage, "virtual machine" is a term that was first used by Sun Microsystems (the developers of the Java programming language and runtime environment), to describe software that acts as an interface between compiled Java bytecode and the microprocessor (or hardware platform) that actually performs the program's instructions.

Once a virtual machine has been written for a particular platform, any program written to run within the specifications of that virtual machine will now run on that platform. Java was designed to allow application programs to be built that could be run on many platforms without having to be rewritten or recompiled by the programmer for each separate platform.

For example, take the Windows OS and Macintosh OS. Both are operating systems with their own very specific instruction sets. The goal behind Java is that a program written and compiled with the Java compiler could be ported from the Windows OS to the MAC OS by simply moving the code.[2]

Virtual machines are what make all this possible. The Java virtual machine has a specification, which is defined as an abstract, rather than a real machine (or processor), which specifies an instruction set, a set of registers, a stack, a garbage heap, and a method area. The real implementation of this abstract (or logically defined processor) is done in other code that is recognized by the real processor. The output of "compiling" a Java source program is called bytecode. A Java virtual machine can either interpret the bytecode one instruction at a time (mapping it to a real microprocessor instruction) or the bytecode can be compiled further for the real microprocessor using what is called a just-in-time compiler.

The output of "compiling" a Java source program (a set of Java language statements) is called bytecode. A Java virtual machine can either interpret the bytecode one instruction at a time (mapping it to a real microprocessor instruction) or the bytecode can be compiled further for the real microprocessor using what is called a just-in-time compiler.

CASL has taken the virtual machine approach and applied it to handheld devices. CASL exists for Windows, Windows CE devices, and Palm OS devices. In the case of CASL, the virtual machine is called CASLrt.prc. If a CASL application has not been compiled using the CASL Pro compiler, the application will require that CASLrt.prc is installed on the target device.

Although you do not need anything except CASL and either a real Palm or the Palm OS Emulator (POSE)[3] to get started, I would suggest that you obtain a copy of the Palm OS SDK, including the latest documentation (available from the Palm Web site). You can also download their Conduit Developers Kit 4.02 for COM, which supports any COM-compliant language, including Visual Basic. This

---

[2] Of course, this is the scenario played out as the ideal. In reality, there are so many steps to port an application written in Java for the Windows OS to the Macintosh OS, it would take another book to explain them all.

[3] See Chapter 2 for instruction on how to obtain and install the Palm OS Emulator.

means that you can now develop custom conduits[4] using Visual Basic. Although CASL ships with a conduit (CASLCn20.DLL), there may be instances where the conduit tool that comes with CASL does not meet your needs. For a complete review of building a conduit using the CASL conduit DLL, see Chapter 9.

The SDK contains three important items:

- *Example code:* You can peruse this code (although it's all in C/C++) to get a feel for how POSE works.

- *Documentation:* Think of the documentation as a dictionary in which you can look up all the possible system functions available for your code. The SDK documentation is not very interesting to read, unless you find reading a dictionary exciting.

- *Palm OS Emulator:* The emulator, shown in Figure 7-2, essentially functions as a virtual Palm on your desktop. POSE allows you to debug and run the programs you develop on your computer, instead of performing a HotSync every time you make a new build. You definitely need the emulator, unless you enjoy resetting your Palm device several times while writing your software. (See Chapter 2 for more information on using the POSE.)

Figure 7-2. The Palm OS Emulator (POSE)

---

[4] A conduit is a means of communication between a Palm OS device and a desktop PC. For a more detailed explanation of conduits, see Chapter 9.

Getting Started

Once you have completed the installation of the CASL compiler (by running the installation program), you will notice that when you start it, it looks more like Microsoft Visual C than Visual Basic. On startup, you'll see the Tips dialog box we've become so familiar with (see Figure 7-3).

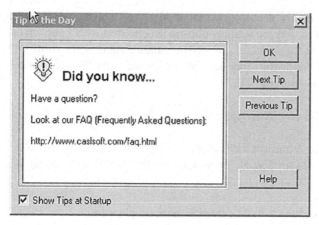

Figure 7-3. The Tips dialog box at CASL compiler startup

Before any application can be built, we should review a bit about the IDE. There are several items that have to be considered. The first is to be aware that CASL is designed to generate applications for Windows, Windows CE (versions 2 and lower—it does not yet support version 3), and the Palm OS. You must take care to configure the IDE properly when building a Palm application. Let's review some of the supported controls provided.

Almost any toolbar can be docked or undocked by double-clicking it. You can feel free to rearrange the CASL IDE as you see fit. One thing you cannot do, however, is dock the toolbars on the sides.

Understanding the Screen Objects

There are currently seven supported screen objects (akin to ActiveX controls in standard Visual Basic). Most of these objects, listed here, are self-explanatory:

- *Buttons:* These are oval-shaped objects that have a label and function very much like their Windows counterparts. When a button is clicked, some associated action is fired.

- *Checkboxes:* These objects indicate a setting of either on or off.

- *Labels:* These objects contain text and function like Windows labels.

- *Text Field:* All I have to say about this object is think textbox. That's what these objects are. They can be single or multiple lines, and you can set the properties of a field so that it does or does not have scrollbars.

- *Selector:* These objects at first appear to be a textbox with a spinner control, but they are actually pop-up lists. To deal with a pop-up list, you must first set the standard properties (name, display, and so on) and then you must define the array size and the list contents. Both can be done at runtime or from the IDE.

- *File Selector:* This object works just like a selector, but only applies to files.

- *Frame:* A frame is a Windows construct that is used in the Palm version for the form surface. All forms in a Palm application need a frame onto which controls can be placed.

There are also two objects for constructing menus:

- *menu_top:* This object is the top level declaration for a menu. You define these objects in source code using the following syntax:

```
menu_top <menuName>;
    display <menuCaption>;
end;
```

- *menu_item:* This object is the actual menu item that is contained by the menu_top object. You define these objects in source code and associate them directly to the named menu_top object using the following syntax:

```
menu_item <menuSubItemName>, <menu_topObject>;
    display <menuCaption>;
end;
```

Building Your First Project

I'll start by taking you step by step through creating a new application so that you can familiarize yourself with the CASL IDE. Begin by selecting File | New Project.

The standard Windows File Open dialog box will appear, prompting you to enter a new project filename. Name the file Project 1. This creates a blank template project with two windows and displays project information in the left-hand Project browser window (see Figure 7-4). A project is a collection of files that make up your application: the main code file (.csl), all the code package files (.cpk), all the form files (.cff), all the bitmaps (.cbm), and the icon file (.cic). With the latest release of CASL Pro, you can now include C code and C header files as part of the project. Essentially, a project in CASL is akin to the project of a Visual Basic program.

Figure 7-4. The Project Browser and New Project 1 windows

NOTE   *A CASL package file is like a child or subfile of the main code file. All projects created in CASL have a main code file. This file can be as big or small as you wish. You can include supplemental files (or packages) within a CASL application using the include statement. Since CASL is a one-pass compiler, the order of functions is important (at least for the CASL code itself). A function that is called by a function being compiled must itself already be compiled, or an error will result. With CASL, it is a good idea to use package files to keep code organized and control the flow of functions. In CASL Pro, using package files is also important because the C build compiler will tag each file so it can reside in its own 64KB memory segment. The GNU C compiler uses tags and you can find more information about this in the CASL manual.*

Before we go much further, let's review what you're seeing in the Project window. The first (topmost) element you see is labeled Project 1. This is actually the Project Settings icon. If you select this icon, the Project Settings dialog box will load (see Figure 7-5).

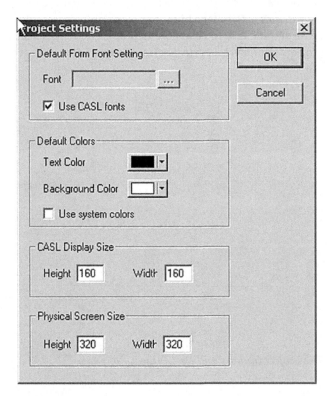

Figure 7-5. The Project Settings dialog box

This form simply presents you with options for changing some of the simple elements of the project, such as font, color, and two very interesting items, display size and physical screen size. For fonts, I suggest enabling the Use CASL fonts option, as these will often translate the best. For the color settings, if your target device supports color, then you are okay designing for a color screen and you can play with the fonts and colors. Otherwise, you should work with the standard default system colors.

The Display Size parameters control the height and width of the final compiled form, whereas the Physical Screen Size attributes control the size of the form within the IDE. This is pretty much a zoom feature. In the Palm world, a screen can be 160 pixels tall by 160 pixels wide. To develop a form for the Palm, you need to set the form Display Size attributes to be 160×160; however, this is very hard to see on the screen, so if you set the Physical Screen Size attributes to 320×320, the form is effectively "zoomed," presenting you with an enlarged screen (or form) to work with.

Language Elements

Although it is quite common for a language to have structure and rules that describe how to write the code (that is, the syntax), as a Visual Basic programmer you have probably become used to the VB syntax and structure. CASL is not VB—it has some language elements that make it similar to C and Delphi. Here are a few of the more common elements:

- For comments, use the pound sign (#).
- All functions in CASL are invoked in response to an event of one sort or another and must have an End statement.
- To declare variables, you include a variables section, and then you declare the type followed by the variable name. These must also end with a semicolon (;).
- Putting text into controls requires the use of the keyword Put (or you can assign a text string to the Display property of the object by using a dot format, similar to VB).
- All CASL statements must end with a semicolon (;).

The second element (also labeled Project 1) is the Project 1 CASL source code section. If you double-click this icon, a code window will open. It is within this window that you will write most of your code (see Figure 7-6).

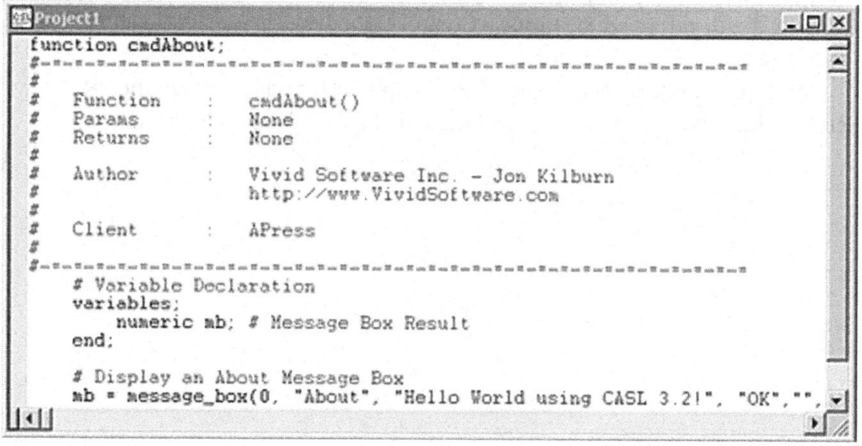

```
function cmdAbout;
#-=-=-=-=-=-=-=-=-=-=-=-=-=-=-=-=-=-=-=-=-=-=-=-=-=-=-=-=-=-=-=-=-=
#
#    Function    :    cmdAbout()
#    Params      :    None
#    Returns     :    None
#
#    Author      :    Vivid Software Inc. - Jon Kilburn
#                     http://www.VividSoftware.com
#
#    Client      :    APress
#
#-=-=-=-=-=-=-=-=-=-=-=-=-=-=-=-=-=-=-=-=-=-=-=-=-=-=-=-=-=-=-=-=
    # Variable Declaration
    variables;
        numeric mb; # Message Box Result
    end;

    # Display an About Message Box
    mb = message_box(0, "About", "Hello World using CASL 3.2!", "OK","",
```

Figure 7-6. The Project 1 CASL Source Code window

NOTE *Unlike VB, the CASL IDE does not have combo boxes to select the control or to locate events associated with the control. Although this does not hinder your development in any way, as a VB programmer, you may find this a bit disorienting at first.*

The third element is the Forms folder. This tree view–like icon will open and expand to show all the forms collected for an application. If you open and expand the Forms folder, you will see the form Project 1. To change the name of the form, you must save the form with another name.

If you look at the IDE, you'll notice that tucked away in the far right-hand side on the toolbar is a combo box that contains four items. These four items are the application build types, listed here:

- Windows Release (this is a Windows desktop or Windows CE 2.11 release, as CASL does not yet support Windows CE 3.0 or higher)

- Windows Debug Release (again a Windows desktop or Windows CE 2.11 release)

- Palm Pilot Release

- Palm Pilot Debug Release

Before you get further into the project, you should select the type of build for this project; for this example, select Pilot Release. Now that you have chosen the Palm OS build, you need to supply a Creator ID, a desktop name and a Palm PRC name.

From the menu, select Project | PRC Settings. This will bring up the PRC Settings dialog box (see Figure 7-7). Fill in the fields in this dialog box.

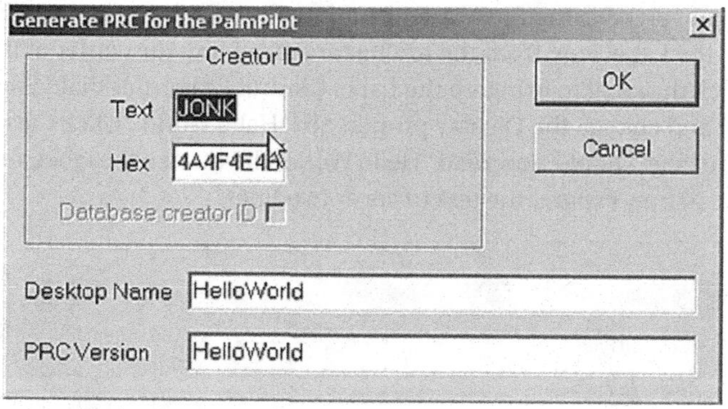

Figure 7-7. The PRC Project Settings dialog box

With the properties for the PRC set, if you double-click the Project 1 form, a blank form will open, waiting for you to begin designing your application. The first thing you should notice is that a group box covers the whole form. This group box is designed to simulate the form surface. When you double-click the control to bring up the Frame Properties dialog box, you will see the name of the frame and the Display property setting (see Figure 7–8). Change the Display setting to change the title in the title bar of your window.

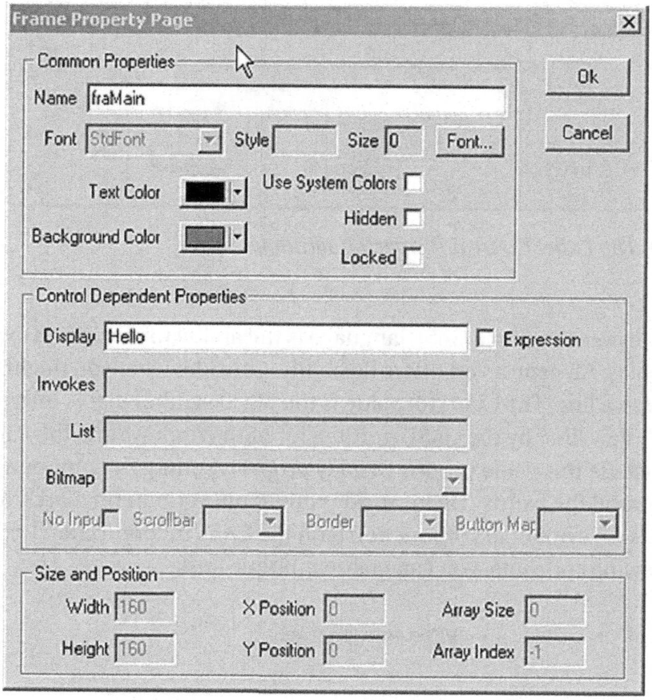

Figure 7-8. The Frame Properties window

Now that you have the form open, continue by adding a couple of lines of text. Select the Label icon from the toolbar and drop it in the center of the form. Double-click the label to bring up the Label Control Properties dialog box (see Figure 7-9) and change the Display property to "Hello World". Click the OK button, and the label should now read "Hello World". If you size the label, making it taller, you can now expand the text to cover two lines.

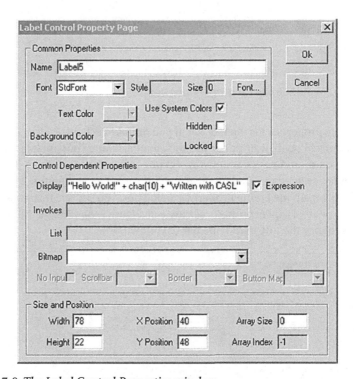

Figure 7-9. The Label Control Properties window

A nice extension of the CASL language is the ability to include an expression for the display. An expression offers flexibility. Consider what you might do if you need to wrap a line. The Char(10) value is the ASCII symbol that is interpreted as a line feed (new line) by the CASL runtime for both Windows and the Palm OS. You can include this value in your Display property setting by combining strings. If you surround the words "Hello World" with double quotation marks, and then use the plus (+) symbol in conjunction with the CASL function char(10) as shown in the following code line, you can create multiple lines.

```
"Hello World" + char(10) + "Written with CASL"
```

Now if you are content with the label, you can "lock" the control in place. This is a nifty feature, as using the Lock option prevents the control from being moved within the IDE.

Finally, add a button along with some action code to your simple form. Another trick, but not one that is instantly obvious, is the linking of an invoker function directly to an object, such as a button. If the button has a name such as cmdAbout, then the invoker function will be named cmdAbout. The killer here is getting the syntax correct. The use of the keyword function requires that it be spelled in all lowercase. CASL, like JavaScript, is case sensitive. "Function" does not mean the same as "function". So when the button is clicked, CASL will locate the function cmdAbout and perform the actions requested (see Listing 7-1).

Listing 7-1. The About Button Click Code

```
function cmdAbout;
#-=-=-=-=-=-=-=-=-=-=-=-=-=-=-=-=-=-=-=-=-=-=-=-=-=-=-=
#
#    Function    :    cmdAbout()
#    Params      :    None
#    Returns     :    None
#
#    Author      :    Vivid Software Inc. - Jon Kilburn
#                     http://www.VividSoftware.com
#
#    Client      :    Apress
#
#-=-=-=-=-=-=-=-=-=-=-=-=-=-=-=-=-=-=-=-=-=-=-=-=-=-=-=
    # Variable Declaration
    variables;
    numeric mb;     # Message Box Result
    end;

    # Display an About Message Box
    mb = message_box(0, "About", "Hello World using CASL 3.2!", "OK","","");

end;
```

The result is a very simple form with an About message box.

Now let's move on to compiling and uploading the project. Since you have specified the Creator ID and application name, you can now proceed to compiling the program. Select Build | Compile. If the application compiles cleanly, you will see the Total Errors = 0 message in the Build tab (see Figure 7-10). When the build completes successfully then we can do the final compile. Select Build | Make PRC to generate the final Palm OS application file.

```
CASL compiler 3.2.0 b6, Professional Edition (Beta 6.17), registered to....
Jon Kilburn
Vivid Software Inc.

Requires CASL runtime version 3.2.0 (or greater)

Total errors = 0

Find In Files 1    Find In Files 2    Build
```

Figure 7-10. The Build tab

With the application successfully compiled, you must now install it. To install the compiled application, first locate the folder labeled Pilot Release, which will have been created under the current working folder. In the Pilot Release folder, you will find the file Project1.PRC.

When installing a CASL application, you must first install the CASL runtime file (CASLrt.PRC). This file is typically located in the Program Files\CASLsoft\CASL32\PilotFiles directory. If you select the Build | PRC Install menu option, you will be guided through creating an installation. If it's your first time using the CASL IDE, this starts with selecting the user for which to install the application (see Figure 7-11). The previous user setting is used for future PRC installations.

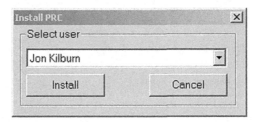

Figure 7-11. The Select User dialog box

Once the user is selected, nothing else will appear on the screen. If you open the Palm Install tool and select the user, you will now see that the application is in the Install tool waiting for the HotSync operation (see Figure 7-12).

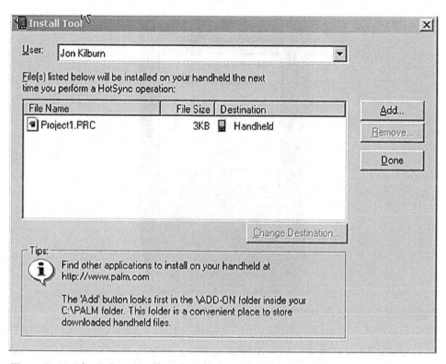

Figure 7-12. The Palm Install tool with the Project 1 application displayed

Now while you have the Palm Install tool open, you can also add the CASLrt.Prc file. Upon your next HotSync, both the runtime and the project will be uploaded. No reset is required for the CASL runtime to be active. If you click the CASL runtime icon on the Palm Device, it will switch to a listbox showing any CASL applications installed on the device to give you the choice of which application to launch (see Figure 7-13).

Figure 7-13. The CASL runtime application listbox

Finally, if you click the "Hello World" application icon, it will open the sample CASL application (see Figure 7-14). If you then click the About button, you'll see the nifty little About message box pop up.

Figure 7-14. The "Hello World" application

Adding an Icon

Although it sounds like a trivial task to do so, adding an icon is a bit tricky. To start with, icon files are not the standard Windows .ico file type. The trick to adding an icon to your application begins with selecting File | New. This will present you with a selection dialog box listing several choices (see Figure 7-15). Two of these choices are for bitmap and icon files. Select the ICON File option.

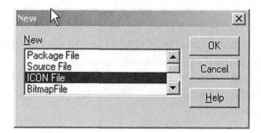

Figure 7-15. Adding an icon

Once you have opened the Icon designer, a new menu option, Image, will appear on the main title bar. At this point, you have two options to create an icon for your application. You can draw the icon using the tools provided and save the icon file, or you can import an image file by clicking the Image menu option and selecting Import Image.

NOTE   *Only bitmap files of pixel size 32 by 22 (or smaller) can be converted to icons. An icon file may be used as the target of a bitmap property for a button or label object.*

The first edit field is for the bitmap image file that is to be converted to an icon file (see Figure 7-16). If you click the button with the ellipsis, you open a Find File dialog box. After selecting the file to be imported, you must then specify an output filename. This file will be stored in the CASL icon format (*.cic).

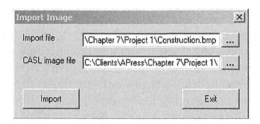

Figure 7-16. Converting a Windows bitmap to a CASL icon

Once the file is converted, it is not automatically added to the project. To add the icon image, you must select Project | Add Files. In the File Open dialog box, select CASL icon file type (*.cic) from the drop-down list.

A new item group named Images will appear in the Project browser. The newly created icon file is now present. If you double-click the icon file, it will open in the Icon editor.

Working with Menus

In Windows, it's a common practice to use a menu for assigning and grouping actions. Not surprisingly, a variation of menus is supported by CASL. It is interesting to note that a menu is really a screen object, yet does not appear within the toolbox as an option, and instead can only be created through code using the menu_top and menu_item language constructs.

Menus provide a way to access multiple commands without occupying too much screen real estate. Each menu should contain one or more menu items, to which commands should be associated. You can visually group items using a separator bar, just like in Windows. Menus themselves are contained within a menu bar, and there can only be one menu bar per form.

To define a menu, you just have to do it the old fashioned way—with code. A menu does not belong to a single frame; it in fact belongs to all frames. Your menu structure will show within any frame that is visible. You can dynamically change menu display properties before showing a frame, which does allow for some customization.

The menu_top construct creates a top-level menu under which menu subitems should be grouped. Under Windows, this would be like the pull-down menus seen across the top of the applications, such as the CASL IDE. On the Palm OS devices, this will create one set of pull-down menus that appears when the Menu button is clicked on the screen. Also, when you do not specify that a menu_top item invokes a function, it just makes the drop-down list of menu items appear.

Be careful: a menu structure is not global. The menu_item requires that you specify the parent_menu, which is really the top-level menu_top item the menu belongs to. Selecting a menu_item will invoke a function—the function that has been associated either through the menu name or by the use of the Invokes keyword.

> **NOTE** *Menu shortcuts can be enabled by prefixing the shortcut character with a carrot (^) symbol. The menu display string must have the same pixel width for shortcuts to line up; this can be done roughly manually, or during startup using the Pixel_width C function in the C library.*

Finally, to make the menu function appear, nothing special needs to be done other than to have a menu_top and at least one menu_item defined. You can then simply call the menu event function by naming the event function the same as the menu option itself (see Listing 7-2).

Listing 7-2. Example of a Cut, Copy and Paste Sample Menu

```
# The parent, top menu item.
# right to left order is determined by the
# order defined starting with the left.
menu_top mtEdit;
    display "Edit";
end;

# When declaring the child menu items the
# top to bottom order is determined by the
# order defined starting with the top.

# Cut Menu Item is "Owned" by the
# Menu Top mtEdit menu object
menu_item miCut,mtEdit;
    display "Cut    ^X"; # 2 extra spaces
end;

menu_item miCopy,mtEdit;
    display "Copy  ^C"; # 1 extra space
end;
```

```
menu_item miPaste,mtEdit;
    display "Paste ^P"; # No extra spaces
end;

# This section will define an Option menu
# with only one element the "About" list.
menu_top mtOptions;
    display "Options";
end;

# The child "About" option
menu_item miAbout,mtOptions;
    display "About";
end;

# This is an example of a function which
# would be invoked by a menu click since
# it is named the same as the menu items definition
function miAbout;
#-=-=-=-=-=-=-=-=-=-=-=-=-=-=-=-=-=-=-=-=-=-=-=-=-=-=-=-=-=
#
#    Function   :   miAbout()
#    Params     :   None
#    Returns    :   None
#
#    Author     :   Vivid Software Inc. - Jon Kilburn
#                       http://www.VividSoftware.com
#
#    Client     :   Apress
#    Notes      :   This function is fired by a menu click
#                       which selects "Options" | "About"
#
#-=-=-=-=-=-=-=-=-=-=-=-=-=-=-=-=-=-=-=-=-=-=-=-=-=-=-=-=-=
    # Variable Declaration
    variables;
        numeric mb;  # Message Box Result
    end;

    # Display an About Message Box
    mb = message_box(0, "About", "Hello World Menu using CASL 3.2!", "OK","","");

end;
```

Putting It All together

Now that you have experimented with menus and learned a bit about the CASL compiler, it's time to write your first program. For the next program, you'll build a simple application to calculate the daily production rate for piecework assembly. I got this idea from a program I wrote for one of my clients, which tracks assembled inventory. Since my client uses robots for product assembly, this program really wouldn't do the client much good, but it would be very useful to help a line supervisor estimate the average assembly time and average daily production for a given product.

This simple application will take the number of pieces that are assembled in a minute and calculate the assembled production estimates for one hour and for a standard eight-hour work day. Begin by creating a new project in CASL:

1. Name the application Product Calculator.

2. Select the option Project PRC Settings and supply the Creator ID of DEMO.

3. Change the Desktop and PRC Versions settings to Production Calculator and Production Calc.

4. Select the frame by double-clicking the body of the form. Change the Display setting to Production Calculator.

5. Select a Label control and drop it on the form layout. Change the Font setting to Large Bold. You can also click the Font button to select from a list of fonts installed on the system and to change the point size. Change the Display property to Assembled Pieces and center the label at the top of the form.

6. Now add three more labels, and change their label display to Per Minute, Per Hour, and Per Shift.

7. Next, insert three corresponding text input fields. For the Per Minute label, name the associated field txtMinute; for the Per Hour field, name the text field txtHour; and for the Per Shift field, name the text field txtShift.

8. For the txtHour and txtShift fields, select the property sheet of each by double-clicking the fields and then checking the No input option. These fields are for display purposes only.

9. Select all the controls using the mouse or right-click while pressing Ctrl. Right-click and from the pop-up menu select Lock controls. This will prevent you from accidentally dragging controls around.

10. Add a button and place it in the bottom-right corner of the screen. Change the name of the button to cmdCalc and the Display property of the button to Calculate.

11. Select the button and right-click. Choose the Lock controls menu option.

Now you are ready to add the calculation code (see Listing 7-3). You know there are sixty minutes in an hour and eight hours in a shift. So to calculate the pieces per hour, you multiply the contents of txtMinute by a value of 60. You then take the resulting value and multiply it by 8, which will yield the number of estimated pieces per shift. Finally, you write the resulting values into the Display property of the two fields, txtHour and txtShift.

Listing 7-3. The Production Calculator Code

```
# This section will define an Option menu
# with only one element the "About" list.
menu_top mtOptions;
    display "Options";
end;

# The child "About" option
menu_item miAbout,mtOptions;
    display "About";
end;

# This is an example of a function which
# would be invoked by a menu click since
# it is named the same as the menu items definition
function miAbout;
#-=-=-=-=-=-=-=-=-=-=-=-=-=-=-=-=-=-=-=-=-=-=-=-=-=-=-=-=
#
#   Function    :   miAbout()
#   Params      :   None
#   Returns     :   None
#
#   Author      :   Vivid Software Inc. - Jon Kilburn
#                       http://www.VividSoftware.com
#
```

```
#    Client     :   Apress
#    Notes      :   This function is fired by a menu click
#                       which selects "Options" | "About"
#
#-=-=-=-=-=-=-=-=-=-=-=-=-=-=-=-=-=-=-=-=-=-=-=-=-=-=-=-=-=-=
    # Variable Declaration
    variables;
        numeric mb;   # Message Box Result
    end;

    # Display an About Message Box
    mb = message_box(0, "About", "Production Calculator Version 1.0", "OK","","");

end;


function cmdCalc;
#-=-=-=-=-=-=-=-=-=-=-=-=-=-=-=-=-=-=-=-=-=-=-=-=-=-=-=-=-=-=
#
#    Function   :   cmdCalc()
#    Params     :   None
#    Returns    :   None
#
#    Author     :   Vivid Software Inc. - Jon Kilburn
#                       http://www.VividSoftware.com
#
#    Client     :   Apress
#    Notes      :   This function is fired by Clicking the
#                       Calculate Button.
#
#-=-=-=-=-=-=-=-=-=-=-=-=-=-=-=-=-=-=-=-=-=-=-=-=-=-=-=-=-=-=
    variables;
        numeric nMin;                # Minutes
        numeric nHour;               # Hours
        numeric nShift; # Shift
        numeric nMb;                 # Message Box Result
    end;

    # Retrieve the Entry from the txtMinutes field
    if txtMinute.display <> "";
        # retrieve the number of pieces assembled
        # in a minute from the text
        nMin = value(txtMinute.display);
```

```
        # calculate
        nHour = nMin * 60;
        nShift = nHour * 8;

        # Display back the calculated values
        txtHour.display = string(nHour, "###");
        txtShift.display = string(nShift, "###");
    else;
        # Display a Message Box Informing the
        # user the calculation can only work
        # against a valid numeric entry
        nMb = message_box(0, "Error", "You must enter a value", "OK","","");
    end_if;
end;
```

Conclusion

In this chapter, I've given you a brief overview of the CASL IDE, how the CASL compiler works, and how to use it to build menus and even a simple application. I've also discussed the basic principals behind how to compile, install, and test your CASL application on the Windows desktop and the Palm environment.

Building the GolfPro Application Using CASL

CASL is not Visual Basic, but then Palm-powered handhelds are not Windows machines. CASL was written with the Palm OS in mind. Let's look at what kind of advantages this has, by building a relational database application.

Most Palm solutions are composed of two pieces: the handheld application portion and the desktop conduit portion (conduits are covered in Chapter 9). In this next section, I'm going to focus on building the handheld application portion of the example Palm application.

As a practical exercise, I will take you step by step through creating an application for keeping track of your golf game at a given golf course. Although I don't play golf much (and I'm certainly not very good at it), I do like to see how much I can improve my game and at which courses I'm shooting the best score—thus the focus of the example application. This simple application will require a few tables, some graphics, and a couple of simple lookups as well as reading and writing to Palm Database files.

The Project Outline

First let's review the basic functionality of what you want to accomplish with what I am calling the Portable GolfPro application. If you don't play the game of golf, or if you do but it doesn't show from your scores (this is the category I fall into), I'll briefly explain the rules of the game, which are quite simple.

Often a game of golf is played at a golf club or at a public golf course. These courses generally have a name and 18 holes. (Although I've heard that some courses have only 9 holes, I've never seen one. And for those of you wondering, *yes*, it would improve my game.) Each hole is then assigned a par. A *par* is the number of shots required to sink the golf ball into the cup on the green. If you can achieve the feat of getting the ball into the cup in the required number of shots, you have achieved par on that hole.

It is from the par on each hole that the figure for *par for the course* is calculated. To determine this number, you add up the number of strokes required to play each course, and that is how you calculate your level of play. If you can complete the course using the same number of strokes as indicated on the scorecard, you have *broken even.* The goal is to save as many strokes as possible and to complete the course at even or perhaps (in the make-believe world where I can actually play this frustrating game) under par.

Okay, so now you know the rules if you hadn't already. Generally speaking, there are a few aspects to the game that you want to include in this application.

- *The courses:* Before you can play a golf game, you have to determine which golf course you will be playing on. Clubs often contain more than one golf course, but, for the purposes of this example, each course is independent of an actual golf club.

- *The course scorecard:* The course scorecard contains the par setting (or number of strokes allowed to put the ball in the hole before applying a penalty of a lost stroke). When you play a hole of golf, you are allowed *x* number of strokes to complete the hole. If you complete the hole before using the allotted number of strokes, you are *under par.* If you sink the ball in the required number of strokes, you have *made par.* And if you sink the ball in two strokes fewer than required, you have made an *eagle.* Finally, if you sink a ball in only one shot, you have made a *hole in one.*

- *Course scoring:* This is the individual scorecard you carry for each course as you play it. When you play a hole, you enter the number of strokes you made to get the ball in the hole. This is also called a *scorecard*, but it refers to each individual's game.

- *Course notes:* When you play a course, you might wish to make notes about a particularly tough hole, say, about a bad dog leg (sharp bend) on the fourth hole. You may want to record that the best way to play this par 4 hole is to get to the green in two strokes, and which particular club you recommend for your tee shot.

On to Palm Database Files

Databases on a Palm device are similar to files on a desktop computer, except that the Palm OS databases reside inside the RAM of the device instead of on a permanent storage media such as a hard drive. Using functions in CASL, you can easily create, open, update, and delete database files and records.

Databases organize related records; every record belongs to one and only one database. A database may be a collection of all address book entries, all date-book entries, and so on. A Palm OS application can create, delete, open, and close databases as necessary, just as a traditional file system can create, delete, open, and close a traditional file.

The GolfPro program will need a simple database. Now I know some of you may read this and later e-mail me a better database design, but I'm not trying to create a great database design. Understand this: Palm Database (PDB) files are essentially the same as good old fashioned DBF files. You may remember them— DBase made them popular in the '80s and early '90s, before SQL came along.

First, let's get some of the basics about PDB files out of the way. Palm Database files are akin to flat files, not relational files. This means, as the programmer, you are responsible for keeping track of relationships and cleaning up after yourself.

Structure of a CASL Database File

If you open a CASL database (CDB) file with a standard text editor, you will see a number of lines at the top that start with a pound sign (#). These are header records, and they describe the file version, number of records, and the record structure. The remaining records are data records. The various header records are described in the following table:

HEADER	DESCRIPTION
#CDBID	CASL file identifier
#MAJREV	Major revision
#MINREV	Minor revision
#FLDCNT	Number of fields per record
#RECCNT	Number of data records following the header records
#SYNCMODE	HotSync mode

The first field in any record is the ID field and is assigned by the PDA. You should not assume anything about the value of this field. When a new record is added on the PC side, its first field is set to zero, 0x00000000. The next field is the status field. This can be a combination of the following values:

FLAG	VALUE
0x0001	Used during HotSync
0x0002	Marks record for deletion
0x0004	Indicates the record has been modified
0x0008	Indicates the record is new

The fields that follow the status field contain the application's data. String fields have double quotes surrounding them. If a double quote is part of the string, then it has double quotes around it (""""). If a field is empty, then it still needs a comma as a placeholder.

The allowed values for #SYNCMODE are listed here:

VALUE	DESCRIPTION
MERGE	Indicates typical transfer
PC_TO_PDA	Specifies PC overwrites the PDA
PDA_TO_PC	Specifies PDA overwrites the PC
NO_SYNC	Indicates no transfer is performed
NOT_SPECIFIED	Specifies external control (same as MERGE for now)

Field definitions are defined as #FLDNUM:N TYPE:T SIZE:S, where N is the field number starting with 1 and ending with the field count specified by #FLDCNT; T is the field type, which can consist of S for a string, N for a number, NA for a number array, and BA for a byte array; and S is the number of elements (if the field type is one of the array types), otherwise this value is zero.

Creating Database Tables

The first table you should create will be the Courses table. This table, which will contain each course and the par value for each hole, has to be created first because you need to use it before all the other related tables. You have several options for creating this table (including using a PDB file creation utility for the PC), but the easiest way to do so is through code using the dbfile object (more on this in a moment).

The second table will be the Players table. The Players table will contain the info for each player and his or her handicap. The Players table and the Courses table are independent of each other but share a relationship in the Scores table.

The third table will be the Score (scorecard) table. The Score table will be related to the Courses table by the field CourseID, and to the Players table via the PlayerID. The idea here is that you can now track a player's score on a golf course based on any given date. Later if you wished, you could then chart a player's improvement (or in the case of my golf game, deterioration).

The fourth and final table is the Notes table. This table is related to the Course table by the CourseID. You will also add the hole as an integer (that is, 1 through 18) to help you read any notes on a particular course hole you may have made (other than the usual "I hate this hole" comment).

For a complete understanding of the table's layouts and relationships, please refer to Figure 8-1.

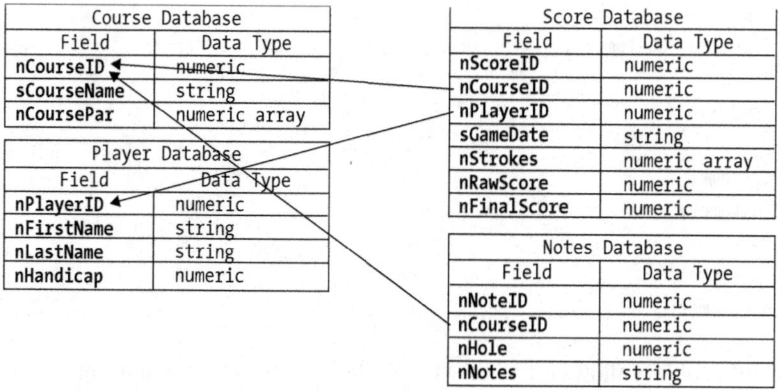

Figure 8-1. The databases in the GolfPro program with their relational links

CASL databases are easily implemented with the dbfile object. The CASL file object also allows data storage, so let's look at both of these options a bit. The dbfile object files and the file object files both represent a collection of data stored in records, which are in a large data file container stored in flash memory. A common set of CASL commands enable you to create, open, close, and delete files of either type.

dbfile Object

A dbfile object defines a record structure, and binds the field data to program variables. This means that you must define program-level variables to serve as the target for the data stored in a record (see Listing 8-1). The first field defines how the records will be sorted in the dbfile object.

Listing 8-1. Code for Opening and Creating a Customer's CDB File

```
dbfile dbCustomer;
      field nCustID; # auto-increment
      field sName;
      field sAddress;
      field sCity;
      field sState;
      field sZipCode;
      sync_pref pda_to_pc;
end;


# Open will Create a file if it does not exist
# using the database design supplied in the dbfile
```

```
# structure
Open dbCustomer, "Customer";

# .. Do some stuff

# Close Customer
close dbCustomer;

# Delete Customer
delete dbCustomer;
```

The dbfile object allows for all the standard record behaviors—adding, reading, writing, and deleting of records using the insert, get_fields, put_fields, and remove functions (see Listing 8-2).

Listing 8-2. Code for Reading, Writing, and Deleting a Customer's record.dbfile

```
dbCustomer;
        field nCustID; # auto-increment
        field sName;
        field sAddress;
        field sCity;
        field sState;
        field sZipCode;
        sync_pref pda_to_pc;
end;

# Open will Create a file if it does not exist
# using the database design supplied in the dbfile
# structure
Open dbCustomer, "Customer";

# Set the values
sName = "Jon Kilburn";
sAddress = "7474 Foxtail Drive";
sCity = "Dallas";
sState = "Texas";
sZipCode = "75287";

# Insert the Record
insert dbCustomer;

# Change Values
sAddress = "7408 Watson Drive"
```

```
sCity = "Plano"

# Update Record
put_fields dbCustomer;

# Delete the Record
remove dbCustomer;

# Close Customer
close dbCustomer;
```

Records are sorted using the first (key) field, which in this case would be the customer number (nCustID). A search command allows random access to a dbfile by matching the key field value (inexact matching is also possible). The CASL conduit allows HotSync operations only on CASL files of type dbfile (see Chapter 9 for more information on the CASL conduit).

A file object can be read and written by a record, but the record is organized as you specify in your code. During a write operation, you must organize your data the way you want. During a read operation, you must parse your data in a manner that is consistent with how you organized it during your write operation.

Error Codes

When using the database functions in CASL, an internal custom error code is generated if any of these functions fail. In CASL, the approach is to set the *errorcode* variable equal to zero before performing a database operation, and then check the value of *errorcode* after the operation (see Listing 8-3). The error codes for the various dbfile functions are listed in Table 8-1.

Listing 8-3. Checking Error Codes

```
# Variable Declaration
variables;
      numeric mb;                 # Message Box Result
end;


# Perform a Search
errorcode = 0;
search dbCustomer, "123";

if errorcode = 0;
      # Display a Message Box
      mb = message_box(0, "Found", "Customer Found!", "OK","","");
end_if;
```

Table 8-1. CASL errorcode *Values*

CODE	NAME	DESCRIPTION
-1	CE_DIV_0	Divide by zero
-2	CE_ARRAY	Invalid array index
-3	CE_NOT_OPEN	File not open
-4	CE_FLD_MIS	Database field mismatch
-5	CE_EOF	End Of File
-6	CE_FMODE	Invalid file mode
-7	CE_FILE_NF	File not found
-8	CE_FILE_DEL	Record deleted
-9	CE_SERIAL_OPEN	Serial port error
-10	CE_SERIAL_COMM	Serial communications error
-11	CE_FILE_OPEN	File already open
-12	CE_REC_NOT_FOUND	Record not found
-13	CE_PUT_RECORD_ERROR	Put record error
-14	CE_FILE_DELETE_ERROR	Delete record error
-15	CE_BAD_NUMBER_ERROR	Bad number error

Let's review a few of the items of interest within the dbfile. The first item of importance is that I used a dbfile object for this file. A good rule of thumb is to name dbfile objects starting with "db" plus the name of the table. In this case, "dbCustomer" was used.

Now let's talk about the code required to open a Palm Database file and work with it inside the CASL version of the Portable GolfPro application.

Defining a CASL Database

When defining a CASL database, you need to define the field variables and then a dbfile record structure, which will bind the field values written to or read from memory with the field variables.

Considering first the course database, you'll need the variables shown in Listing 8-4.

Listing 8-4. Variables Used for the Course Table

```
variables;
      numeric nCourseID; # auto-increment
```

```
      string sCourseName;
      numeric nCoursePar[18];
end;
```

Notice variables are defined by using a variables block. You're defining a numeric CourseID, a string CourseName, and a numeric array of single dimension with the size 18 (offsets of 0 through 17). CASL allows fields to be numeric arrays, but not string arrays. The first field (which will be the key) cannot be an array.

> **NOTE** *In CASL, numerics are numbers stored in IEEE 8-byte floating-point format, and can represent values in the range of 10E+38 to 10E-38, with 16 digits of decimal precision. This is a native Palm OS format for numbers.*

Next, all you have to do is use those variables for defining the record structure. Using a dbfile declaration, you include the variables and link them to the table via the keyword "field" (see Listing 8-5).

Listing 8-5. Creating the File Object

```
dbfile dbCourse;
      field nCourseID; # auto-increment
      field sCourseName;
      field nCoursePar;
      sync_pref pda_to_pc;
end;
```

What you have now is a dbfile object named dbCourse. The record has three fields. The first field is the course ID and will be the sort key; the other fields are linked to the record, and the final parameter is the sync preference. This defines for the CASL conduit how to interact with the data when performing a HotSync operation. Notice that, for a field array, you leave off the index, signifying the whole array.

Organizing Code

For this application, you're going to define an appreciable amount of code. This being the case, it's wise to think about code organization. Proper code organization will facilitate debugging, but it's also a way to tell the CASLpro compiler in which memory segment you'd like code stored. Each memory segment can hold a maximum of 32KB of code.

You're going to have four databases (Course, Player, Score, and Notes), so you need to define package files for each database. I'll also instruct you as to how to put the auxiliary form actions such as the Splash form code and About form code in a fifth package file.

To create a package file, use the CASLide menu command, File | New, and specify a file type of package for your new file. Use the File | Save As menu command to give the file a name. If you were creating the Course database package file, you might use the name "Course." The folder by default will be the project folder, with the extension .cpk (which stands for CASL package file). To get the file to appear in your project window, you put an include statement in your main code module:

```
include "Course.cpk";
```

As you'll want the compiler to "see" the dependent variables, objects, and functions you'll be defining before your event functions, you want to put the include statement in the main code module before any of the event functions.

> **NOTE** *The reason that you must use "forward" function calls is because the CASL compiler is a one-pass compiler. This means that the compiler will attempt to resolve references to functions and variables when they are encountered.*

Once you've added an include statement in your code, select Project | Update Includes to add the package files to your project window.

In a similar manner, you'll need to run through the same steps to create package files for the Players, Score, and Notes databases.

Since all event functions will be the top-level functions called as a result of program startup, user interaction with display objects, and program shutdown, you'll keep all event functions in the main code module.

User Interface Design

As is the case with most Palm OS applications, there is a list view form and a record view form for each database. This makes eight forms for the four databases of this example application.

I also mentioned that you would want an About form, and for this application you'll include an About CASL form, and a fatal error form. The fatal error form will be used to disable the program in the event of an unexpected database access problem.

Figure 8-2 shows the forms for each of the files needed by the GolfPro program.

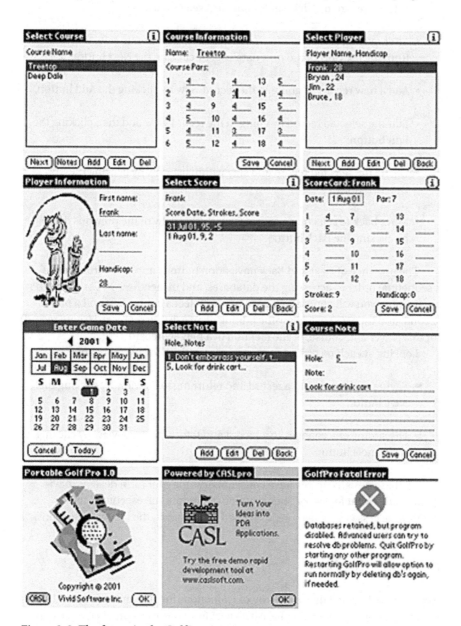

Figure 8-2. The forms in the GolfPro program

Looking at each database-related form, you can see that each list view includes options that let users perform the following actions:

- Select a record by clicking its name in a selector list.

- After making a selection from this database, move on to selecting a record from the list view of the next database by clicking the Next button.

- Add a new record by going to the record view by clicking the Add button.

- Edit the selected record by going to the record view and then clicking the Edit button.

- Delete the selected record and stay within list view by clicking the Delete button.

- Move back to selecting a record from the list view of the previous database by clicking the Back button.

The presence of Next and Back navigation buttons implies there must be a sequential order to accessing the databases, and in fact there is. For the GolfPro application, you will choose to force a user to select a course first and a player second, and then you will allow the editing of an existing scorecard (score record) for this player and course, or the creation of a new scorecard.

Looking at each record view, you see user options for the following:

- Saving any changes to a record and returning to list view by clicking the Save button

- Discarding any changes to a record and returning to list view by clicking the Cancel button

All these design choices have consequences for your form designs, navigation code (what forms are shown after user options are executed), and database access code. These are discussed separately in the following sections.

Program Startup

Now let's start adding the code to invoke functions for all events associated with the SelectCourse (Course database list view) form. Concentrate first on displaying the intended form when object events are invoked. This is normally called *program navigation.* You will add code to realize the intended database operations later.

In this design, the SelectCourse form is the first shown, since a record from this database will be the first selected. The actual task the user will want to do is track scores, but I've decided for the purposes of this example that each score record will be related to a course and player record; therefore you will force the user to make a course and player record selection by taking him or her sequentially through the database list views as previously described.

This program has many forms, and each form has a hidden property. When a CASL program starts up, the program will attempt to show each form with the hidden property cleared (set to show). Obviously the display can physically show only one form, so you will want to manage the hidden properties in order to show only the desired form. When you initialize your forms, you initialize all hidden properties so the forms are hidden. In the startup function, if you clear the hidden property of the SelectCourse form, you'll achieve the desired result (see Listing 8-6).

Listing 8-6. Startup Function

```
function startup;
        # all forms hidden, show main form
        # alternative syntax, frGolfPro.hidden=false;
        show frCourseList;
end;
```

Looking at the Course List form, the first thing you might consider is the selector event. This is intended to signify a choice has been made from displayed records—the event has no effect on the displayed form. Since you're concentrating on form navigation, and you don't have databases defined yet, just make a placeholder for this event, as shown in Listing 8-7.

Listing 8-7. Adding Placeholder Code

```
# this is a compiler instruction to compile all CASL code in this file now,
# and when finished, return to compiling code in this file
include "..\library\sml_ShowMsgLite.cpk";

function cl_slCourseList;
        # note new selection
        sml_ShowMsg(0,"New selection "+string(cl_slCourseList.selected,"")+
  " noted");
end;
```

The sml_ShowMsg() function is a wrapper around the CASL function message_box(). Its operation is left to the reader. The CASL function message_box() is a modal dialog box that allows up to three user inputs. Its syntax is explained in the CASL Reference Manual.

> **NOTE** *By clicking the sml_ShowMsgLite.cpk file in the project window, placing your cursor on the message_box function, and then pressing the F1 key, you can open the CASL Language Manual and display the message_box entry. This is true of any CASL function.*

The next thing you might consider are the action buttons along the bottom of the form. Look at each from left to right.

Begin by designing the Course List form (see Figure 8-3). The Course List form will be the central focal point of the GolfPro application.

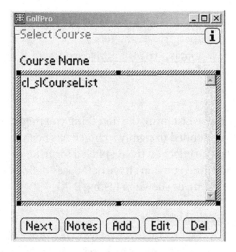

Figure 8-3. The layout of the Course Form in the CASLide

Now that you have the form designed, you need to add the code to load the course data from the Courses database file into the List control (see Listing 8-8).

Listing 8-8. Adding the Course Records to the List Control

```
function ffFillCourseList as numeric;
#-=-=-=-=-=-=-=-=-=-=-=-=-=-=-=-=-=-=-=-=-=-=-=-=-=-=-=-=-=
#
```

```
#    Function     :    ffFillCourseList()
#    Params       :    None
#    Returns      :    None
#
#    Author       :    Vivid Software Inc. - Jon Kilburn
#                      http://www.VividSoftware.com
#
#    Client       :    Apress
#    Purpose      :    Loads the Course List
#
#-=-=-=-=-=-=-=-=-=-=-=-=-=-=-=-=-=-=-=-=-=-=-=-=-=-=-=-=
        # fill course list
        nLastCourseI=0;

        # point at bof
        seek_start dbCourse,0;

        # attempt to read first record
        errorcode=0;
        get_fields dbCourse;

        # read all records until error
        while errorcode=0;
                nCourseKeys[nLastCourseI]=nCourseID;
                sCourseList[nLastCourseI]=sCourseName;
                nLastCourseI=nLastCourseI+1;
                get_fields dbCourse;
          end_while;

        # nLastCourseI is 1-based count of db records and list size
        # remember last course id
        if nLastCourseI=0;
                nLastCourseID=0;
        else;
                nLastCourseID=nCourseID;
        end_if;

        # return false if not eof
        ffFillCourseList=errorcode=ce_eof;
end;
```

Now try running the program by selecting the Windows Release (or Windows Debug) option on platform drop-down list, and then selecting Execute | Run or clicking the Run toolbar.

Figure 8-4. The Course List form running in Windows

The Portable GolfPro Project

Following the instructions for creating a new CASL application presented in the previous chapter, you will create a new CASL application and name it GolfPro. Start by modifying the startup function so the Splash form is first shown, and then after two seconds the main Course List form appears. You will do this by using the CASL timer function, which will call the function given as its first parameter after the number of milliseconds specified as its second parameter (see Listing 8-9).

Listing 8-9. The Modified Startup Function

```
function HideSplashShowMain;
      # hide splash form and show course list form
      hide frSplash;
      show frCourseList;
end;

function startup;
      # all forms hidden, show splash for 2 s, then show main form
      ShowSplash;
      timer HideSplashShowMain, 2000;
end;
```

Building the Splash Form

Now it's time to build the Splash form.

1. Open the blank form and select the frame. Double-click the frame to bring up the Properties page. Change the frame's name to frSplash and change the display option to Portable GolfPro 1.0.

2. Add a button. Drag it to the lower-right corner and name it sp_btOK. Change the button's display option to read "OK".

3. Add another button. Drag it to the lower-left corner and name it sp_btCASL. Change the button's display option to read "CASL", and also change the button's background color to blue.

4. Now add two labels. Change the first label's display property to "Copyright "+char(169)+" 2002" and click the Expression checkbox. This will cause the copyright symbol to appear in the text. Change the display property of the second label to read "Vivid Software Inc."

Adding a Bitmap to Your Splash Form

At this point, you are ready to add a bitmap to your Splash form. Bitmaps are an optional property of a label or button object. When a bitmap is already provided, the easiest way to import the bitmap into the CASLide is to use the Import tool. To do this, select Image | Import Image. The Import Image dialog box appears, as shown in Figure 8-5.

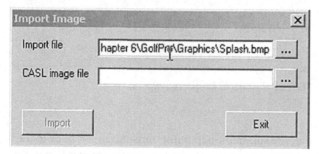

Figure 8-5. The Import Image dialog box

Use the ". . ." button to specify the provided bitmap. To specify a CASL file-name, enter the name you want for your file in the CASL display image textbox.

This file can be new, as is the case here. The .cbm (CASL bitmap) extension will be added automatically. When completed, a CASL image will have been created at the same size, and the colors automatically translated to the closest 256 colors that the Palm OS supports.

To add the image file to your project, use the Add Files menu command. Be sure to specify file type cbm. You should be able to find the file you just created. Clicking OK will add this image to your project.

You now need to add this image to the bitmap property of the label or button on which you wish to display the image. On the Splash form, you need to define a label with the same size dimensions, and assign the bitmap to the bitmap property of the label, as shown in the Label Control Property page for the Splash form label in Figure 8-6.

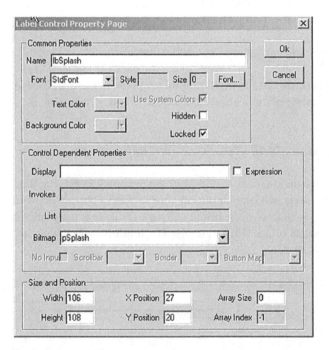

Figure 8-6. The Label Control Property Page

Notice that the splash bitmap is not transparent. Go back to the image file by clicking its name in the project window, under the Images folder. The transparent color is the blue-green color. Click the blue-green color box on the Color Selection tool, and select the Fill tool. Clicking the image in the background area will fill the background with the transparent color. Save the image, and the image on the Splash form will now be transparent (see Figure 8-7).

Figure 8-7. The final Splash form

You're not quite done. You now have a color image, but what if your user has a monochrome Palm handheld? This is where image families come in.

Creating Image Families

CASL programs that have image families will display the appropriate image during program execution. To create an image family, select Image | New Image Type. This will create a blank monochrome image the same size as your color image. You can cut and paste the color image here, but in the GolfPro example, this will not create a presentable image, since all colors except white are translated to black.

To create a good monochrome image from the provided image, you'll need to use your favorite image editor, and reduce the color count to 2. You can then cut the original image and paste it into the monochrome image.

 NOTE *CASL comes with a complete set of image drawing tools for creating your own images, should an image not be provided. You can also cut an image from any bitmap editor and paste it into a CASL image of the same size.*

About Box Navigation

An about box and a splash screen are both ways to show your users something about your program. The main difference between the two is an about box normally has an OK button to dismiss the form, and a Splash form normally shows for only a given period of time, therefore not requiring an OK button. You will use the same form for both the about box and the splash screen, so I'll show you how to write some show functions for the About form and the Splash form to accommodate this difference. In addition to an OK button, the About form also has an About CASL button you'll need to hide when you're showing the form as a splash screen.

Listing 8-10. Code to Hide/Show Buttons on the Splash Form Based on the Action

```
function ShowAbout;
      # show about form with ok and casl buttons
      show sp_btOK;
      show sp_btCASL;
      show frSplash;
end;

function ShowSplash;
      # show splash form with no ok and casl buttons
      hide sp_btOK;
      hide sp_btCASL;
      show frSplash;
end;
```

You are going to have an about box form shown whenever the "i" icon button is clicked. Note that, because you have an "i" icon button on multiple forms (all the list forms and the score record form), you need a means of knowing which is the calling form so that it will be redisplayed once the About form is dismissed. Use the frame's object_string property to do this. The calling code for each frame's "i" button will look similar to the template code shown in Listing 8-11.

Listing 8-11. About Button Code, which Calls the Splash Form

```
function cl_btAbout;
      hide frCourseList;
      frSplash.object_string="cl"; # use pl, sl, nl and sr for other frames
      show frSplash;
end;
```

The OK button on the About form will then determine the return code. The nested if-then blocks are used to determine the value of the object_string property, and therefore the calling form (see Listing 8-12).

Listing 8-12. Determining the Calling Form

```
function sp_btOK;
    hide frSplash;
    # determine which was calling frame and reshow
    if frSplash.object_string="cl";
        show frCourseList;
    else;
        if frSplash.object_string="pl";
            show frPlayerList;
        else;
            if frSplash.object_string="sl";
                show frScoreList;
            else;
                if frSplash.object_string="nl";
                    show frNotesList;
                else;
                show frScoreRecord;
                end_if;
                end_if;
            end_if;
    end_if;
end;
```

Now that you know how to open the forms, load the program into the POSE and run it to test the timer delay and the display of the About form into the Course List form.

Figure 8-8. The Splash form running in the POSE

Manipulating CASL Database Files

Now that you have successfully gotten to the Course List form, it's time to load the course list so you can select which course to begin working with. The first item to deal with is the Courses database file not being present on the Palm Device.

Start by creating a new package file for the Course form. Once you have created the package file, you need to add the information for the dbfile (see Listing 8-13).

Listing 8-13. The Code from the Course Package File

```
# course data
variables;
      numeric nCourseID; # auto-increment
      string sCourseName;
      numeric nCoursePar[18];

      numeric nLastCourseID; # last id counter value, next is +1
      string sCourseDBName="gpCourse";

      numeric nLastCourseI; # 1-based size of lists
      numeric nMaxCourseI=32; # 1-based max size of lists
      numeric nCourseKeys[nMaxCourseI]; # list of all key values
```

```
        # already defined in cff file
        # string sCourseList[nMaxCourseI]; # display list
        numeric nSelectedCourseID;
end;


# course db
dbfile dbCourse;
        field nCourseID; # auto-increment
        field sCourseName;
        field nCoursePar;
        sync_pref pda_to_pc;
end;


# course list functions
function ffFillCourseList as numeric;
        # fill course list
        nLastCourseI=0;

        # point at bof
        seek_start dbCourse,0;

        # attempt to read first record
        errorcode=0;
        get_fields dbCourse;

        # read all records until error
        while errorcode=0;
                nCourseKeys[nLastCourseI]=nCourseID;
                sCourseList[nLastCourseI]=sCourseName;
                nLastCourseI=nLastCourseI+1;
                get_fields dbCourse;
        end_while;

        # nLastCourseI is 1-based count of db records and list size
        # remember last course id
        if nLastCourseI=0;
                nLastCourseID=0;
        else;
                nLastCourseID=nCourseID;
        end_if;

        # return false if not eof
        ffFillCourseList=errorcode=ce_eof;
end;
```

```
# before calling assumes that course list and related size
#   variables are already defined
function ShowSelectCourse;
     variables;
               numeric i;
               numeric found;
     end;
     if nLastCourseI=0;
               # disable buttons
               hide cl_btNext;
               hide cl_btNotes;
               hide cl_btEdit;
               hide cl_btDel;
               # hide empty list
               hide cl_slCourseList;
     else;
               # enable buttons
               show cl_btNext;
               show cl_btNotes;
               show cl_btEdit;
               show cl_btDel;
               # display list
               cl_slCourseList.list_size=nLastCourseI;
               # try to find match with selected id
               found=false;
               i=0;
               while i<nLastCourseI;
                         if nCourseKeys[i]=nSelectedCourseID;
                              cl_slCourseList.selected=i; # default to selected id
                                   found=true;
                                   i=nLastCourseI;
                         end_if;
                         i=i+1;
               end_while;
               if not found;
                         # default to first item if no match
                         nSelectedCourseID=nCourseKeys[0];
                         cl_slCourseList.selected=0;
               end_if;
               show cl_slCourseList;
     end_if;
     show frCourseList;
end;
```

```
# intended to call in startup function
function InitCoursePrompts;
     variables;
               numeric i;
     end;
     i=0;
     while i<18;
               cr_lbParPrompt[i].display=string(i+1,"");
               i=i+1;
     end_while;
end;
```

In the sections of code listed earlier (specifically the ffFillCourseList function), you do not have to move the record pointer to the first record. When you call get_fields, the variables defined in the dbfile will receive the values from the first record (in the sorted order).

Next, you simply start walking the file by using a while loop in conjunction with a call to the get_fields function. This function will read the next record in the file into the supplied dbfile. You can see that the code loads each record into the sCourseList array structure, defined earlier, and then loads the course name into the cl_slCourseList List control in the ShowSelectCourse function.

Now in the main GolfPro CASL file, which forms should be shown and what functions should be executed need to be defined in the function Startup (see Listing 8-14). If you look closely, you'll see another function, the OpenDBs function. This function will be responsible for opening all the databases used by the GolfPro application. Once the databases are opened, you can move on to filling the list.

Listing 8-14. Startup Code

```
function startup;
     # all forms hidden, show splash for 2 s, then show main form
     ShowSplash;
     timer HideSplashShowMain, 2000;

     # initialize form displays
     InitCoursePrompts;
     InitScorePrompts;

     # recursively try to open db's until success or user aborts
     fDeletedDBs=false;
     OpenDBs;
end;
```

```
            function OpenDBs;
            # check if all db's already exist, or all db's don't exist
            if ffDBsExist or ffNoDBsExist;
                        # can rely on integrity of db's, try to open each
                        #  and if problem, delete all, then open all initialized as new
                        if dbn_ffOpenDB(dbCourse,sCourseDBName) and
                         dbn_ffOpenDB(dbPlayer,sPlayerDBName) and
                         dbn_ffOpenDB(dbScore,sScoreDBName) and
                         dbn_ffOpenDB(dbNotes,sNotesDBName);
                                    # ok all db's open
                                    # read all course records and fill selector
                                    if ffFillCourseList;
                                            # ok, select course form will display when
                                            #  splash times out
                                            if fDeletedDBs;
                                                    # experienced prior db open problems, when
                                                    #  initial splash screen timed out, no new
                                                    #   screen was shown
                                                    fDeletedDBs=false;
                                                    ShowSelectCourse;
                                            else;
                                                # no prior db open problems, when splash screen
                                                 #  timed out, select course screen shown, this
                                                    #  function takes much less than time out
                                                    #  period
                                            end_if;
                                    else;
                                            # unexpected error
                                        DeleteDBsAndReopen(sCourseDBName+" must be corrupt, "+
                                            "must delete all and restart");
                                    end_if;
                        else;
                                    # one or more db must be corrupt, must delete
                                    DeleteDBsAndReopen("One or more db must be corrupt, "+
                                        "must delete all and restart");
                        end_if;
            else;
                        # at least one db existed, but not all did, assume
                        #  all corrupt, delete all, then open all initialized as new
                        DeleteDBsAndReopen("One or more db is missing, "+
```

```
                    "must delete all and restart");
        end_if;
end;


# Call this function to load the course lists both into the control
# and into an array (nCourseKeys)
function ffFillCourseList as numeric;
        # fill course list
        nLastCourseI=0;

        # point at bof
        seek_start dbCourse,0;

        # attempt to read first record
        errorcode=0;
        get_fields dbCourse;

        # read all records until error
        while errorcode=0;
                nCourseKeys[nLastCourseI]=nCourseID;
                sCourseList[nLastCourseI]=sCourseName;
                nLastCourseI=nLastCourseI+1;
                get_fields dbCourse;
        end_while;

        # nLastCourseI is 1-based count of db records and list size
        # remember last course id
        if nLastCourseI=0;
                            nLastCourseID=0;
        else;
                            nLastCourseID=nCourseID;
        end_if;

        # return false if not eof
        ffFillCourseList=errorcode=ce_eof;
end;
```

The final result of this startup code is a grid of courses waiting to be played (see Figure 8-9).

Figure 8-9. Browsing the Course List form running in the POSE

Getting Your GolfPro Program to Run

Now there are several things that have to take place to make the GolfPro program work. First you must set up the course on which you want to play. As explained earlier, a course has a given number of strokes, which are assigned to all 18 holes. If the course is completed in this number of strokes, a player is considered to have played an even game (this comes up later).

So each course has a total number of strokes required for each hole, which is why you have created the Course table. So let's consider what the Course database holds. It holds the name of the golf course and the number of strokes allotted to each hole for par. That means each record requires an ID, course name, 18 holes, and the strokes (or par) for each hole (see Figure 8-10).

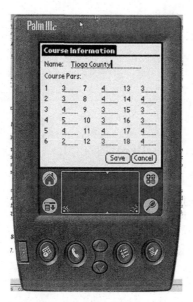

Figure 8-10. The Course Information screen

So now let's take a look at the code to save a new record and modify an existing record. When you click the Add button, you want to display the Course form but you want to default to the par for each hole. This will save the user time when creating a new course record. You'll add an invoker function named cl_btAdd to be run when the user clicks the Add button. This function will call a form setup function, ShowNewCourse, to format the Course form before it's displayed (see Listing 8-15).

Listing 8-15. The Code to Add a Course Record

```
function cl_btAdd;
      # make sure not over limit
      if nLastCourseI<nMaxCourseI;
              # ok, show new default record
              hide frCourseList;
              ShowNewCourse;
      else;
              sml_ShowMsg(2,"Courses are at limit of "+string(nMaxCourseI,"")+
               ", delete one to add one");
      end_if;
end;
```

```
# called by Add button, frame tagged so know what kind of save to do
function ShowNewCourse;
      variables;
                numeric i;
      end;
      cr_txName.display="";
      i=0;
      while i<18;
                cr_txPar[i].display=string(4,"");
                i=i+1;
      end_while;
      frCourseRecord.object_string="a";
      show frCourseRecord;
end;
```

Saving the Course Record

So now that you've seen how to set up the display of the Add portion of the Course form, let's think about what you have to do to save the course record. Saving the course record requires several elements:

- Making sure a valid course name has been supplied.

- Checking the frame's object string to determine the type of operations (a = add, e = edit), and then acting accordingly: if in add mode, write a new record, and if in edit mode, write to the current record.

- Updating the key column.

- Refilling the course list.

Now that you have determined the save actions, you need to write the database access code. For this application, a generic set of database functions is created and placed in the package file dbn_DBNAccess. In this file, the code to insert, update, and delete records is consolidated to minimize the code (see Listing 8-16).

Listing 8-16. The Write Record Functions

```
# db bound variables already have field data
# given dbfile object, and key field data string,
# side effect: if key is new insert new record, if key
#  already exists return false,
```

```
#  errorcode has error status
# returns true/false on success
function dbn_ffWriteNewRecord(object dbobj,numeric key) as numeric;
      if dbn_ffRecordExists(dbobj,key);
              # don't create record with duplicate key
              dbn_ffWriteNewRecord=false;
      else;
              # add new record
              errorcode=0;
              insert dbobj;
              dbn_ffWriteNewRecord=errorcode=0;
      end_if;
end;


# Code to write existing record

# db bound variables already have field data
# given dbfile object, and key field data string,
# side effect: if key is new return false, if key
# already exists writes new data for existing record,
# errorcode has error status
# returns true/false on success
function dbn_ffWriteExistingRecord(object dbobj,numeric key) as numeric;
      if dbn_ffRecordExists(dbobj,key);
              # write existing record
              errorcode=0;
              put_fields dbobj;
              dbn_ffWriteExistingRecord=errorcode=0;
      else;
              # don't create new
              dbn_ffWriteExistingRecord=errorcode=false;
      end_if;
end;
```

Now that the records have been properly added, let's look at what has to be done to edit an existing record. The trick here is to get the current course ID and work with it. To get the current course ID, you have to do several things. The first item was already handled in the ffFillCourseList function noted earlier; in this function, the course ID value is stored in an array (nCourseKeys), which directly corresponds to the values displayed on the screen.

Next the List controls' invoker function is used to link the course ID to an event.cl_CourseList. In the cs_CourseList event, the selected ID is stored to a variable, nSelectedCourseID, which you can later use to search through the database.

Now you simply attach the code to read the record to the invoker function of the cl_btEdit button (see Listing 8-17). The code will find the record that matches, and then load the value from the database directly into the text controls.

Listing 8-17. Code to Store Course ID and Edit a Course

```
# Function Linked to List Control Event
function cl_slCourseList;
      # Store Current Selection ID
      nSelectedCourseID=nCourseKeys[cl_slCourseList.selected];
end;


# Code Invoked by the Edit Button
function cl_btEdit;
      # attempt to read existing record
      if dbn_ffReadExactRecord(dbCourse,nSelectedCourseID);
              # ok, show existing record
              hide frCourseList;
              ShowExistingCourse;
      else;
              sml_ShowMsg(2,"Unable to read course record "+cl_slCourseList.display);
      end_if;
end;


# Reprinted here for Clarity is the dbn_ffReadExactRecord function
function dbn_ffReadExactRecord(object dbobj,numeric key) as numeric;
      if dbn_ffRecordExists(dbobj,key);
              # found
              errorcode=0;
              get_fields dbobj;
              dbn_ffReadExactRecord=errorcode=0;
      else;
              # not found
              dbn_ffReadExactRecord=false;
      end_if;
end;


# called by Edit button, frame tagged so know what kind of save to do
function ShowExistingCourse;
      variables;
              numeric i;
```

```
    end;
    # assign field variables to display objects
    cr_txName.display=sCourseName;
    i=0;
    while i<18;
            cr_txPar[i].display=string(nCoursePar[i],"");
            i=i+1;
    end_while;
    frCourseRecord.object_string="e";
    show frCourseRecord;
end;
```

Deleting a Record

This brings you to the final piece of the puzzle. You need to know how to delete
a record, and when you delete a course you must take care to delete any records
that may be related to this course. If you do not delete related records, then you
risk leaving orphan records in your databases. Ultimately, this could consume
quite a bit of space.

So the key is to first confirm that the user wishes to delete the course, and if
he or she does, then based on the success of each sequential delete you will
remove the scorecards and notes associated with this course (see Listing 8-18).

Listing 8-18. Code to Delete a Course and Related Records.

```
# Delete Button Click Event
function cl_btDel;
    # Confirm Delete
    if sml_ffConfirmYes("Delete course "+cl_slCourseList.display+
        " and related notes and score cards?");
            if dbn_ffRemoveRecord(dbCourse,nSelectedCourseID);
                    if ffDeleteRelatedNotesRecords(nSelectedCourseID);
                        if ffDeleteCourseRelatedScoreRecords(nSelectedCourseID);
                                # updated course list
                                if ffFillCourseList;
                                        ShowSelectCourse;
                                else;

                    DeleteDBsAndReopen(sCourseDBName+" must be corrupt, "+

"must delete all and restart");
```

```
                                                    end_if;
                                else;
                                            # problems with scores db
                                DeleteDBsAndReopen(sNotesDBName+" must be corrupt, "+
                                                    "must delete all and restart");
                                    end_if;
                        else;
                                    # problems with notes db
                                DeleteDBsAndReopen(sScoreDBName+" must be corrupt, "+
                                                    "must delete all and restart");
                            end_if;
                else;
                        # no remove
                        sml_ShowMsg(2,"Delete of course "+cl_slCourseList.display+
                         " unsuccessful");
                    end_if;
            end_if;
    end;


    # Delete and Record Exists Functions reprinted
    # here for convenience, the Notes Delete function
    # and the Course Score Delete Function both reside
    # in there respective Notes and Course Package files
    function dbn_ffRemoveRecord(object dbobj,numeric key) as numeric;
            if dbn_ffRecordExists(dbobj,key);
                    errorcode=0;
                    remove dbobj;
                    dbn_ffRemoveRecord=errorcode=0;
            else;
                    dbn_ffRemoveRecord=false;
            end_if;
    end;


    function ffDeleteRelatedNotesRecords(numeric coursekey) as numeric;
            variables;
                    numeric abort;
            end;
            # read all notes records and delete those that have coursekey
```

```
        # point at bof
        seek_start dbNotes,0;

        # attempt to read first record
        errorcode=0;
        abort=false;
        get_fields dbNotes;

        # read all records until error
        while errorcode=0 and abort=false;
                if nCourseID=coursekey;
                        # this is record that matches course id
                        if not dbn_ffRemoveRecord(dbNotes,nNotesID);
                                abort=true;
                        end_if;
                end_if;
                get_fields dbNotes;
        end_while;

        # return false if not eof
        ffDeleteRelatedNotesRecords=errorcode=ce_eof and abort=false;
end;

function ffDeleteCourseRelatedScoreRecords(numeric coursekey) as numeric;
        variables;
            numeric abort;
        end;

        # read all score records and delete those that have coursekey
        # point at bof
        seek_start dbScore,0;

        # attempt to read first record
        errorcode=0;
        abort=false;
        get_fields dbScore;

        # read all records until error
        while errorcode=0 and abort=false;
                if nCourseID=coursekey;
                        # this is record that matches course id
                        if not dbn_ffRemoveRecord(dbScore,nScoreID);
                                abort=true;
```

```
                    end_if;
            end_if;
            get_fields dbScore;
        end_while;

        # return false if not eof
        ffDeleteCourseRelatedScoreRecords=errorcode=ce_eof and abort=false;
end;
```

Adding Course Notes

When you have finished adding a course and assigning the scorecard, then you can look at adding the course notes. Course notes are notes that an individual player may make about a particular hole or area of the golf course.

A typical example of a course note would be to detail the way a ball might break on a green or even the speed of a green. Adding a course note is simple: pass the course ID on to the Notes browse, and from there you can pass this value to the Notes edit form (see Figure 8-11).

Figure 8-11. Browsing the Notes database

In the Notes browse, you must check the current course ID against the course ID in the Course Notes database to make sure that they match, since you really want to see only those notes that pertain to the selected golf course. In the Notes Package File Event of frmNotesBrowse, you will filter against the records to make sure you load only the notes that belong to the selected course (see Listing 8-19).

Listing 8-19. Code to Fill the Notes Browse

```
# Notes list functions with notes records with selected course id

function ffFillNotesList as numeric;
      variables;
              numeric dbsize;
      end;

      # keep current selected course id
      nSelectedCourseID=nCourseID;

      # fill Score list with only records having same
      #   course id as that selected
      # fill Notes list
      nLastNotesI=0;
      dbsize=0;

      # point at bof
      seek_start dbNotes,0;

      # attempt to read first record
      errorcode=0;
      get_fields dbNotes;

      # read all records until error
      while errorcode=0;
              if nCourseID=nSelectedCourseID;
                      nNotesKeys[nLastNotesI]=nNotesID;
                      sNotesList[nLastNotesI]=string(nHole,"")+", "+
                        left(sNotes,27)+"...";
                      nLastNotesI=nLastNotesI+1;
              end_if;
              dbsize=dbsize+1;
              get_fields dbNotes;
      end_while;

      # dbsize is 1-based count of db records
      # remember last Notes id
```

```
        if dbsize=0;
                nLastNotesID=0;
        else;
                nLastNotesID=nNotesID;
        end_if;

        # reestablish the course id to selected id
        nCourseID=nSelectedCourseID;

        # return false if not eof
        fffFillNotesList=errorcode=ce_eof;
end;
```

There are a few things you have to do along the way. In order to work with Courses, Players, and Scorecards, you will need to pass variables between forms. You can create separate Global variables for this.

Applying Actions to Action Buttons

The next step to working with the course notes is to determine what action to take when a user selects one of the buttons.

The first action you'll tackle is the Add option. Adding a new course note is handled in virtually the same way that you added a course. This time, however, you need only two fields: one for the hole on the course, and one for the note about that hole. As you can see in Listing 8-20, the functions to add, edit, and delete a course note are clearly related to similar functions for a golf course.

Listing 8-20. The Code to Add, Edit, and Delete a Note

```
# Code for Add, Edit and Delete of a Course Note
# show new notes record

function nl_btAdd;
    # make sure not over limit
    if nLastNotesI<nMaxNotesI;
            # ok, show new default record
            hide frNotesList;
            ShowNewNotes;
    else;
            sml_ShowMsg(2,"notes are at limit of "+string(nMaxNotesI,"")+
              ", delete one to add one");
    end_if;
end;
```

```
# show selected notes record

function nl_btEdit;
      # attempt to read existing record
      if dbn_ffReadExactRecord(dbNotes,nSelectedNotesID);
              # ok, show existing record
              hide frNotesList;
              ShowExistingNotes;
      else;
              sml_ShowMsg(2,"Unable to read notes "+nl_slNotesList.display);
      end_if;
end;


# delete selected notes record

function nl_btDel;
      if sml_ffConfirmYes("Delete notes "+nl_slNotesList.display+"?");
              if dbn_ffRemoveRecord(dbNotes,nSelectedNotesID);
                      # updated Notes list
                      if ffFillNotesList;
                              ShowSelectNotes;
                      else;
                          DeleteDBsAndReopen(sNotesDBName+" must be corrupt, "+
                              "must delete all and restart");
                      end_if;
              else;
                      # no remove
                      sml_ShowMsg(2,"Delete of notes "+nl_slNotesList.display+
                       " unsuccessful");
              end_if;
          end_if;
end;


# Reprinted from the Notes Package file

# called by Add button, frame tagged so know what kind of save to do
function ShowNewNotes;
      nr_txHole.display="";
      nr_txNotes.display="";
      frNotesRecord.object_string="a";
      show frNotesRecord;
end;
```

```
# called by Edit button, frame tagged so know what kind of save to do
function ShowExistingNotes;
      nr_txHole.display=string(nHole,"");
      nr_txNotes.display=sNotes;
      frNotesRecord.object_string="e";
      show frNotesRecord;
end;
```

The final result is a form that loads with or without information based on the flags that are set in the Notes Browse form (see Figure 8-12).

Figure 8-12. Editing course notes

Saving the Record

The final piece of the puzzle comes with saving the record. To save a record, you will need to do several things based on the Modify settings. The first decision you must make in the Save routine is to determine if you are adding a new record or editing an existing one. Again, to accomplish this, you use the object_string member of the frame.

The insert function used for adding a new record, and for modifying a record you would use a combination of search and put_fields. Both functions accept the database handle as a parameter (see Listing 8-21).

Listing 8-21. Code to Save a Course Note

```
# save changes to notes record, return to select notes screen

function nr_btSave;
     if nr_txHole.display="";
             sml_ShowMsg(0,"Notes not saved since no hole given");
     else;
             FillNotesFields;

             # Add or Edit? Compare Object String
             if frNotesRecord.object_string="a";

                     # auto increment id counter
                     nNotesID=nLastNotesID+1;

                     # Write the Record
                     if dbn_ffWriteNewRecord(dbNotes,nNotesID);

                             # Save Last Notes ID
                             nLastNotesID=nNotesID;

                             # updated Notes list
                             if not ffFillNotesList;

     DeleteDBsAndReopen(sNotesDBName+"
must be corrupt, "+
                                                     "must delete all and
restart");
                                     end_if;
                     else;
                             # no save
                             sml_ShowMsg(2,"Save of new notes for hole "+
                              string(nHole,"")+" unsuccessful");
                     end_if;
             else;
                     # Record exists, so find and overwrite
                     if dbn_ffWriteExistingRecord(dbNotes,nNotesID);

                             # updated Notes list
                             if not, ffFillNotesList;
                         DeleteDBsAndReopen(sNotesDBName+" must be corrupt, "+
```

```
                                              "must delete all and restart");
                          end_if;
                          else;
                          # no save
                          sml_ShowMsg(2,"Save of edited notes of hole "+
                            string(nHole,"")+" unsuccessful");
                          end_if;
                end_if;
        end_if;

        # Hide Form
        hide frNotesRecord;

        # Back to Select Notes Form
        ShowSelectNotes;
end;
```

Working with Players

Whenever a golfer actually plays the game of golf he or she generally carries a handicap (unless he or she is a pro golfer). A *handicap* is a method for improving a player's score. The concept is that by giving the player a handicap, you can level the playing field. This means that if I have a handicap of 12, when I have finished playing a course I can subtract 12 strokes from my golf game, and I should be close to even. The higher the handicap, the more a player needs to improve his or her game. (Yes, I have a *very* high handicap, now let's get back to the example application, shall we?) Every player that the GolfPro system has can have a handicap. If a player has no handicap, then just leave the value 0.

Once the user has selected a course to play on, then he or she must add a player or select an existing one. Working with players is handled in much the same manner as working with course notes. You pass the course ID and load the list of players, but do not actually use the value until the user begins the process of adding a scorecard (see Figure 8-13).

Figure 8-13. Browsing Players

Working with players is essentially the same as working with course notes. The only real difference (besides the file structures) is that for this section I opted to use a graphic in the Players form (see Figure 8-14).

Figure 8-14. Combining an image with a form

Although having a graphic on the form does not actually do much in the way of improving the ease of use of the GolfPro program, it does help to take up some of the extra space and give the form a more completed look.

Calculating the Score

Finally, let's take a look at how to calculate your score while playing a course. Generally this is achieved by comparing the number of strokes you have against the number of strokes required to maintain par and then subtracting your handicap. There are several pieces to this puzzle that you need to figure out:

- Loading the values for the course into an array so you can calculate the current score for each hole against the par (nCoursePar)

- Calculating scoring on the fly

- Dealing with a player's handicap

- Dealing with an incomplete score card (in other words, calculate the par as you play) and a 0 value, since 0 is referred to as even

Okay, now let's handle each item one at a time. First, let's deal with the value for each hole. You've already loaded each hole's par into an array element (nCoursePar) so later on you can calculate your score against it (see Listing 8-22).

Listing 8-22. Code to Calculate Score

```
# Fill a Score Card
function FillScoreFields;
     variables;
               numeric i;
     end;

     # Save Course
     nCourseID=nSelectedCourseID;

     # Save Player
     nPlayerID=nSelectedPlayerID;

     # Initialize Loop Counter
     i=0;
```

```
        # Initialize Strokes, Par for Holes played
        # and Strokes for Holes Played.
        nRawStrokes=0;
        nParPlayed=0;
        nHolesPlayed=0;

        # loop through holes array
        while i < 18;

                # If it's a null string will convert to 0 value
                nStrokes[i]=value(sr_txHoleStrokes[i].display);


                # Stroke > 0 indicates hole has been played
                if nStrokes[i] > 0;

                        # Add up only non-zero strokes
                        nRawStrokes=nRawStrokes+nStrokes[i];

                        # Add up pars for only non-zero holes
                        nParPlayed=nParPlayed+nCoursePar[i];

                        # Increment Number of Holes Played
                        nHolesPlayed=nHolesPlayed+1;

                end_if;

                # Increment hole counter
                i=i+1;

        end_while;

        # final score deducts par for only the holes played, and
        #  normalizes course par for 72 and number of holes played
        nHandicapPlayed=((nParPlayed/72)*(nHolesPlayed/18)*nHandicap);
        nFinalScore=nRawStrokes-nParPlayed-nHandicapPlayed;

end;

# Called by Add Button
function ShowNewScore;
        variables;
                numeric i;
```

```
        end;
        frScoreRecord.display="ScoreCard: "+sFirstName+" "+sLastName;
        sGameDate=gdt_sfToday;

        # don't need to define nHolesPlayed=0, since will be calculated
        #   by FillScoreFields during save
        i=0;
        nParPlayed=0;

        while i < 18;
                sr_txHoleStrokes[i].display="";
                i=i+1;
        end_while;

        # Initialize vars
        nRawStrokes=0;
        nParPlayed=0;
        nHandicapPlayed=0;
        nFinalScore=0;

        # Set Object String to "Add Mode"
        frScoreRecord.object_string="a";

        # Display the fields
        DisplayScoreFields;

        # Show the Score card
        show frScoreRecord;
end;

# called by Edit button, frame tagged so know what kind of save to do
function ShowExistingScore;
        variables;
                numeric i;
        end;

        frScoreRecord.display="ScoreCard: "+sFirstName+" "+sLastName;
        sr_btDate.display=fdt_sfFormatDate(sGameDate,"");

        # assign field variables to display objects
        i=0;
        nRawStrokes=0;
        nParPlayed=0;
        nHolesPlayed=0;
```

```
    while i<18;
            sr_txHoleStrokes[i].display=sfStrokesString(nStrokes[i]);
            if nStrokes[i]>0;
                    # add up only non-zero strokes
                    nRawStrokes=nRawStrokes+nStrokes[i];

                    # add up pars for only non-zero holes
                    nParPlayed=nParPlayed+nCoursePar[i];

                    # increment holes played
                    nHolesPlayed=nHolesPlayed+1;
            end_if;
            i=i+1;
    end_while;

    # final score deducts par for only the holes played, and
    #   normalizes course par for 72 and number of holes played
    nHandicapPlayed=((nParPlayed/72)*(nHolesPlayed/18)*nHandicap);
    nFinalScore=nRawStrokes-nParPlayed-nHandicapPlayed;

    frScoreRecord.object_string="e";
    DisplayScoreFields;
    show frScoreRecord;
end;

# Code Reprinted here for convenience.

# updates the strokes dependent display objects with
# new field variable data
function DisplayScoreFields;
    sr_btDate.display=fdt_sfFormatDate(sGameDate,"");
    sr_lbPar.display="Par: "+string(nParPlayed,"");
    sr_lbTotalStrokes.display="Strokes: "+string(nRawStrokes,"");
    sr_lbHandicap.display="Handicap: "+string(nHandicapPlayed,"");
    sr_lbFinalScore.display="Score: "+string(nFinalScore,"");
end;
```

Now let's tackle the on-the-fly scoring. Pay close attention here. The CASL TextBox controls support control arrays. So now all you have to do is set all 18 holes to call the same invoker event (see Listing 8-23).

Listing 8-23. Code to Calculate On-the-Fly Scoring

```
# when update hole strokes, update display with holes played
# depended tallies as course par, handicap, and final score
function sr_txHoleStrokes;
      FillScoreFields;
      DisplayScoreFields;
end;
```

Compiling

Now that you have the application developed, compile it. Get used to using the Compile option. Since CASL is designed to build applications to run on both the Windows and Palm OS environments, the only way to thoroughly test your application is to compile it and then test it using POSE.

After completing your compilation of the GolfPro program, you are now ready to upload the compiled GolfPro program to your Palm device.

Conclusion

CASL is an excellent choice for building Palm-based applications. It offers a great deal of functionality at a price that will not break your bank, even if you splurge for the Pro version.

After reading this chapter and working through the GolfPro sample application (the full source code of which is provided on the CD-ROM included with this book), you should have a good grasp of CASL's functionality and how to use it to develop Palm-based applications.

Technical support for CASL is excellent, and there is a great support Web ring on Frank O'Brien's home page (http://frankscaslpage.home.att.net/home.htm), which you can go to for help if you need it. (Frank O'Brien is the primary contact for CASL technical support, by the way.) CASL is evolving and continues to improve every day. It shows tremendous potential, and in its latest release has a very user-friendly IDE. With the onset of CASLPro, this product promises to be a very powerful application development tool for the Palm.

Overall the product is a solid and inexpensive way to provide highly functional software with a quick turn around time. Programmers using CASLPro will soon be competing against C programmers to provide effective solutions with all the power and speed of C-based development at a fraction of the cost.

CHAPTER 9

Developing Conduits

WHAT EXACTLY ARE CONDUITS? Well, a conduit is a piece of software by which applications and data are synchronized between the Palm OS handheld device and a user's desktop computer. Sound confusing? It's not really. After I finish walking you through conduits, you'll have a pretty good understanding of what a conduit is, what your options are for writing a conduit, and how to build a conduit based on one of the tools I'll review and discuss in this chapter.

A Simple Conduit Example

Let's say that you have just written the next killer app, a program that will scan a user's body for any illnesses or diseases. The medical community is about to be revolutionized! You go around and scan several people, building a database of illnesses. Now, how do you get this very important information off of your handheld device and onto a PC where you can analyze it and send it to a medical professional for review? This is where the conduit comes into the picture. It permits you to transfer all of this data from your handheld to your desktop computer. Okay, great! Your application is getting rave reviews and you are about to release it to the masses when a new, dangerous virus has been discovered. How do you get the new virus information to everyone's handhelds? Again, the conduit comes to the rescue. You can build a conduit that does more than one thing: transfer data from the handheld to the PC and transfer data from the PC to the handheld. Every time the user performs a HotSync operation, they get the latest information on their handheld.

An easy way to think of a HotSync operation is to compare it to database replication, which is the process of copying records from one database to another to create a "mirrored" image or backup. This process is often accomplished by the use of an internal key, known as the replication key. A replication key can either be supplied by the database engine or created by a program. In the case of Palm databases, a field already exists as part of the record, which contains a unique record ID. Palm database files also contain a bit value, which is set when the record is updated or created. This bit is referred to as the "Dirty" flag. When a record is flagged as dirty, the Conduit Manager will then know to interact with this record based on the requested conduit action.

The Basic Conduit Operation

Conduits connect pieces of equipment (desktop PCs and handheld devices) and then move data between them. That's it in its simplest form. Data goes from point A to point B, or vice versa. A conduit can be simple or complex depending on the job it has to do. No matter what the conduits' complexities, all conduits conform to a single way of interacting with the desktop PC (see sidebar).

NOTE   *For the purposes of this book, I am focusing on Windows PC-based solutions. All references to behaviors are in the context of a Windows-based application.*

Standard Conduits

The conduits that ship with all Palm devices are the standard conduits for communicating with the Palm Desktop software. These standard conduits include the Date Book, Mail, Address Book, To Do List, Memo Pad, Expense, and a few system conduits such as System, Backup, Install, Install to Card, and Install Services Template.

NOTE   *Several of these conduits were introduced with the Palm Desktop version 4.*

Are there conduits for other hardware/OS that work with Palm OS? Yes and no. A conduit is really OS specific. A conduit written to run on a Mac runs on a Mac, but still communicates with Palm devices. The conduit's interaction with a software program on the desktop is really the key. The controlling PC's OS determines how you (the programmer) build the conduit.

Conduit actions are controlled by the HotSync Manager, which controls the entire HotSync process. This program runs in the background on a Windows-based PC. (Generally, you can see the little icon in the task bar.) The HotSync Manager serves two main purposes:

- It contains a listing of all the conduits installed on your system. This allows you to execute each conduit separately or all of them at once.

- Based on the rules defined by a specific conduit, data is moved or matched against a corresponding database. This means that I can have data in an Access database file on my desktop and use a conduit to move the data to a PDB file on the Palm device.

What Does a Conduit Do?

A conduit is responsible for the application's data during a synchronization process. A conduit needs to perform the following actions:

- Open and close databases on the Palm device.

- Determine what action it should perform (upload data to the device, download data from the device, or some combination of both).

- Appropriately add, modify, or delete records either on the handheld or on the desktop.

- Be able to work within a multiuser environment in which more than one Palm handheld device may be syncing to the same network or desktop computer (although not at the same time).

- Convert the data into the appropriate database structures, either on the desktop or the Palm device.

- Optionally, although generally recommended, compare records so that only modified records are synced.

The conduit is responsible for saving the data to your desktop in whatever format you decide is appropriate. Optionally, you may also sync to a database server engine such as SQL Server. If your conduit is going to interact with files on your desktop, it must also be able to read and write to that file's format. In other words, if I use an Access MDB file on my desktop, the conduit should understand how to open the Access MDB file. As a result, each conduit often handles storing and retrieving data differently.

The three basic categories of conduits are as follows:

- *Upload or download only*. These are conduits that simply copy data from one device to a single destination, overwriting any data that already exists.

- *Mirror-image record synchronization*: These conduits are designed to mirror the data from either the PC or the handheld device by performing a two-way sync. An example of this would be the Address book.

- *Transaction processing:* These conduits do some type of processing of records but aren't doing a mirror-image synchronization. A good example of this might be a multiuser order entry application that sends transactions (such as inventory movements) out the conduit to be processed on the desktop.

Transaction Processing

It is during Page: 1 transaction processing that the concept of a replication key comes into play. For example, if I have 200 order takers carrying Palm devices through a crowd, and they're all entering multiple orders, how do we maintain a unique ID so that, when the upload occurs, there are no duplicates?

The answer is to create a device seed table. Each device contains a table, which has the "seed" for all records it will create. For example:

Device 1 – Seed 1000

Device 2 – Seed 2000

Device 3 – Seed 3000

And so on. . .

This will allow the users of each device to generate up to 999 orders before they approach the point of overwriting other record IDs.

So what about the locally generated unique ID (such as Autonumber columns in an Access database) that may be referenced on the Palm device itself? We need a method for relating records, and the use of a key is often required. Well, the answer to that is to have a master seed table that controls the record keys, not just the keys on the PC but also the seed keys uploaded to the Palm devices.

How do we maintain referential integrity when performing a HotSync? We, the programmers, must take care when inserting and modifying records to update all the required records and tables. Which brings us to the question of constraints. Constraints that have already been set in the target database may cause problems when the data is uploaded. Unfortunately, this is an issue that is dependent upon the database design.

NOTE *Because conduit development centers around developing software to run on the desktop rather than the Palm device, this section focuses on the Visual Basic-centric solutions that offer the quickest results and the best control.*

Understanding How Conduits Work

A standard Windows conduit is really just a DLL (Dynamic Link Library) with an entry point that is called by the HotSync Manager. A conduit is the only piece of software that must cooperate with a number of other programs to transfer data between a handheld and a desktop computer. We've already discussed the HotSync Manager and its general purpose as well as the conduits themselves, but here for your reference are all the items that you as a programmer should be aware of:

- *HotSync Manager*: Discussed earlier, this program is the meat of any conduit or sync process. This program controls what conduits are executed and in what order.

- *Conduits*: This is the plug-in component, which is executed by the HotSync Manager.

- *Notifier DLLs*: If both a conduit and a desktop application can modify the same data, it may be necessary to tell the desktop application to leave the data alone (or to lock it) during the course of the actual sync process. This is to prevent data loss, duplicate records, or any other mangling of data that could result from trying to access files during this process.

- *Handheld applications*: Obviously you know what a handheld application is, but what you may not know is that you don't have to do much of anything to make your application work with the standard HotSync process. In fact, if all you need to do is back up your program and database, the default backup conduit will handle that for you. It's only when you get into passing data elements (such as records entered on the handheld into a SQL Server database on the PC) that you need to concern yourself with writing a conduit.

- *Desktop applications*: Because of the flexibility of conduit design, almost any desktop application can share data with a Palm device.

- *The Sync Manager API*: This application programming interface (API) allows conduits to communicate with the handheld regardless of how the handheld is connected to the PC. The Sync Manager API can directly read and write data on the handheld, and it forms the basic underlying layer in conduit development.

Just so everyone is clear on this, we are going to review only those conduit development tools that can assist the Visual Basic developer. The idea is that, because these tools integrate with Visual Basic (a language we know), then there should be an easier learning curve than if we were writing a conduit in C, for instance. If you are familiar with C and you want to know more about the underlying architecture of conduit development, a trip to Palm.com is in order. There you can find many examples of conduit development using the CDK (Conduit Developers Kit) in C and C++. Although we will be using the CDK later in this chapter, we will focus on the ActiveX COM implementations and stick to using Visual Basic as our tool for conduit development.

Let's start by stepping through a basic HotSync operation, as this will help some of the beginners get a better understanding of how HotSync works.

 NOTE   *At the current time, a HotSync operation may only be initiated by the Palm device. Because of limitations with the current cradle hardware, there is no way to start the sync process from the desktop using software.*

1. *User validation and location:* Each Palm OS device has a unique user ID associated with it. When the user synchronizes the handheld device for the first time, the HotSync Manager assigns a number to that particular handheld device, which allows a single desktop computer to synchronize with multiple handheld devices and still keep the data separate. At the beginning of the sync operation, the HotSync Manager makes sure the user ID on the handheld device is valid, and then locates the path to that particular user's data on the desktop.

2. *Determination of synchronization type:* The HotSync process is designed for maximum efficiency, which means minimizing the data that needs to be transferred whenever possible. The HotSync Manager application accomplishes this by using two forms of record-level synchronization.

    These two types of syncs are a *SlowSync* and a *FastSync*. In a SlowSync, the conduit compares each record in the handheld database file with each record on the PC in its corresponding data source.

    In a FastSync, the conduit compares only those records with the modification flag set. The HotSync Manager determines which type of synchronization to perform by looking at the PC ID stored on the handheld from its last HotSync operation. Like a user ID, the PC ID is a number generated by the HotSync Manager to uniquely identify the PC (see Figure 9-1).

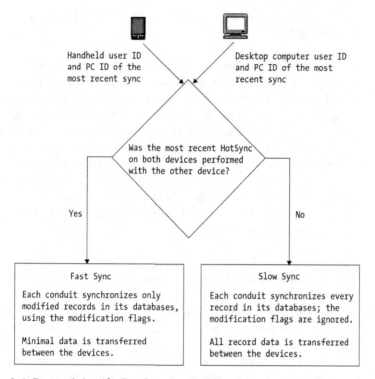

Figure 9-1. Determining if a FastSync is possible

Whenever a HotSync operation takes place, the HotSync Manager stores, on the device itself, the PC ID of the last desktop machine that the handheld was synchronized with. If the handheld was last synchronized with the same machine that is currently performing a sync operation, then a FastSync will occur. If the PC ID is different, the HotSync Manager will tell the conduit to perform a SlowSync. This is because the conduits cannot rely on the modification flag of each record to be valid.

3. *Desktop application modification*: The HotSync Manager calls one of the appropriate notifier DLLs to let the desktop PC know that it is about to modify the data shared between the desktop and the handheld device.

4. *Conduit setup*: Once the notification is out of the way, the HotSync Manager will retrieve the CreatorID of all the applications stored on the device. (They have a type of appl.) If a conduit is installed for a particular CreatorID, the HotSync Manager adds that conduit to the list of conduits to execute. The HotSync Manager will also look at all the databases on the handheld that are of the type DATA to determine if the backup bit is

set. If a database has the backup bit set, it is added to the list of files to be synchronized.

5. *Installation*: Now the HotSync Manager uses the built-in Install conduit to install any applications and databases that are sitting on the PC in the Install directory. Generally, these databases and applications were added using the Palm Install tool. In Windows, the HotSync Manager knows there are applications and databases to install when a particular registry key is present (\HKEY_CURRENT_USER\Software\U.S. Robotics\Pilot Desktop\HotSync Manager\Install XXXX, where XXXX is the pseudo-random user ID assigned to the handheld). The Palm Install tool creates this registry key when it queues up an application for installation, and then copies the program or database into the Install subdirectory of the appropriate user's data folder.

6. *Conduit execution*: The HotSync Manager cycles through the list of conduits that it assembled (in step 4), calling each in turn to sync data.

7. *Second installation*: Starting with version 3.0.1 of the HotSync Manager, a second call is made to the install conduit. This happens so that the HotSync Manager can pick up any databases that were set for install by any of the other conduits. This step allows a conduit to generate a database and "push" it onto the "stack" (that is, Install Tools list of queued files) and then have it uploaded to the device.

8. *Database backup*: The HotSync Manager calls the Backup conduit to copy the databases (which were queued up in step 4). These databases are stored in a Backup subdirectory off the current user's data directory.

9. *Synchronization information update*: Now that the HotSync Manager has completed most of its tasks, it updates the sync time, PC ID, and user ID (if needed), in the HotSync application on the device. It is at this point that the HotSync Manager also uploads an abbreviated version of the HotSync log.

10. *Second desktop notification*: The HotSync Manager calls the appropriate notifier DLLs a second time to alert the application that the sync operation has been completed.

11. *Handheld application notification*: The Palm OS itself gives notification of a finished HotSync operation to newly installed handheld applications, and those whose data was modified during the sync process.

Conduit Design Goals

Each conduit can synchronize data with a single application on the handheld, or perhaps with a desktop application or one of half a dozen different variations of the two. Given that different databases can synchronize with each other, four different types of syncs also can be performed. Each of these four syncs falls into one of the three categories of synchronization that we discussed at the beginning of the chapter:

1. *Transaction based*: These conduits center on some process, such as a real-time stock quoting system. In other words, some action must take place between each record being processed. This type of approach should be used only when absolutely necessary as it can slow the HotSync process considerably.

2. *Mirror image*: The goal of these conduits is to leave the desktop and the handheld with a set of data that is exactly mirrored between the two. This can get tricky because the conduit must resolve conflicts such as when a user modifies a record on the handheld and another user may have modified the same record on the desktop.

3. *One directional*: Only one side of the connection is receiving data. In other words, the contents of a file are moved either to the PC from the handheld or from the handheld to the PC.

4. *Backup*: If an application does not have a desktop component, it can rely on the standard Backup conduit to move itself and any of its data to a backup folder on the user's PC.

HotSync technology has been a very important part of the success of the Palm platform. One of the reasons for this is that the conduits called by the HotSync Manager run quickly and adhere to a strong set of design goals. Consider that the primary focus of your conduit should always be speed. Try not to overengineer your conduit and always use the simplest form of synchronization to get the job done.

 NOTE *Most HotSync operations take place via the serial port on the Palm device. Because this is a major drain on batteries, you should keep the synchronization time as short as possible. However, do not skimp on testing the process. A fast but inaccurate conduit does no one any good.*

You need to develop your conduit with these same goals in mind, as described in Table 9-1.

Table 9-1. Conduit Design Goals

DESIGN GOAL	DESCRIPTION
Fast execution	The main goal for the HotSync process is that a complete synchronization should be performed very quickly. Conduits need to be designed for optimal processing speed and minimal data transfer.
Zero data loss	A conduit must take the measures required to prevent data loss under any circumstances, including loss of connection during a synchronization process.
Good conflict handling	Conduits that perform mirror-image synchronizations must be able to gracefully handle conflicting modifications. This occurs when the user modifies a record on both the desktop computer and the device. In addition to managing the conflict, the conduit should add an entry to the log to notify the user of this situation.
No user interaction	The user expects to be able to press the HotSync button on the device cradle and have synchronization proceed without any required interaction.

Choosing a Development Option

Although there are many different platforms for conduit development, for the purposes of this chapter I will focus on three different, yet very powerful approaches to conduit development. I will start with the simplest method of developing a conduit, one that requires none or very little code, to a middle-of-the-road solution using a set of COM objects, and finally using the Palm Conduit Development Kit (CDK).

Each of these tools is unique and has something to offer for different situations. It has always been my philosophy that one should choose a tool that fits the job and the budget. In this chapter, we will review four products:

- The AppForge Universal Conduit

- EHAND's Palm Access COM Objects

- Palm's own CDK.

- The CASL Conduit

When we have finished reviewing how to build a conduit with each of these tools, I hope that you will have not only a better understanding of conduits and how they work, but how to build your own. So, let's get started, shall we?

The AppForge Universal Conduit

When it comes to building a conduit, the people at AppForge did their home-work. They knew that having a platform for developing Palm OS applications using Visual Basic[1] would not be much of a success without the ability to develop a conduit. After all, building a Palm application is often only half the battle. Enter the Universal Conduit.

The AppForge Universal Conduit (UC) can be configured using two tools, the first is the graphical wizard that you use to develop the conduit and the second is the command-line program UCConfigCmd.exe, which is how you can create and control the conduits on the end user's system.

NOTE   *The Universal Conduit is available only to those who have purchased the Professional Edition of AppForge.*

Let's start by building a conduit to move data from the PC to a handheld device. Consider the scenario of a teacher who may want to have the relevant information she has on each of her students in her Palm device. We begin by opening the Universal Conduit Manager (see Figure 9-2).

---

[1] See Chapters 2 and 3 on AppForge.

Figure 9-2. The Universal Conduit Manager

Once we have opened the UC, we need to create a new conduit. When you select "New" or "Configure" a wizard starts that will walk you through a series of screens to design and configure a conduit. You must do three things before you can build a conduit using the Universal Conduit:

1. Create an ODBC data source name (DSN) for the application.

2. Have selected a Palm CreatorID for your application.

3. Identify at least one unique sync key field in each table.

When you select to create a new Universal Conduit, the wizard will remind you of these items at the first screen (see Figure 9-3).

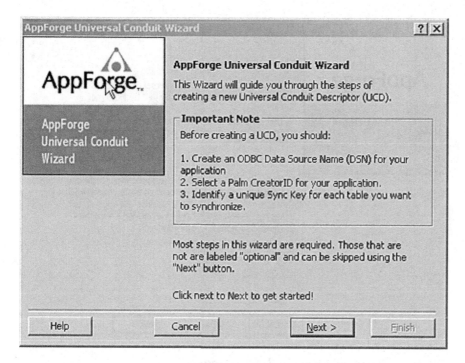

Figure 9-3. Starting the AppForge Universal Conduit wizard

The next two items to be entered within the UC wizard are the name of your conduit (this is the name that will appear in the HotSync Manager) and the Palm CreatorID (see Figure 9-4).

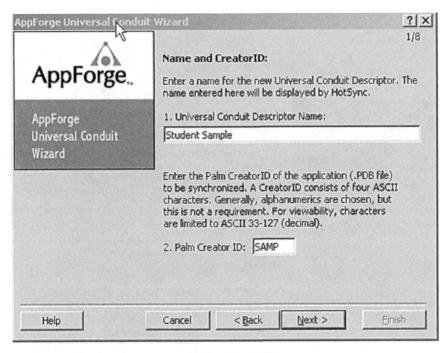

Figure 9-4. Entering the name and Palm CreatorID

Next we move on to selecting the source of our conduit sync. In our example, we did not need to create a DSN because we are going to use one of the installed system DSNs (in this case the Microsoft Access). Select the data source and then click the Next button (see Figure 9-5).

 NOTE *To connect to SQL Server or another SQL-based database engine, you should configure a DSN that has all the required login parameters. However, because the Microsoft Access engine does not (in the standard default mode) require a login or any other special parameters, we are going to use it for our example.*

For the purposes of this example, I chose to use one of the installed DSNs for the sake of simplicity, but I would always recommend creating a DSN for the database, regardless of the type of database. This ensures that the conduit always connects to the correct database. Also, the generic DSNs can be changed easily without one knowing that they could be screwing up an installed conduit.

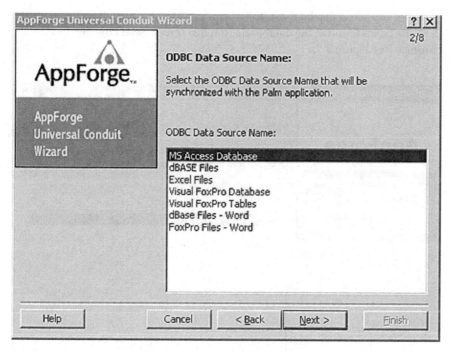

Figure 9-5. Selecting an ODBC data source name (DSN)

When you select the MS Access database DSN, you will be prompted for the
location of the MDB file with which to sync your data (see Figure 9-6).

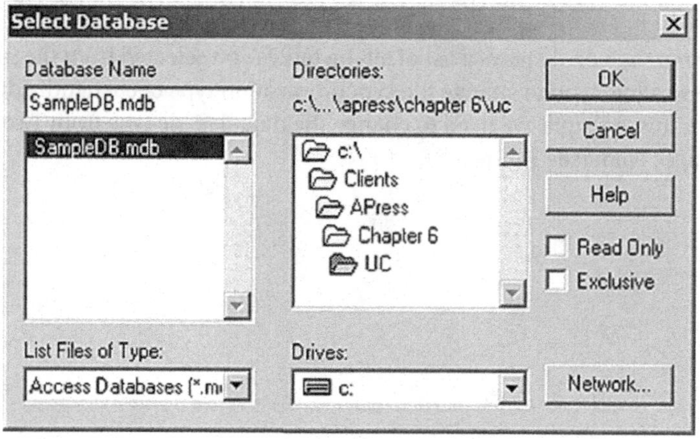

Figure 9-6. Selecting the MS Access file to use

After you select the database, the wizard moves to a screen that displays a list of all the tables found in the database. From this screen, select the files to synchronize (see Figure 9-7).

Figure 9-7. Selecting the tables to synchronize with the Palm device

The next screen displays a list of all the tables you selected from the prior screen and allows you to change the synchronization type of each individual table. For this example, we need to change the default sync type from Two-Way to PC Replaces Palm (see Figure 9-8).

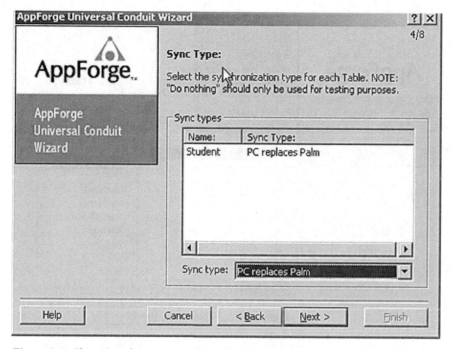

Figure 9-8. Changing the sync type from Two-Way to PC Replaces Palm

In the next screen, all of the fields are displayed; so, had we left the sync type as Two-Way, we would be prompted to select a sync key field (see Figure 9-9).

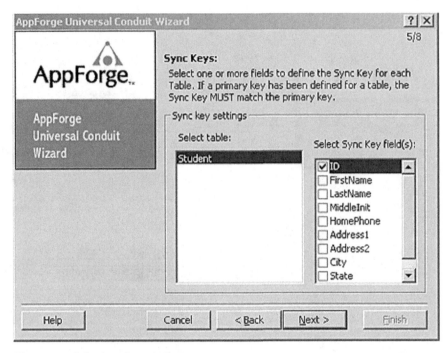

Figure 9-9. Selecting the sync key

A sync key field should be a key that is unique between the two databases and one that would not normally change. For the most part, a standard Access AutoNumber or an Identity column will work. However, in the cases in which an ID value must be assigned on the Palm device, you should use a table to contain the key values, which can also be synchronized (see sidebar).

Creating Your Own Identity Values

Most of us have used AutoNumber columns in Access or Identity columns in SQL Server, and so we are comfortable with the concept of letting the PC assign the next identifier. Well, this brings us to an interesting crossroads, in the world of Palm database files (PDBs), the concept of an Identity or AutoNumber column does not exist. So, how then should we create one?

The answer is simple but requires that it be enforced on both the PC and on the handheld device. What you do is create a table (I usually use the name Next_Identity) and use the table to feed the "identity" column. The Next_Identity column consists of two columns (see Table 9-2).

Table 9-2. Next_Sequence Database Fields and the Purpose of Each

COLUMN NAME	COLUMN VALUE
Key	A name such as StudentID that is used by the lookup routine to "seek" out the next available identity
Next_Key	The next key sequence number, such as 34 or A34. This field can contain anything that your increment routine can increase to a unique value.
Locked	This field is set to "true" or "false" so that we can determine if an update is taking place so as not to create duplicate keys.

Once the table has been created, you need to create a routine to get the next available routine. The routine should be simple and direct, and perform the following actions:

1. Find the requested key.

2. Get the next sequence number.

3. Lock the record.

4. Increment the Key value.

5. Update the Next_Key field.

6. Unlock the record.

The GetNextSequence function can then be used with both the handheld application and the PC application, allowing for a unique key to be generated at both locations (see Listing 9-1).

Listing 9-1. Code to Create a New Sequence Number in AppForge

```
Function GetNextSequence(ByVal cSeekKey As String) As Long
'-=-=-=-=-=-=-=-=-=-=-=-=-=-=-=-=-=-=-=-=-=-=-=-=-=-=-=-=-=-=
'
'    Function    :    GetNextSequence( cSeekKey )
'    Params      :    cSeekKey - Lookup Key
'    Returns     :    LONG - New Key
'
'    Author      :    Vivid Software Inc. - Jon Kilburn
'                     http://www.VividSoftware.com
'
```

```
'   Client      :   Apress
'   Purpose     :   Generate an "Autonumber"
'
'-=-=-=-=-=-=-=-=-=-=-=-=-=-=-=-=-=-=-=-=-=-=-=-=-=-=-=-=

    Dim ReturnKey As Long
    Dim nHandle   As Long
    Dim rec       As tNextSequenceRecord

    ' Open Next_Sequence Table
    #If APPFORGE Then
        nHandle = PDBOpen(Byfilename, "Next_Sequence", _
                0, 0, 0, 0, afModeReadWrite)
    #Else
        nHandle = PDBOpen(Byfilename, App.Path & "\Next_Sequence", _
                0, 0, 0, 0, afModeReadWrite)
    #End If

    If nHandle = 0 Then
        'We failed to open the database
        GetNextSequence = -1
        Exit Function
    End If

    ' Find this Record
    Call PDBFindRecordByField(nHandle, 0, cSeekKey)

    ' Lock Record
    If PDBReadRecord(nHandle, VarPtr(rec)) <> 0 Then
        ' Error!
        GetNextSequence = -1
        Exit Function
    Else
        ReturnKey = rec.Next_Key
        rec.NextKey = rec.NextKey + 1

        ' Edit this Record
        Call PDBEditRecord(nHandle)
        Call PDBWriteRecord(nHandle, VarPtr(rec))
        Call PDBUpdateRecord(nHandle)
    End If
```

```
' Close Database
Call PDBClose(nHandle)
nHandle = 0

GetNextSequence = ReturnKey
End Function
```

This process is not without a few drawbacks; for example, on the PC you could use an Access table, but on the handheld you would use a PDB so the two sets of code would be different but produce the same result.

Another way to create identity values can be achieved in Oracle with *sequences*. Unlike Access, a sequence is independent of any one table and simply serves as a source for unique, sequential numbers. Therefore, if you do not need to have sequential numbers on a particular table, only one sequence is needed to serve as a source for all unique numbers for every table in the database. Listing 9-2 is an example on how to create and use a sequence.

Listing 9-2. Code to Create a Sequence Table in Oracle

```
CREATE SEQUENCE EmployeeSeq START WITH 10000;

Dim snpNextSeq As Recordset
Dim lNextSeq As Long

If iAddMode Then
    Set snpNextSeq = dbMainData.OpenRecordset("SELECT employeeseq.nextval FROM
dual", dbOpenSnapshot, dbSQLPassThrough)

    lNextSeq = snpNextSeq.Fields(0)

    cSQL = "INSERT INTO bibliography (code, description) VALUES (" & lNextSeq &
", '" & txtDescr & ")"
Else
    cSQL = "UPDATE bibliography SET description = " + Chr(34) + txtDescr +
Chr(34) + " WHERE code = " & lCode
End If
```

So, now you have a couple of choices and some examples to help you create unique sequence numbers.

The next screen is optional and allows for creation of the PDB file and a corresponding Visual Basic module at this point (if you haven't already done so using the AppForge Database Converter as discussed in Chapter 2 and 3). The final screen displays all of your selected choices for your review. From this screen (see Figure 9-10), the conduit will be created when you select "Finish".

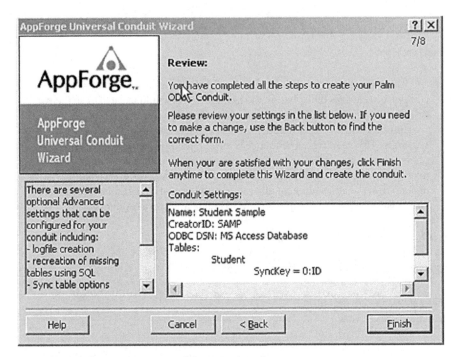

Figure 9-10. The review screen of the UC wizard

When the wizard has been completed, you need to restart the HotSync Manager to see your newly created conduit. Once you have restarted the HotSync Manager, if you right-click on the HotSync Manager icon and select the Custom option, a list of installed conduits will appear. You should see in this list our newly created Student Sample conduit (see Figure 9-11).

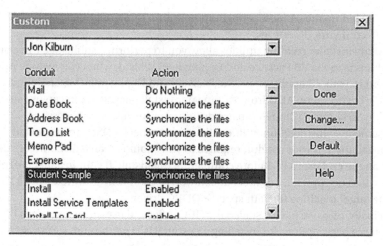

Figure 9-11. The newly created conduit displayed in the HotSync Manager

Installation of a UC Conduit on an End User's System

The Universal Conduit wizard included with the UC package is a great tool for developers because it allows for easy configuration and reconfiguration for testing purposes. It is not, however, an appropriate answer to install the UC wizard on an end user's machine. For this, AppForge has created a special set of installation instructions that can be found in the AppForge UC help file.

To make the installation process as easy as possible for the end user, you may wish to create a custom setup package that copies the application's files and configures the Universal Conduit and UCDs for the application. For this, I suggest that you use the install tool of your choice (such as Install Shield Express, or WISE).

Some simple preliminary installation steps that should always be followed (and can be configured by your installer) are to check the target system for the following elements:

- ODBC 3.5 or later (for best Unicode support)

- HotSync Manager 3.0 (or higher)

Once this has been done, AppForge created a utility named the Universal Conduit Runtime (UCRunSetup.exe), which we can use to configure the UC on the end user's machine. The Universal Conduit Runtime, which can be distributed, is a completely self-contained setup program file named UCRunSetup.exe. This program can be included with your application's installer and must be installed before the conduit configuration utility (UCConfigCmd.exe) can be used to configure UC entries.

Many installer creation utilities allow you to perform a subinstall. (An example of this is in the VB Package and Deployment Wizard, when you include ADO support in your VB applications, the Package and Deployment wizard launches MDAC_TYP to set up ADO from within your install package.) You can use such a facility to launch UCRunSetup.exe during your installation process.

Some installer creation utilities allow you to specify DSNs to be created during installation. If your conduit requires it, you should create and configure the DSN on the end user's PC before completing the install. If your installer creation utility does not provide this mechanism, you need to find a way to create a DSN on the target machine for your specific ODBC driver.

Finally, once we have installed the UCConfigCmd.exe on an end user's PC, we have three basic options for installing a custom UCD on the end user's system:

- Deploy UCConfigCmd.exe temporarily onto the end user's system. It is recommended that you use UCConfigCmd.exe to create UCDs if you create an installer to deploy your own UC-based applications. This command-line tool allows for easy configuration from .bat files, scripts, and almost any install program, all without having to write any code. (See the Reference section of the UC help file for the command-line specifics.)

- Deploy UCConfig.dll temporarily onto the end user's system. UCConfig.DLL contains code to help you configure your UCD. The easiest way to interface with the DLL is to write a Visual Basic application containing modUCConfig.bas. This module can be found in the Universal Conduit's installation directory and contains a well-documented API for UCConfig.DLL. (It is possible to use this API from C/C++, but this is generally not recommended because it was designed for use with Visual Basic.)

- You can also write custom code to directly modify the proper registry entries. This is generally not recommended because one mistake or missed key could cause your conduit to not function or possibly cause another conduit to cease functioning.

NOTE   *Visit the AppForge Developer Sector at* http://www.appforge.com *for registry information.*

EHAND's Palm Access COM Objects

If you get right down to it, although the people at AppForge did an excellent job with the UC, in quite a few places you still will often need to write your own code or perhaps even an SQL query to retrieve the information you need for your sync.

Consider this interesting scenario: a customer has a desktop application that receives data from a Web application in the form of text files. These text files must interact with data on a Palm device. However, the application written on the Palm device uses a control file to determine what action to take. That action can be one of several choices:

- Upload new orders from the PC to the Palm device (UPLOAD).

- Download orders from the Palm device to the PC (DOWNLOAD).

- Move a piece of equipment's physical location (MOVE).

These actions are controlled by a command file on the Palm device (CmdAction.Pdb). The command file has only one field and contains the values (as a string) of "UPLOAD", "DOWNLOAD", or "MOVE".

CAUTION   *Palm filenames are case sensitive! I cannot stress this enough. Checking for the existence of a file named "cmdaction" is not the same as checking for a file named "CmdAction".*

Which brings us to EHAND's Palm Access DLL.

What Is EHAND PalmAccess?

When I was faced with the need to write a conduit for my application (which was too complicated for the UC), I decided to investigate the option of using something other than the CDK. My research led me to EHAND PalmAccess, a product offered by EHAND AB, a company in Sweden. EHAND PalmAccess is a COM-based product that allows you to write conduits with every Windows development tool that can create automation objects. The price for EHAND PalmAccess is free for testing and developing applications, but $390 for distribution (for up to 500 users). The manual that comes with the product provides Visual Basic samples, which makes developing your first conduit rather easy.

NOTE *When I began using EHAND PalmAccess, a new product appeared on the company's Web site. Lo and behold, it was EHAND's new EHAND Connect SDK for AppForge. It was listed on the Web site, but I could not find a copy of the EHAND Connect SDK for downloading and testing. For more information, check out the PDF whitepaper at* http://www.ehand.com.

Where EHAND falls down is on the installation side (more on this later). Developing and creating the conduit is easy for the programmer, but installing the finished conduit on an end user's system was an exercise all unto its own.

A conduit written with EHAND PalmAccess will interact with the HotSync process to perform its tasks. When the user is synchronizing a Palm device, the HotSync process is initiated and iterates through the conduits defined in HotSync Manager, launching each one. When it encounters a conduit developed by EHAND PalmAccess, you will see a small popup window indicating that your custom conduit has been launched.

NOTE *The conduits that are created with Microsoft Visual Basic 6.0 and EHAND PalmAccess will be ActiveX DLL projects. This basically means that they will not be standalone programs that can be started from within Windows; rather, they will be objects that are created only from the HotSync process.*

Installing EHAND PalmAccess is simple and straightforward. Simply launch the EHAND PalmAccess application and it unpacks itself and starts the install. For the most part, all the default settings work fine. Now the only thing that has to be set up in your development environment is a reference to the EHAND PalmAccess type library.

A type library is a file that contains information about what different methods and properties a specific COM object can handle. In this case, you want Visual Basic to be aware of the capabilities of EHAND PalmAccess; therefore, you need to set up this reference.

For every Microsoft Visual Basic conduit project that you will be working with, you have to open Visual Basic 6.0 and create a new ActiveX DLL project or load an existing one (see Figure 9-12).

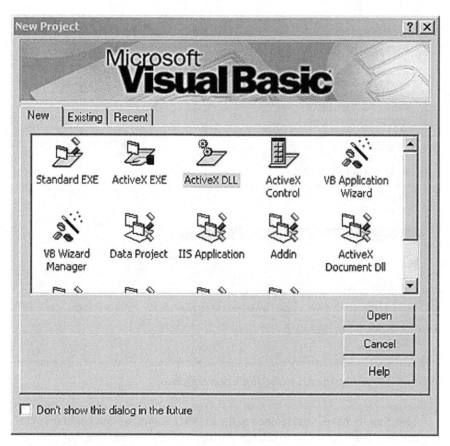

Figure 9-12. Creating a new Visual Basic ActiveX DLL

The next thing you will be presented with is a blank code window in VB. This code window is named Class1 and is part of the default project Project1. Let's add the EHAND PalmAccess Type Library now. We do this by selecting Project | References. When the References window appears, click the Browse button. We must locate the EHAND type library file (*.tlb). Once the file is found, change directories to the EHAND PalmAccess folder and select the file PalmAccess.tlb. When you have done so, a reference to the EHAND PalmAccess Library appears in your list of references (see Figure 9-13).

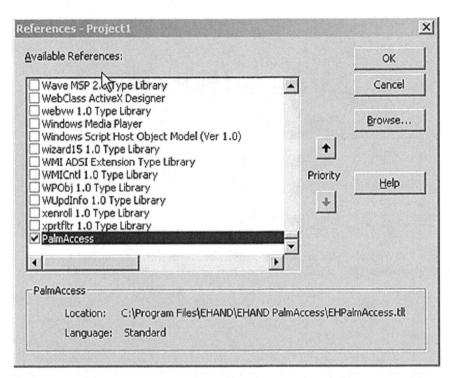

Figure 9-13. Adding the EHAND PalmAccess reference

Now that we have the reference to the EHAND library, we can begin to build the conduit. The first step is to change the name of the project. This will ultimately become the name of the ActiveX DLL. Change the name of the project to EHTest. Next, change the name of the class to clsTestConduit.

The first section of code that we must add is the "entry point" at which the conduit can be loaded. EHAND will pass to this method an object, which is the EHAND conduit object. Using the EHAND conduit object, we can now interact with the Palm device. In this first example, let's begin by writing a simple log entry into the HotSync log (see Listing 9-3).

Listing 9-3. The Code to Open an EHAND Conduit and Make a Log Entry

```
Public Sub OpenConduit(oConduit As PalmAccess.Conduit)
'-=-=-=-=-=-=-=-=-=-=-=-=-=-=-=-=-=-=-=-=-=-=-=-=-=-=-=-=-=-=-=-=-=
'
'   Sub         :   OpenConduit()
'   Params      :   oConduit - EHAND PalmAccess Conduit Object
'   Returns     :   None
'
```

```
'    Author      :   Vivid Software Inc. - Jon Kilburn
'                    http://www.VividSoftware.com
'
'    Client      :   Apress
'    Purpose     :   Initialize the Conduit and do the Work.
'
'-=-=-=-=-=-=-=-=-=-=-=-=-=-=-=-=-=-=-=-=-=-=-=-=-=-=-=-=-=-=-=

     oConduit.AddLogEntry "Hello EHAND PalmAccess World"

End Sub
```

This is all the code needed to set up a link between HotSync and Visual Basic, but we need to do some additional configuration. The next step is to register the new conduit so that HotSync knows that it should be called during the sync process.

Registering the EHAND Conduit

The easiest way to register a new conduit is to use a utility distributed with EHAND PalmAccess called CondCgf.exe, but other ways are available. (We'll explain how to do this later on when describing the installation process on an end user's machine.)

To make a conduit run during a HotSync, two things are required. The first is that you have registered the conduit on the host computer with a specific CreatorID. (There can be only one conduit with the same CreatorID.) The second is that the handheld has to have an application with the same CreatorID on it. One very common mistake made by conduit developers is that they place a normal database on the device with the correct CreatorID, but what is really needed is an application with the correct CreatorID. To get this simple conduit running, there's really no need to install a specific application just to test if things are working. We're going to use the CreatorID of the calculator that is present on virtually every Palm-powered device.

To register the conduit with the CondCfg.exe program, we need to first locate the CondCfg.exe program. This program is generally installed in the EHAND PalmAccess bin folder. The source for the CondCfg.exe program is located in the subfolder source. (If you get a chance you may want to play with this, as EHAND ships some neat controls along with the EHAND PalmAccess.)

1. Start CondCfg.exe.

2. Choose Add. . .

3. At the CreatorID prompt, enter "calc".

4. For Conduit, type the path to PalmAccess.DLL that is distributed with
    the EHAND PalmAccess package (generally C:\Program
    Files\EHAND\EHAND PalmAccess\EHPalmAccess.dll). For Class name,
    type in EHTest.clsTestConduit (see Figure 9-14).

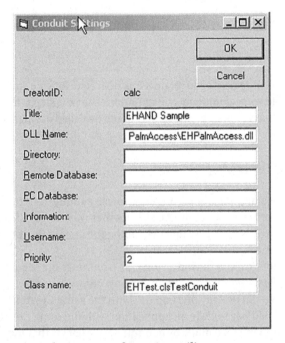

Figure 9-14. EHAND PalmAccess configuration utility

Your new conduit should now appear in the list of conduits that was first
displayed when you opened CondCfg (see Figure 9-15). To see your new conduit
in the list of custom conduits, select the Restart HSM button to restart the
HotSync Manager.

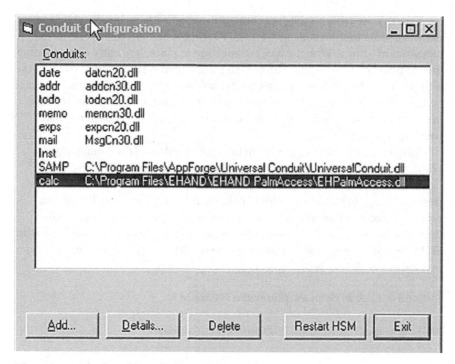

Figure 9-15. The list of installed conduits

Now, if we right-click on the HotSync Manager icon in the system tray and select the "Custom. . ." option (as we did for the UC student sample), a list of installed conduits will appear. You should see in this list our newly created "EHAND Sample" conduit (see Figure 9-16).

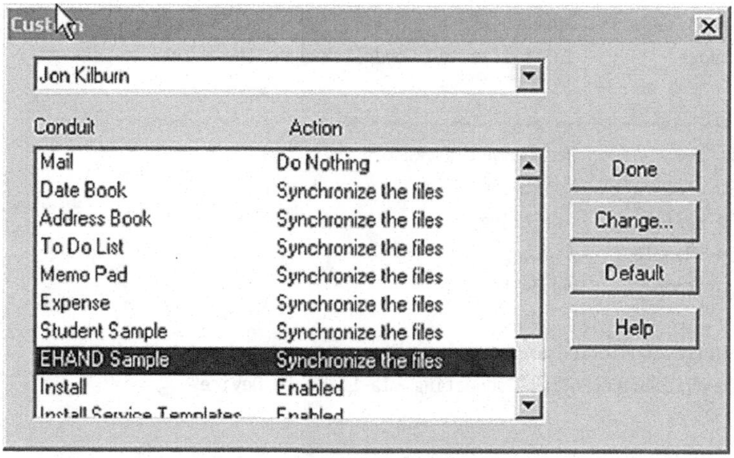

Figure 9-16. The newly installed EHAND Sample conduit

Now that we have established communications with the handheld device, we can write some custom code in our EHAND Sample conduit to perform an action or a series of actions. With the basic connection in place, let's move on to creating the template for our conduit. The next step after opening the conduit connection is to check for the existence of the CmdAction databases (remembering that the name is case sensitive). Once we have located the command database, we need to open the file and read the first record to see what action has been requested (see Listing 9-4).

To open a database, use the OpenDatabase() method of the conduit object. With the database open, you must then define the field layout for the database via the conduit object's DefineFields() method. The final trick is to read the actual record. We need to create a variable to hold the record information. EHAND has provided a record object (PalmAccess.Record) for this purpose. After you define the fields, you can read the record (I used ReadRecordByIndex(nRecNum)) into the EHAND record object. Finally, you access the fields by using the GetField(nIndex) method of the EHAND record object.

Listing 9-4. Code to Open the Command Database

```
Public Sub OpenConduit(oConduit As PalmAccess.Conduit)
'-=-=-=-=-=-=-=-=-=-=-=-=-=-=-=-=-=-=-=-=-=-=-=-=-=-=-=-=-=-=
'
'    Sub        :    OpenConduit()
'    Params     :    oConduit - EHAND PalmAccess Conduit Object
'    Returns    :    None
'
'    Author     :    Vivid Software Inc. - Jon Kilburn
'                    http://www.VividSoftware.com
'
'    Client     :    Apress
'    Purpose    :    Initialize the Conduit and do the Work.
'
'-=-=-=-=-=-=-=-=-=-=-=-=-=-=-=-=-=-=-=-=-=-=-=-=-=-=-=-=-=-=
    Dim rec        As PalmAccess.Record
    Dim cAction    As String
    Dim buffer     As String
    Dim nHandle    As Long
    Dim iLoop      As Integer

    ' Write Connection Entry
    oConduit.AddLogEntry "Connecting via EHAND to Device"
```

```
' Set Product Name information
oConduit.SetProductName "EHAND Palm Access Sample"

' Open the Conduit
If oConduit.OpenDatabase("CmdAction") Then

    ' Define Fields
    oConduit.DefineField "Field0", eString, ""

    ' Open the Control file and determine what to do
    Set rec = oConduit.ReadRecordByIndex(0)

    ' Retrieve Action Byte
    cAction = rec.GetField(0)

    ' Done so close file
    oConduit.CloseDatabase True

    ' Determine what to do
    Select Case UCase(cAction)
        Case "UPLOAD"
            ' Perform Upload
            oConduit.AddLogEntry "UPLOAD Requested."

        Case "DOWNLOAD"
            ' Perform Download
            oConduit.AddLogEntry "DOWNLOAD Requested."

        Case "MOVE"
            ' Move the data
            oConduit.AddLogEntry "MOVE Requested."
    End Select
Else

    ' File Does not exist.
    oConduit.AddLogEntry "EHAND Sample Command File Not Found."

End If
End Sub
```

Check for the existence of CmdAction so our new EHTest DLL will now connect to the Palm device, and then read the first record and determine what action was requested. Once the record has been read and the action determined, a log entry will be written based on the requested action.

For the final step, we have to do several things. First, as I mentioned earlier all database created on a Palm device require a CreatorID, and a Type ID. Since we know that we will have to create new databases we need to write a function that will convert a string CreatorID into the required Palm Format (see Listing 9-5).[2]

Listing 9-5. Code to Convert a String to a Palm Long Value

```
Public Function CreatorID(sValue As String) As Long
'-=-=-=-=-=-=-=-=-=-=-=-=-=-=-=-=-=-=-=-=-=-=-=-=-=-=-=-=-=
'
'    Function    :    CreatorID(sValue)
'    Params      :    sValue - String to Convert
'    Returns     :    LONG - Creator ID
'
'    Author      :    Vivid Software Inc. - Jon Kilburn
'                     http://www.VividSoftware.com
'
'    Client      :    Apress
'    Purpose     :    Converts a passed string to the Hex value
'                     for a Creator ID. PDB functions require a
'                     CreatorID and TypeID in long format, but most
'                     developers don't know the string version of
'                     IDs. This function performs the conversion.
'
'    NOTE        :    This function does not protect against invalid
'                     IDs. Please refer to Palm OS documentation for
'                     more specific information about Creator and
'                     Type IDs.
'
'-=-=-=-=-=-=-=-=-=-=-=-=-=-=-=-=-=-=-=-=-=-=-=-=-=-=-=-=-=
    Dim PalmLng As Long
    Dim iLoop    As Integer

    ' Only convert if length is four chars
    If Len(sValue) = 4 Then
```

---

[2] Both the EHAND documentation and AppForge include code to convert a passed string to a CreatorID. This code was modified from the AppForge example that can be found in the AppForge Users Guide under the Extended functions library.

```
        ' Walk the string
        For iLoop = 1 To Len(sValue)
            PalmLng = PalmLng * 256 + Asc(Mid(sValue, iLoop, 1))
        Next iLoop
    End If


    ' Return the value
    CreatorID = PalmLng
End Function
```

Now that we have the code to build a CreatorID value, we need to write the final code to move the data from the desktop to the Palm device and from the Palm device to the PC. In my example, I have hard-coded a path of C:\EHTest. You can modify this in the EHTest code or you can create the folder to test this conduit. Generally, you should not include hard-coded paths, but this is simply an example.

As we noted earlier, what has to happen will be controlled by the CmdAction database. Here is each process broken down:

- *UPLOAD*: To perform the upload of a new order, we need to open the ASCII file (C:\EHTest\orders.txt), check the Palm device for the existence of the Orders table, and then write each order in the ASCII file to the Palm device.

- *DOWNLOAD*: To perform the download of a processed order, we need to open an ASCII file on the desktop (C:\EHTest\completed.txt), then check for the existence of the Orders table, and finally write each order from the Orders table that is marked as shipped (Shipped = 1) to the ASCII file.

- *MOVE*: To perform the move of an inventory item, we need to open an ASCII file on the desktop (C:\EHTest\inv_move.txt), and then check for the existence of the MoveInventory table, and finally write each record in the MoveInventory table to the ASCII file.

Now that you understand how the process works, let's review the code. See Listing 9-6 for the final EHTest Conduit code.

NOTE   *I have not used any new functions but rather have simply continued using the functions from the EHAND PalmAccess library that we reviewed earlier.*

Listing 9-6. The Completed EHTest Conduit

```
Option Explicit

Const fldOrderNo = 0
Const fldCustNo = 1
Const fldInvNo = 2
Const fldQty = 3
Const fldShipped = 4


Const fldMoveInvNo = 0
Const fldMoveLocation = 1


Public Sub OpenConduit(oConduit As PalmAccess.Conduit)
'-=-=-=-=-=-=-=-=-=-=-=-=-=-=-=-=-=-=-=-=-=-=-=-=-=-=-=-=-=-=
'
'   Sub       :   OpenConduit()
'   Params    :   oConduit - EHAND PalmAccess Conduit Object
'   Returns   :   None
'
'   Author    :   Vivid Software Inc. - Jon Kilburn
'                 http://www.VividSoftware.com
'
'   Client    :   Apress
'   Purpose   :   Initialize the Conduit and do the Work.
'
'-=-=-=-=-=-=-=-=-=-=-=-=-=-=-=-=-=-=-=-=-=-=-=-=-=-=-=-=-=-=
    Dim rec         As PalmAccess.Record
    Dim cAction     As String
    Dim buffer      As String
    Dim nHandle     As Long
    Dim iLoop       As Integer

    ' Write Connection Entry
    oConduit.AddLogEntry "Connecting via EHAND to Device"

    ' Set Product Name information
    oConduit.SetProductName "EHAND Palm Access Sample"

    ' Open the Conduit
    If oConduit.OpenDatabase("CmdAction") Then
```

```
' Define Fields
oConduit.DefineField "Field0", eString, ""

' Open the Control file and determine what to do
Set rec = oConduit.ReadRecordByIndex(0)

' Retrieve Action Byte
cAction = rec.GetField(0)

' Done so close file
oConduit.CloseDatabase True

' Determine what to do
Select Case UCase(cAction)
    Case "UPLOAD"
        ' Perform Upload
        oConduit.AddLogEntry "Performing Upload of New Orders"

        ' Do the Upload of this data to the Palm Device
        nHandle = FreeFile

        Open "C:\EHTest\orders.txt" For Input As #nHandle

        ' Upload the records
        If Not oConduit.OpenDatabase("Orders") Then
            ' Create File
            Call oConduit.CreateDatabase("Orders", _
                    CreatorID("SAMP"), CreatorID("DATA"))
        End If

        oConduit.DefineField "OrderNo", eString, ""
        oConduit.DefineField "CustNo", eString, ""
        oConduit.DefineField "InvNo", eString, ""
        oConduit.DefineField "Qty", eInteger, ""
        oConduit.DefineField "Shipped", eInteger, ""

        ' Read in the data and pass it into the Orders file
        Do While Not EOF(nHandle)
            buffer = Space(255)
            Line Input #nHandle, buffer

            buffer = Trim(buffer)
```

```
                        ' Check for empty CrLf which leaves a blank record
                        If Len(buffer) = 0 Then
                            ' Do nothing, because we are really at the EOF
                        Else
                            ' Create new reocrd
                            Set rec = oConduit.GetEmptyRecord

                            ' Set first Field Value, write the Order Number
                            rec.SetField "OrderNo", Left(buffer, _
                                InStr(1, buffer, ",", vbTextCompare) - 1)

                            ' Trim buffer, Write Customer Number
                            buffer = Mid(buffer, _
                                InStr(1, buffer, ",", vbTextCompare) + 1)

                            rec.SetField "CustNo", Left(buffer, _
                                InStr(1, buffer, ",", vbTextCompare) - 1)

                            ' Trim buffer, Write Inventory Item Number
                            buffer = Mid(buffer, _
                                InStr(1, buffer, ",", vbTextCompare) + 1)
                            rec.SetField "InvNo", Left(buffer, _
                                InStr(1, buffer, ",", vbTextCompare) - 1)

                            ' Trim buffer, Write the Quanity
                            buffer = Mid(buffer, _
                                InStr(1, buffer, ",", vbTextCompare) + 1)
                            rec.SetField "Qty", CInt(Left(buffer, _
                                InStr(1, buffer, ",", vbTextCompare) - 1))

                            ' New entry so shipped is 0
                            rec.SetField "Shipped", 0

                            ' Write this record
                            Call oConduit.WriteRec(rec)
                        End If
                    Loop

                Case "DOWNLOAD"
                    ' Perform Download
                    oConduit.AddLogEntry "Performing Download of Finished Orders."
```

```
' Do the Upload of this data to the Palm Device
nHandle = FreeFile

Open "C:\EHTest\completed.txt" For Output As #nHandle

' Load the records
If Not oConduit.OpenDatabase("Orders") Then
    ' Create File
    Call oConduit.CreateDatabase("Orders", _
        CreatorID("SAMP"), CreatorID("DATA"))
End If

oConduit.DefineField "OrderNo", eString, ""
oConduit.DefineField "CustNo", eString, ""
oConduit.DefineField "InvNo", eString, ""
oConduit.DefineField "Qty", eInteger, ""
oConduit.DefineField "Shipped", eInteger, ""

' Read in the data and if the record has the shipped
' flag set to 1 download the order
For iLoop = 0 To oConduit.GetDBRecordCount - 1
    Set rec = oConduit.ReadRecordByIndex(iLoop)

    ' Return Shipping Field
    buffer = rec.GetField(fldShipped)

    If CInt(buffer) = 1 Then
        ' Item has shipped, so write out the line
        buffer = rec.GetField(fldOrderNo)
        buffer = buffer & "," & rec.GetField(fldCustNo)
        buffer = buffer & "," & rec.GetField(fldInvNo)
        buffer = buffer & "," & rec.GetField(fldQty)
        buffer = buffer & "," & rec.GetField(fldShipped)

        Print #nHandle, buffer
    End If

Next iLoop

' Close ASCII File
Close #nHandle
```

```
                              ' Close Database
                              oConduit.CloseDatabase True

                              ' Write Log Entry
                              Call oConduit.AddLogEntry("Download of Shipped Orders Complete")


                    Case "MOVE"
                         ' Move the data
                         oConduit.AddLogEntry "Performing Move Inventory Location"

                         ' Do the Download of this data from the Palm Device
                         nHandle = FreeFile

                         Open "C:\EHTest\inv_move.txt" For Output As #nHandle

                         ' Load the records
                         If Not oConduit.OpenDatabase("MoveInventory") Then
                              ' Create File
                              Call oConduit.CreateDatabase("MoveInventory", _
                                   CreatorID("SAMP"), CreatorID("DATA"))
                         End If

                         ' Define the field
                         oConduit.DefineField "InvNo", eString, ""
                         oConduit.DefineField "NewLocation", eString, ""

                         ' Write out the inventory item
                         For iLoop = 0 To oConduit.GetDBRecordCount - 1
                              Set rec = oConduit.ReadRecordByIndex(iLoop)

                              ' Build Buffer
                              buffer = rec.GetField(fldMoveInvNo)
                              buffer = buffer & "," & rec.GetField(fldMoveLocation)

                              ' write out the buffer
                              Print #nHandle, buffer
                         Next iLoop

                         ' Close ASCII file
                         Close #nHandle
```

```
        ' Close Database
        oConduit.CloseDatabase True

        ' Write Log Entry
        oConduit.AddLogEntry "Move Inventory Location Complete"

    End Select
Else

    ' File Does not exist.
    oConduit.AddLogEntry "EHAND Sample Command File Not Found."

End If

End Sub
```

Installation of EHAND on an End User's System

To get your PalmAccess conduit working on an end user's system, you must install several files, including a very important INI file, to the same directory. This is most easily accomplished with an installation packager tool, such as InstallShield Express. Some of the files must be registered in Windows, so the packager must be able to do this.

PalmAccess requires the following files be installed into the same directory:

- Condmgr.dll (located in <Program Files>\EHAND\EHAND PalmAccess\bin)

- EHAConf.ini (a template is located in <Program Files>\EHAND\EHAND PalmAccess\bin which can simply be modified for usage, see below)

- EHAutoReg.dll (located in <Program Files>\EHAND\EHAND PalmAccess\bin)

- EHPalmAccess.dll (located in <Program Files>\EHAND\EHAND PalmAccess)

- Your conduit DLL file

EHAConf.ini contains the information required to install your conduit and is in the following format:

```
[Conduit]
CreatorId = calc (your app's creator id)
Override = 1
Path = %CurDir%\EHPalmAccess.dll
Title = Test (whatever you want to appear in HotSync manager's list
Prio = 2
ClassName = USCO_Conduit.clsConduit (your dll name and function)
```

EHAutoReg.dll must be registered during the installation process. Registering it is what actually adds your conduit to HotSync Manager and restarts HSM for you. This is very nice and saves a lot of work. Just remember that your conduit DLL file must also be registered for it to work properly (see Figure 9-17).

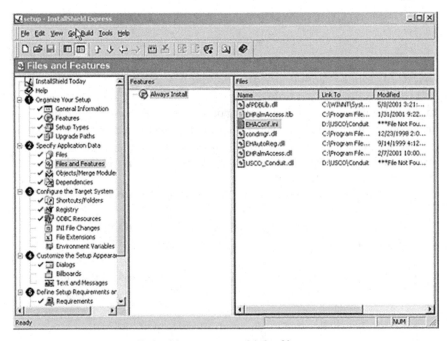

Figure 9-17. Using Install Shield Express to add the files

The only bad things I have to say about the EHAND product are:

- The Web site is terrible to navigate. Many links appear broken, and it is very hard to determine the current product.

- There is no real documentation on installing the finished conduit onto an end user's system. It's alluded to in the supplied documentation, but it was a matter of trial and error and knowing someone who had done it before to get the installation to work properly.

The Palm Conduit Developers Kit (CDK)

Getting started with the Palm CDK requires two things: a cup of coffee (or some other beverage you can sip while you wait) and a high-speed Internet connection. Even when zipped, the CDK is a beefy 53MB download. (For those of you with a dialup, aren't you lucky we put it on the CD?) So sip that cup of coffee and wait on the download, but I've got another surprise for you. Even after you download the CDK, you need to spend some more time checking the Palm Web site for documentation updates. Once you have everything downloaded, you can install the Palm CDK.

After completing the installation you have the option to register the installed software package. I recommend that you take the time to fill out the rather simple form; Palm will send you email notification when updates and changes to the CDK occur. Once the installation has completed, you'll find a new program group has been created for the Palm CDK. Under this, you'll find tons of information (much of which has been summarized by this chapter); unfortunately, not very much of it is written for the Visual Basic Developer. Most of the information contained within the CDK pertains to developing conduits in C/C++[3]. It took several hours to distill most of the information into usable chunks, and I hope that you find this section an easier read than the Palm CDK documentation.

Getting Started with the Palm CDK in Visual Basic

As a beginning, I thought I'd share a few thoughts on what it takes to set up a sample application using COM in Visual Basic, and to point out a few of the more serious pitfalls for beginning developers. Although the CDK is well written, it is a bit skimpy in a few critical parts. And it's really skimpy when it comes to examples using the COM interface with Visual Basic.

Before you begin, be aware that, unlike EHAND and the AppForge UC, you are now playing around with the conduit system directly. Mistakes you make can alter your Palm databases and cause strange behavior. Make sure that you have backed up everything that is critical (and print out anything really critical that you may need) before you begin altering your conduits.

After you have installed the Palm CDK, if you are running the HotSync Manager you should exit it, as it is a good idea to make a backup of your current

---

[3] It was this lack of information for the VB programmer that helped prompt me to write this book.

Palm data. You can accomplish this by either opening a DOS command window (in NT/2000, select Start | Run and type "cmd"; in 98/95, select Start | Run and type "command"), or by opening the Windows Explorer. Locate the directory that the CDK was installed into (C:\CDK402) and then locate the Common\Bin\C4.02 subdirectory. In this subdirectory, you will find a copy of the HotSync Manager and all the DLLs required to start it. Now we need to start the HotSync Manager while identifying this directory as the new backup directory. If you are in DOS, you can start the HotSync Manager by typing HOTSYNC.EXE –D. If you are using the Windows Explorer, you need to select Start | Run and then browse until you have the entire path in the Run Command dialog box. Add to the end of the directory path "HOTSYNC.EXE –D" and this will set the HotSync Manager's backup directory.

 CAUTION *Any backups are saved to the 4.02 directory only until you reboot your computer. Once the computer has rebooted, the default (usually C:\Palm) will once again be set to the backup directory.*

Put your Palm device into its cradle and press the HotSync button. You will receive the prompt "Would you like to create a new user?" Click the Yes button. In the dialog box, enter the user name you wish to use. A full synchronization will run for enough time to drink yet another cup of coffee. (You can even brew a fresh pot if you have a particularly full Palm.) The contents of your Palm will be freshly backed up into the C4.02 directory in a folder labeled with the user name you supplied.

Now that we have restarted the HotSync Manager, we are ready to begin creating a new conduit. The first thing to do is open the conduit configuration manager program supplied by Palm (CondCfg.exe)[4]. This file should be in the same subdirectory as the HOTSYNC.EXE file we used earlier. You can either run the program from DOS or the Windows Explorer (see Figure 9-18).

---

[4] This program looks remarkably like the one we used while developing our EHAND conduit.

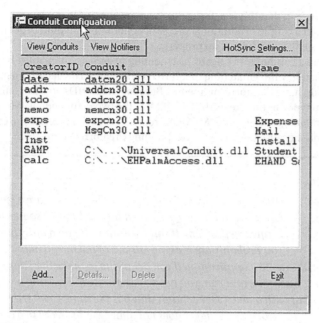

Figure 9-18. The conduit configuration manager

We are now going to create a simple COM-based conduit that will interface with the SimpleDB application. (The SimpleDB application is supplied with the Palm CDK and is located in C:\CDK402\Com\Samples\Tutorial\SimpleDb.) It's easy, but you need to follow a couple of essential rules to get the SimpleDB app to work. (These rules are present, but not obvious, in the CDK documentation.) The same rules that I mentioned when we were developing a conduit using EHAND also apply here (as these are universal Palm conduit development rules).

- Conduits cannot share the same CreatorID.

- HotSync will run only those conduits that have applications with matching CreatorIDs on the Palm device.

Incorrect Information in the CDK

If you were following the directions in the CDK guide to set up the SimpleDb conduit, you probably typed in the CreatorID "MEMO" for SimpleDB (because this is what the instructions instruct you to do). After you finished setting up the conduit and clicked the HotSync button, nothing happened. Bit of a surprise there, huh? You would think that the Palm documentation would be correct. Well, it is, sort of. . .

It turns out that this is a misleading section of the CDK guide, and that you have to add a couple of additional pieces of conduit information to get the Visual Basic IDE conduit set up properly.

To run a conduit (once again, as I mentioned earlier), there must be an application with a matching CreatorID on the Palm. The default memo pad application has a CreatorID of "memo". Because CreatorIDs are case sensitive, when you typed in the CreatorID of "MEMO", the two do not equal. When the HotSync Manager selects the "MEMO" CreatorID that you created, the conduit will not run because there is no corresponding CreatorID on the Palm.

 NOTE *Remember that no two conduits can share a single CreatorID. This brings us to an interesting and somewhat confusing problem. If you use your Palm on a daily basis, you probably are making fair use of the memo pad (CreatorID "memo") application. If you are trying to make the SimpleDB application compile and run, you need to overwrite the existing memo pad conduit with a new COM conduit that has the same CreatorID ("memo"). The HotSync Manager does not allow you to create two conduits that share the same CreatorID (CondCfg.exe will not allow this either). As a sidenote, it doesn't really matter what CreatorID you actually use (it can be "memo" or "date", for instance); it just has to be an ID that is present on your Palm so that HotSync Manager will run the conduit.*

Which brings us to setting up a conduit that will actually work properly. The first thing you should do before we go any further is open up Notepad (or get a piece of paper and write this down) and open the memo conduit. Make sure you record all of the information about the conduit before continuing (see Figure 9-19).

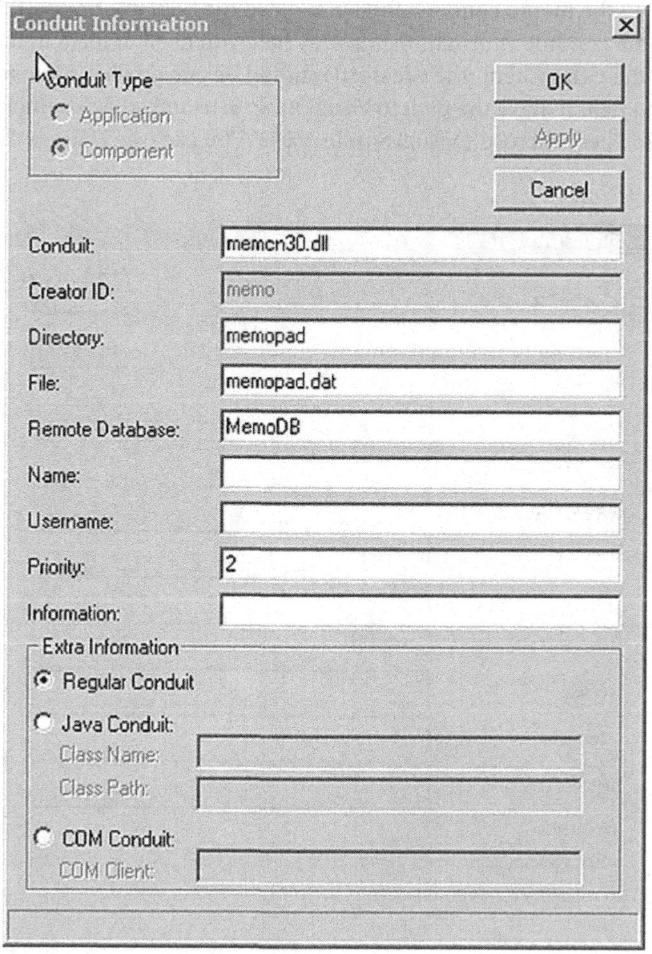

Figure 9-19. The memo pad conduit

Now that you have made a backup of the memo pad conduit we can continue. We are going to set up a very basic conduit in Visual Basic, so you can fool around with that and do general EXE / Conduit debugging on the SimpleDB application. We will be overwriting some of the information in the memo pad conduit, so make sure you have recorded and stored all the information about the memo conduit.

Open up the memo conduit, and write down the field information. After recording the conduit information, the only field you need to fill in in the memo conduit is the COM Client (the CreatorID should be grayed out). Change the COM Client field to have the path to Visual Basic 6; usually this is something like C:\Program Files\Microsoft Visual Studio\VB98\VB6.exe (see Figure 9-20).

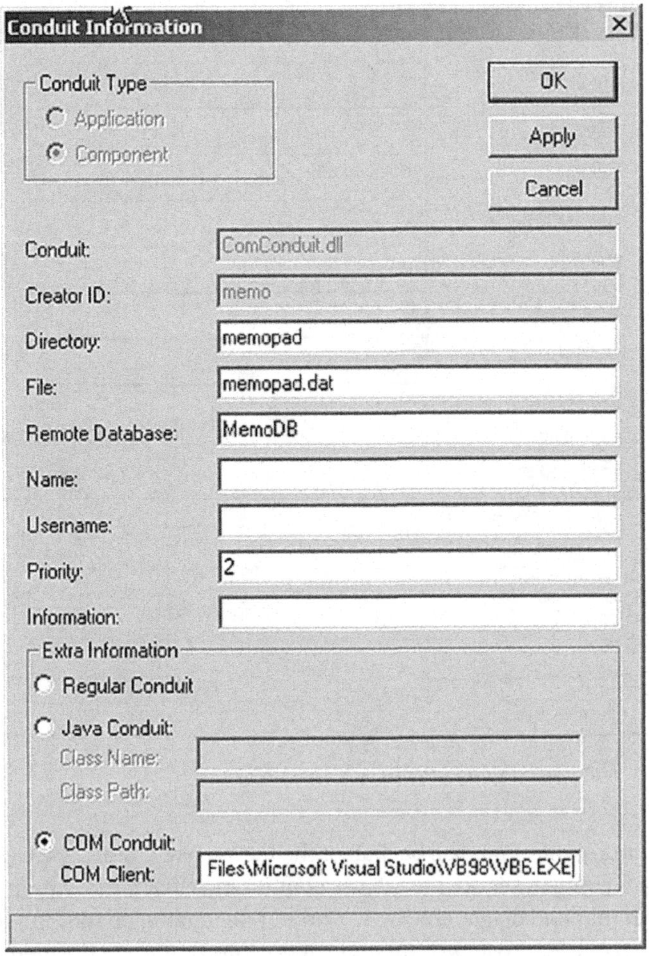

Figure 9-20. Changing the COM client setup

You can leave the other fields alone or delete them. You do not need to fill in any of the other fields for this conduit to work properly because the only activity SimpleDB engages in is to read information from the MemoDB database on the Palm (and this information is specified in the SimpleDb application itself). The other fields listed (Directory, File, Remote Database, Name, and Username) are optional fields that are primarily used to store default values for the client PC.

We are just about ready to run a test using the SimpleDB application. Open SimpleDB application in VB. Once the application is open, you can see the references that you need to add to any VB COM conduit you may want to build (see Figure 9-20).

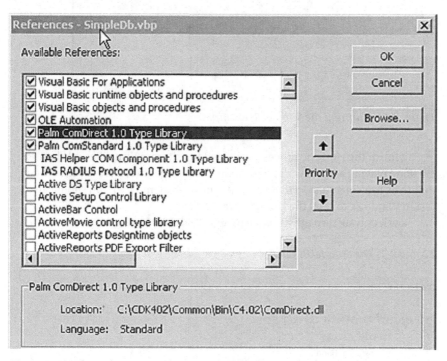

Figure 9-21. The Palm COM references used by the SimpleDB VB sample

Now that we know what references are needed, we can use them again when we are writing another COM-based conduit. For right now, go ahead and close the References window and shut down VB. Place your Palm device in its cradle and press the HotSync button. The HotSync Manager should start and run through all the conduits just like usual until it encounters the memo pad conduit. At this point, the HotSync Manage will appear to freeze. You should notice that Visual Basic has been launched and is waiting for you to do something.

That something is loading the SimpleDB example and running it. After filling in the search field, SimpleDB now iterates through the memo pad, searching for your string that you typed into the search field (see Figure 9-22).

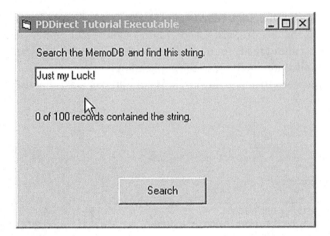

Figure 9-22. Running the SimpleDB example

To finish the HotSync process, you need to exit from Visual Basic. When you are done playing around with the conduit, don't forget to restore the memo conduit to its previous state so that you can sync your memo pad. You should also restart Windows to reset the HotSync Manager.

Now let's walk through the code in SimpleDB (see Listing 9-7).

Listing 9-7. The SimpleDB Code

```
Option Explicit

Private Sub btnSearch_Click()
    '   Handle errors
    On Error GoTo Handler

    '   Let the user know we're processing
    lblCount = "Please wait....."

    '   Declare the PDDatabaseQuery object
    Dim pDbQuery As New PDDatabaseQuery

    '   Declare the PDRecordAdapter object
    Dim pMemo As PDRecordAdapter

    '   Open the Memo database
    Set pMemo = pDbQuery.OpenRecordDatabase("MemoDB", _
        "PDDirect.PDRecordAdapter", eRead Or eWrite Or eShowSecret)
```

```
'    Declare the record header and data
Dim nIndex As Long
Dim vUniqueId As Variant
Dim nCategory As Long
Dim eAttributes As ERecordAttributes
Dim vData As Variant

'    Declare the PDUtility object
Dim pUtility As New PDUtility

'    Declare the Memo string
Dim sMemo As String

'    Declare the count of records containing the string
Dim nCount As Long
Dim nTest As Variant

'    Read the first record
pMemo.IterationIndex = 0
vData = pMemo.ReadNext(nIndex, vUniqueId, nCategory, eAttributes)

'    Loop and search each Memo record for the string
Do While Not pMemo.EOF
    '    Convert the Memo record to a string
    '    ByteArrayToBSTR returns the next offset
    '    We don't need it
    pUtility.ByteArrayToBSTR vData, 0, 32767, sMemo

    '    See if the search string is in the Memo record
    nTest = InStr(sMemo, txtSearch.Text)
    If VarType(nTest) <> vbNull And nTest > 0 Then nCount = nCount + 1

    '    Read the next record
    vData = pMemo.ReadNext(nIndex, vUniqueId, nCategory, eAttributes)
Loop

'    Prepare the result
lblCount.Caption = Str(nCount) & " of " & Str(pMemo.RecordCount) & _
                   " records contained the string."

'    Don't need the objects anymore
Set pDbQuery = Nothing
Set pMemo = Nothing
Set pUtility = Nothing
```

```
'   Normal exit
    Exit Sub

Handler:
    MsgBox "There was an error performing the search." & vbNewLine & _
           Err.Description & vbNewLine & _
           "Number = " & Hex(Err.Number)

'   Don't need the objects anymore
    Set pDbQuery = Nothing
    Set pMemo = Nothing
    Set pUtility = Nothing
End Sub
```

We will begin by discussing two objects, the first of which is the PDDatabaseQuery object. The PDDatabaseQuery[5] object is used to connect to any database on the handheld and represents the master collection of all the databases.

The next object is the PDRecordAdapter, which represents a single open database. You can use the PDBRecordAdapter[6] object to read database records. The process of reading database records can be accomplished in one of two ways:

- Records can be accessed serially using the iterator methods. The iterator methods are named ReadNext*, and require you to set the IterationIndex before using them. You should use the EOF property to determine when there are no more records in the iteration.

- Records can be randomly accessed using the direct methods. The direct methods are named ReadBy*. Because you are reading a direct index, you do not need to check the EOF method.

The process works like this. Connect to the database master list using PDBDatabaseQuery. Once connected, select which database to work with using the Open() method of the PDBDatabaseQuery object. Using the Open method will return a PDRecordAdapter object. Using the PDRecordAdapter object, we can now perform actions against the memo database stored on the Palm device.

---

[5] The supported methods and functions can be found in the COM Sync Reference help file provided with the CDK.
[6] The supported methods and functions can be found in the COM Sync Reference help file provided with the CDK.

You will notice the use of a user-defined type (ERecordAttributes). The ERecordAttributes type will store one of the values from Table 9-3. You may need this variable later to store the record attributes so you can perform comparisons.

Table 9-3. ERecordAttribute Values

CONSTANT	VALUE	DESCRIPTION
eDelete	0x80	Record has been deleted
eDirty	0x40	Record has been modified
eSecret	0x10	Record is private
eArchive	0x08	Record has been archived

The last object is the PDUtility object, which is used to manipulate strings, byte arrays, and integers. In the SimpleDB example, it is used to manipulate string values by converting them from a ByteArray to the VB sting datatype (BSTR). First, the ReadNext method of the PDRecordAdapter object is used to return the value of the current record. This value is then converted into a VB recognizable BSTR variable (sMemo), which is then searched using InStr().

As you can see, you can do many things with the Palm CDK. I've simply explained one of the examples that comes with it. The CDK is very big and contains functions to do just about anything you could every want. The only problem seems to be finding the documentation to explain how. I expect that, as more VB developers use this very new tool, more and better documentation and samples will become available.

Installation of a COM Conduit Developed with the CDK on an End User's System

This section describes general tips for writing an installer and uninstaller for your COM-based conduit. Palm's documentation that comes with the CDK (COMSyncCompanion) includes an entire section on dealing with building conduit installs and installation scripts. For this section, I'm going to review a few things, but for the most part the Palm documentation is quite good, and a good article on creating install scripts is available at http://oasis.palm.com/dev/kb/manuals/conduit_win/CComp_Install.cfm#939054.

The PalmCOMInstaller.exe (located in C:\CDK402\Com\Installer) executable helps with the installation and registration of the Palm COM components. The PalmCOMInstaller.exe is a self-extracting file that can be used for the installation and uninstallation of the Palm COM objects required on the end user's machine. This executable installs the COM object required by conduits written using the Palm COM API (see Table 9-4 for the list of files needed for an install) so you do not have to do it manually.

NOTE *You can redistribute the PalmCOMInstaller.exe as part of your conduit distribution.*

Table 9-4. List of Files to Install

FILE	DESCRIPTION
MyConduit.dll	This is the conduit you have developed
COMStandard.dll	Client support DLL[7]
COMDirect.dll	Client support DLL
COMConduit.dll	Control Server DLL

COM Sync Suite DLLs

The COM Sync Suite is composed of several DLLs that act as the client and server during the HotSync process. The server is a single DLL (which is itself a standard C-based conduit).

The client consists of several DLLs that combine to communicate with the server, providing you a level of abstraction above the HotSync Manager API. The server DLL "wraps" the Sync Manager API with a COM interface, and the client exposes that COM interface through an object model.

Because the COMConduit.dll is a standard C-based conduit, it is activated and executed during a normal HotSync operation. COMConduit.dll, which acts as the server, handles all Sync Manager API execution. The two client DLLs, COMDirect.dll and COMStandard.dll, communicate with COMConduit.dll while supplying a programming interface for you to use when developing your applications or conduits.

Once the COMConduit.dll is launched during the HotSync process, like any other standard conduit, the COM Sync Suite activates a client process referred to as the *client module.* The client module then uses the COM Sync Suite object model to communicate with the Palm device.

The PalmCOMInstaller.exe helps with the installation of the required COM objects and aids in simplifying your installation program. Your conduit installation

---

[7] See sidebar.

program should invoke this executable with the appropriate command-line options to install and uninstall the Palm COM objects (see Table 9-5).

Table 9-5. Commands to Install and Uninstall the Palm COM Objects

COMMAND	DESCRIPTION
/s -a /s	This set of parameters suppresses or silences all dialog boxes associated with the installation execution.
-a –uninstall	This set of parameters uninstalls PalmCOMInstaller.exe from the user's system.
/s -a -uninstall /s	This set of parameters uninstalls PalmCOMInstaller.exe from the user's system while suppressing or silencing all dialog boxes.

NOTE   *For those of you familiar with prior versions of the Palm CDK, PalmCntl.ocx is now included in the PalmCOMInstaller.exe. You do not have to specifically include that file in your conduit installation packages.*
If PalmCntl.ocx is used during your Visual Basic installation script to register a conduit, for example, include it in your installation package. PalmCOMInstaller.exe installs that file onto the end user's machine.

The CASL Conduit

As with most tasks in CASL, the most challenging part of using the CASL conduit is first finding the documentation and then understanding it. Once you get past this though, using the CASL conduit is very straightforward.

This section assumes that you have a working knowledge of CASL syntax and commands. (For a more complete understanding of CASL, refer to Chapter 7 and 8.) CASL provides an easy-to-use, command-line tool to install and register (with the Windows registry) the conduit. This tool can be readily built into any install script using a batch file, Install Shield, or your favorite install tool.

The sources in the CASL documentation are the Language Reference Help for information on how to prepare your dbfile definition for use with a conduit, and the CASLide Manual for information on how to use the conduit setup tool.

The CASL RAD tools (both normal CASL and CASLpro) come with a CASL conduit that serves as a common conduit for all CASL databases. The way that the conduit is registered, and the way that the database files are created, defines how the CASL conduit will behave with each database. The following configuration options are possible with the CASL conduit:

- Databases can be synchronized one-way (PC to PDA, or PDA to PC), two-way, or not at all.

- Databases can be a format supported by the ODBC object (such as Access, SQL Server, Oracle, or an Excel spreadsheet).

- Databases can be the CASL database format (text file with header information, followed by data record information in a comma-separated value (CSV) format).

 NOTE *The CASL conduit works only with Windows. CASLsoft does not provide a conduit option for other platforms, such as Mac and Linux. For other platforms, you'll need to write your own conduit using any of the conduit development tools available, such as those already mentioned in this chapter.*

The PDA data must be a CASL database file defined using a dbfile definition. A dbfile definition has the following syntax:

```
dbfile name;
    { field field_var, . ... }
    { sync_pref orientation; }
    { data_source_name string_expression; }
end;
```

The sync_pref parameter defines the type of synchronization, which will be performed between your PDA and the PC application (see Table 9-6).

Table 9-6. Constants supplied by CASL for conduit actions

CONSTANT	DESCRIPTION
pda_to_pc	Replaces PC data with PDA data
pc_to_pda	Replaces PDA data with PC data
merge	New records from either are transferred to the other.
none	No synchronization take place in either direction.

CASL Conduit Merge Ambiguities

When the CASL conduit performs a merge operation, it looks at the record status on each platform and takes appropriate action. CASL database files have a unique record ID and status field to keep track of a record on each platform and its status. Possible record status values include not modified, modified, tagged for deletion, and new. The not modified, tagged for deletion, and new status indicators are handled by the CASL conduit in a straightforward way, as implied by the status indicator's name. However, handling the modified status indicator can lead to ambiguities.

The modified status results in the corresponding record on the other platform being replaced with the modified record. However, consider the case in which the record on each platform has been modified between HotSync operations. In this case, each record will have a modified status indicator. Which record should be replaced? In this situation, the CASL conduit duplicates the record. It is then the programmer's responsibility to resolve the ambiguity when the program starts up the next time. Because the CASL search command, which allows random access to a database file, assumes all records will have a unique key field value (the first field), it's advisable to resolve duplicate records into a single record. For an excellent example of one way to do this, see the Password sample application that comes with the CASLide installation.

The data_source_name parameter is optional, and defines the name of the ODBC link you created on your PC. This often confuses users because you are defining within your CASL database file the name of the OBDC link you have created on your PC for communicating with your PC database.

The name can be up to 31 characters long and may contain spaces. If an equals sign is found in the data_source_name string, it is assumed that the string is the full connect string. If not, it will be used as a DSN in the default connect string "DSN=<name>;UID=;PWD=".

You will need to use the full connect string syntax if you have protected your PC database with a password, as is common, for example, with Access databases:

```
"DSN=myODBClink;UID=username;PWD=myPassword".
```

By leaving the data_source_name specification out of the dbfile definition, you'll be specifying that your CASL database will be saved on the PC using the CASL database format. This is a text file with header information, followed by data record information in a CSV format. For details, see the CDB format specified in the CASLide manual.

A completed dbfile definition might look like:

```
dbfile dbMydata;
    field myField1;
    field myField2;
    sync_pref merge;
    data_source_name "myODBClink";
End;
```

The variables myField1 and myField2 should have been previously defined (or you will get a compile error), and the type definitions used should be consistent with the field definitions of the ODBC data source. For example:

```
variables;
    string myField1;
    string myField2;
end;
```

When using the data_source_name specification, the path location of the database on the PC is clear. But what about the case in which we're using the default CASL database format? There are two answers.

The database's CreatorID defines where the database will reside on the PC. Databases created with normal CASL (the entry-level version) always have the CreatorID, "CASL". With CASLpro (the high-end version), CASL databases have the default CreatorID "CASL", or can be programmed to use their program's CreatorID. (This is done with the CASLide by using the Project | PRC Settings dialog box.)

Databases with CreatorID "CASL" always reside in a "casl" subfolder off the Palm user's HotSync folder. The full path specification will be of the form "C:\Palm\User \Casl\", depending on each PC's individual configuration.

Databases with the CreatorID of their program will reside in a subfolder off the casl HotSync folder. You define the name during conduit registration (more on this in a minute). The full path specification will be of the form "C:\Palm\User\Casl\Your_App\", depending on each PC's individual configuration.

Installing and Registering the CASL Conduit on the End User's PC

Consider first the case in which the CreatorID of the database is the same as the program's CreatorID, as allowed by CASLpro. With your CASL datafile properly defined, and any link to your ODBC data source properly referenced, you can now install and register the conduit itself. CASL provides two command-line programs to accomplish this:

1. *CondReg.exe*: Installs the CASL conduit and enables it for use on the next HotSync.

2. *RemCond.exe*: Removes the CASL conduit completely from the system or disables it for a specific use.

CondReg requires the CASL conduit DLL file (CASLcn20.dll) to be available, so this file must be installed by your install script or program, before attempting to install and register the conduit. You should also ensure that two standard Microsoft files, MFC42.DLL and MSVCRT.DLL, are installed in the user's Windows folder as well. These files are generally present.

To install and register the conduit, the normal procedure is to copy CASLcn20.dll and CondReg.exe to the user's system. This can be in a temporary folder because, once CondReg installs the conduit file, CASLcn20.dll, into the Palm folder, the temporary folder can be removed from the user's system.

The syntax of CondReg is:

```
CondReg DLLpath -Appname "name" -CreatorID id -Directory "dir"
```

- *DLLpath*: This is the full path to the CASLcn20.dll file that we previously referred to.

- *Appname*: This is the application name, which is displayed during the HotSync operation and in the Custom window of the Palm HotSync Manager.

- *CreatorID*: This is the CreatorID of the application with which you are performing HotSync operation.

- *Directory*: This is a subfolder under the user's HotSync folder where databases are read from and written to during the HotSync operation. If you're synchronizing to an ODBC source, it can be considered a temporary folder and is not the location of the PC database itself, which is defined by the ODBC link. If you're synchronizing to a CASL database file, this is the location of the CASL database on the user's PC.

NOTE   *When specifying the DLLpath, there is no trailing backslash. If the path name contains spaces, it will need to be enclosed in quotes.*

You should be careful not to use the same folder name for applications with different CreatorIDs.

An example of a full command string as used from an install script might be:

```
CondReg "C:\temp" -Appname "My App" -CreatorID ABCD -Directory "My App"
```

This command will copy the CASLcn20.dll file from a temporary folder and create a HotSync Registry entry called "My App". The CreatorID is set to "ABCD", and the databases will be written to the My App folder under the user's HotSync folder (normally C:\Palm\User\My App).

Now consider the case in which the CreatorID of the database is the default "CASL" CreatorID. The process of installing and registering the conduit is the same as before, except most of the CondReg command options are not needed. The following command string will copy the conduit DLL from a temporary folder to the Palm folder, and register the CASL conduit with the HotSync Manager.

```
CondReg "C:\temp"
```

And that's it! After installing and registering the conduit, you should (as with any conduit) exit and restart HotSync Manager. Thereafter, the conduit will function automatically and, in my experience, very reliably.

Removing a CASL Conduit

It is good practice when installing your application on the user's machine and creating a conduit to provide a convenient means for the user to remove the conduit later on. To do this, install the RemCond.exe program to the user's system and create a Start menu item with the following shortcut command:

```
Remcond -CreatorID id  -KeepDLL
```

- *CreatorID*: This is the application's CreatorID.

- *KeepDLL*: If specified, the CASL conduit DLL (CASLcn20.dll) will not be deleted.

CASL Desktop Version of Palm OS Application

The easiest way to provide a desktop version of your Palm OS application is to compile your CASL program for the Windows target platform and use the CASL database format. The Windows-targeted application is compiled to pseudo-code, which is interpreted by the CASL runtime, CASLwin.exe. CASLwin programs can easily access a CASL formatted database. If you use this strategy, your installation program will also need to install the Windows version of your CASL program, the CASLwin.exe runtime, and the runtime's associated DLL files. For details you can refer to the CASLide manual.

A more sophisticated strategy would be to create a Windows version by using Visual Basic. Your VB application could be easily programmed to access the ODBC database or third-party ActiveX objects, which allow access to the CASL database format. SingeDB is one such object, provided by LFS Informatica (`http://www.singera.com/Palm/`). Because the CASL database format is basically a text-based CSV format, manually coding access isn't that difficult either.

For installing a CASL-formatted database file to your user's Palm device for the first time, you use the .cdi extension. The CASL conduit will install database files with this extension onto a user's Palm device. More details about this can be found in the CASLide manual.

Your installation program can be as easy as writing a batch file. Because you'll need to know certain paths that are in the Windows and/or Palm user registries, CASL provides a CASLcopy utility on the beta page (accessible to all registered users). This utility allows all PRC executable files, and their associated CDI database files to be installed on a user's Palm device, after performing a HotSync operation (or two). Your batch file could be as simple as calling the CondReg and CASLcopy utilities.

CASLsoft will be integrating a distribution wizard into the CASLide with CASL 3.3. The wizard will create a Windows executable for installing CASL applications. CASL 3.3 will be a free upgrade for CASL 3.2 owners.

Conclusion

Well, there you have it in a nutshell. You should now have a more robust understanding of conduits and what it takes to build one. A number of other conduit development tools are available; however, I've taken the time here to review and explain how to use each of the ones that I feel have the best potential. These tools should help you build any manner of conduit you wish. I recommend that you review any conduit task you have to perform and determine which of these tools is the best one to use on a case-by-case basis.

CHAPTER 10

Web Clipping

A FEW SHORT YEARS AGO, browsing the Web on a wireless handheld computer was
nothing short of a Star Trek fantasy. How quickly times change. Today this isn't
a dream, but a reality being put into effect by manufacturers of wireless products
and computer companies alike. In the rush to move the Web to our pocket giz-
mos, developers have to deal with a whole new set of problems, including
squeezing the graphics-rich Web into a 5-by-3 inch screen, and getting all that
data across low bandwidth. As you'll see, these problems are actually not all
that difficult to solve—they just require you to approach your creation of Web
content and code with a different set of goals in mind.

Understanding Web Clipping

Though Palm is by no means the first company to offer a Web-based service
around a wireless PDA device, they are thus far the most successful. In this chapter, you'll get a chance to explore the different approach taken by Palm as well as
the nuts and bolts behind Web Clipping.

NOTE   *Building a Palm Query Application (PQA) and Web
Clipping requires a basic knowledge of Hypertext Markup
Language (HTML). There is really no programming involved
with the development of the Web pages (they are pure
HTML), but some familiarity with CGI scripting is helpful if you wish to
generate dynamic Web content.*

First let me explain a term that I'll be using throughout this chapter. The
typical term associated with an application developed for the Palm wireless environment is *Palm Query Application* (PQA). A PQA file is not really an application,
rather it is really just a set of HTML pages, links, and graphics stored on the local
devices in a compressed database format. Just like any other database, PQA
databases contain records. In the case of a PQA, each record represents an
HTML page.

HTML is itself not a form of executable code. It is simply a series of tags used to describe a formatting action associated with a piece of content. On a PC system, a Web browser will interpret the HTML codes and display the requested content in a readable format. Since you really can't do general-purpose browsing on a Palm, you need a way to interpret HTML codes on the Palm OS device.

For this Palm has developed a program known as Clipper. Clipper can be considered the Palm device's browser. Its job is to load, decompress, and render the HTML stored in your PQA database on the Palm device. Clipper is free with the purchase of any Palm VII device, and for an extra charge will run on other Palm devices such as a Palm V.

Bandwidth and display issues inspired Palm Computing to develop Web Clipping. The PQA is only half the picture, with the rest of the content still on the actual Web site. The goal of Web Clipping is to minimize both display requirements (to fit on the Palm's screen) and bandwidth usage. Although there's always a lot of talk in the Web development world of reducing page load times and trying to keep them fast for users with slow connections, in this case the need is urgent.

As with developing an application to run on the Palm OS, the limited processor power and tight screen size are major constraints when developing a PQA application. Flashy, image-laden Web sites just won't fit onto the 160×160 pixel screen, even if the organizer's processor could download and display them in a reasonable amount of time.

There is another reason that a PQA application is somewhat restricted, and that's the expense of wireless bandwidth. That's right—wireless connections are not cheap. Unlike the typical modem connection, which is billed at a flat rate, wireless connections are billed based on the number of byes sent across the network.

NOTE   *Another issue with connections is that a lengthy connection will consume large amounts of battery power, significantly reducing the battery life of an organizer.*

To deal with this bottleneck of getting Web content to a handheld Palm device over a wireless network, Palm uses an approach it refers to as Web Clipping. The concept is simple. Imagine that you have a family member who just did something that got his or her name in the paper. You want to save the article, but you don't really need or want the entire newspaper. So you get out a pair of scissors and cut out, or clip, the article. Get the idea? Web Clipping delivers only the content you want, reducing the amount of wasted bytes of data.

There are two important concepts that make up Web Clipping:

- *Query and response:* Web Clipping focuses on a simply query that generates a response (the clipping). This is different from a traditional browser, which focuses on using hyperlinks between documents. A query is defined in an HTML form, and the clipping is usually generated dynamically with a CGI script running on a server. Instead of plodding through links to get to the information you want, a single query is sent and a single answer containing all the relevant requested information is returned. The query-and-response design speeds up the process by giving you only the data you want more quickly than if you had to browse for it. Limiting the amount of data sent in both directions helps keep the wireless costs down. Size is of the essence here—Palm recommends that the query sent up to the server be kept to about 40 bytes, and that the Web Clipping sent back is under 360 compressed bytes.

- *Partitioning:* A Web Clipping solution is partitioned between the client and a host. The query part of the application (the PQA) is stored on the client's Palm OS device. The Web application is stored on the host server. Unlike normal Web applications in which a form is downloaded to a browser for display and entry, in a PQA the form is already present on the Palm device. When the user has entered the request information into the local Web page, a query is sent off. The results of the query, called a Web Clipping, are small and compact since they do not contain formatting and display information.

A key element in Palm's Web Clipping solution to the problems of wireless Internet is to use a special architecture that is designed to compensate for the low bandwidth and poor reliability of connections. Also, the content that handheld devices are able to receive and correctly interpret is not the same as that included in most Web pages.

The architecture used by the Web Clipping system is not as simple as merely connecting a Palm OS–powered device directly to the Web sites that it wants to browse. Instead, a system involving the use of special, intermediate servers called Web Clipping Proxies is used. A proxy receives a query request from a handheld device via the User Datagram Protocol (UDP).[1] Next, the proxy communicates with the HTML server via an Internet standard protocol (such as HTTP) to retrieve the information requested by the query. The proxy server then compresses the data and sends it back to the handheld over the wireless network.

---

[1] Use of the simple UDP protocol on the wireless network means that only two small packets are exchanged between the handheld and the proxy, one for the query and one for the clipping.

Understanding Web Clipping Security

Web Clipping has been designed to be secure enough to perform online banking or Internet shopping. Secure connections between a Palm OS handheld and the wireless network are protected using Certicom's elliptic curve encryption. This is a small, but highly efficient, secure public key encryption–based system.

 NOTE *For a complete tutorial on elliptic curve encryption, you can visit Certicom's Web site at* http://www.certicom.com/resources/ ecc_tutorial/ecc_tut_1_0.html.

Messages sent over the wireless network are also protected using a message integrity check (MIC). MICs can detect both transmission errors and message tampering. This helps to ensure that the data you send in a secure transmission is untouched on its journey from your handheld device to the wireless network.

Once a Palm proxy server has received a secure query, the connection between the proxy server and the server that contains the requested query information is protected using standard Secure Socket Layer (SSL) encryption and authentication. To perform authentication, the Web Clipping application should request a username and password when submitting a secured query. Each Web Clipping–enabled Palm Device has a unique identifier embedded in the ROM, which may also be sent with the query to enhance the level of security.

Features Missing from Web Clipping

As you probably noticed in the preceding section, one of the most important things that the Web Clipping Proxy servers do is to strip unsupported content out of target Web sites. So before you get too excited about Web Clipping, this seems like a good place to tell you what parts of HTML are not supported by Web Clipping.

To begin with, Clipper expects any links within a page to come in the form of simple anchor tags, as in this example:

```
<a href="http://www.Vividsoftware.com">A Dallas Based Consulting Firm </a>
```

This requirement makes the use of image maps impossible. For this reason, any image maps that are included in your Web pages will either be converted to a standard image or, more likely, be completely removed.

Unlike a standard Internet browser, Clipper is not equipped to interpret scripts and binaries that are downloaded onto the Palm client. For this reason, JavaScript and client-side VBScript on Web pages are completely ignored. Similarly, any kind of Java applets or ActiveX controls will likewise be ignored.

Some of the standard HTML formatting is also unsupported. This is because of Clipper's need to operate well within the reduced screen space. An example of an unsupported display feature would be the inclusion of frames. Frames are commonly used on the Web to aid in navigation by locking a part of the display so that it will remain constant—even as other parts of the screen change. Another example of unsupported display features is the ability to nest HTML tables within one another. Tables are commonly used in this manner to provide a more in-depth level of page formatting. The good news is that you are still free to use standard non-nested tables in your pages.

Probably the most important feature that is not supported by Clipper is the use of cookies. Often cookies are used to speed up a user's navigation of a Web site by "remembering" key elements of the user's profile. So if your site uses cookies to track from one page to the next if a user has already logged in, then it will simply not work with Clipper. The user will be prompted to log in on every page, because the cookies that identify the user will be lost after each visit.

Features Supported in Web Clipping

The good news is that there are also some features supported by Clipper that are otherwise unknown to the world of HTML. You can build a Web Clipping application that exists entirely on the Palm OS device and never have it call out to the Web. In fact, some of the features offered by Web Clipping make this a very real scenario.

The most minor application of this technology is to use a special meta tag to reference client-side images from your HTML pages. These pages may either be located on the client or the server. Here's an example of this meta tag:

```
<meta name="LocalIcon" content="JonPicture.gif">
```

This command tells Clipper to load an image named JonPicture.gif from the local device rather than from whatever server this current page is located on. This improves the display of pages in Clipper. Since the image is retained locally, Clipper will not have to wait for the image to be transferred over the wireless network.

There are four important meta tags you will want to learn and become familiar with when building Web Clipping applications:

- *PalmComputingPlatform:* This tag identifies your page as Palm friendly. A Palm-friendly page is one that has been designed to work well on the small screen and isn't wasteful of bandwidth. When you include this tag, images will be rendered and the entire text will be displayed on the device. If you do not use this tag, then images will be stripped out and only the first 1024 bytes of your page will display. You should use this meta tag, an example of which follows, on all of your local pages and clippings.

```
<meta name="PalmComputingPlatform" content="true">
```

- *HistoryListText:* This tag specifies the user-visible string for each clipping displayed in the History pop-up menu. You should use this meta tag, as shown in the example that follows, on all of your Web Clipping applications if you wish them to be added to the History pop-up menu.

```
<meta name="HistoryListText" content="true">
```

- *LocalIcon:* This tag identifies HTML documents and graphic images not otherwise referenced that should be stored locally within your Web Clipping application. It is for use in local pages only, and it is suggested that LocalIcon meta tags be placed in the root page of the Web clipping application. Use the following format for LocalIcon tags:

```
<meta name="LocalIcon" content="JonPicture.gif">
```

- *PalmLauncherRevision:* This tag sets the version string for your Web Clipping application. This tag is to be used on the main index (or root) page of your Web Clipping application, following this format:

```
<meta name="PalmLauncherRevision" content="1.0">
```

Another way in which Clipper improves the display of pages is by allowing Web site designers to specify portions of their pages that should not be displayed by Clipper. In this way, a single page may be used both for PQA and for other normal Web browsers. If there is content on this page that shouldn't be sent to Clipper, the Web designer can tell Clipper to skip a piece content by enclosing it in the SmallScreenIgnore tag.

There are several helpful "special" values that can be used with Web Clipping. For example, there is a Web Clipping application available from Starbucks that can tell a Palm OS user where the nearest Starbucks is without ever asking for that user's current location. How does it do this? Through the use of the special value %ZIPCODE. If you embedded this value in your page, the Web Clipping Proxy server will substitute the zip code of the Palm OS user who registered this device.

One cool addition is the ability to link to "real" Palm applications directly from Web Clipping pages. Using special tags you can launch and interact with other applications (those resident on your Palm device) such as another PQA or the Address Book application, or even launch an action such as sending mail. There are three special tags for performing these functions: file:, palm:, and mailto:.

For example, let's say you have a Web page where a user must agree to certain terms before he or she can enter your site (we've all seen these, especially when signing up for Palm's Resource Pavilion). Rather than require the user to click an Agree button every time he or she visits this site, by including the following link in your page, you could call an application stored on the user's Palm device to check the Preferences database on the device to see if the page should be skipped.

```
<A HREF="PALM:CHECKPREF.APPL"></A>
```

What if you needed to check the weather from your current PQA application? You could launch another PQA application, such as the Weather Channel:

```
<A HREF="FILE:WEATHER.PQA"></A>
```

Or suppose you needed to send an e-mail from inside your PQA application (we've all seen these pages on Web sites for sending mail). You can simulate the same process from inside the PQA by invoking the iMessenger application:

```
<A HREF="MAILTO:JKILBURN@VIVIDSOFTWARE.COM"></A>
```

Steps to Create a PQA Application

Creating a PQA application is really quite easy. There are just a few simple (and free, I might add) tools that you need to do the job:

- *An HTML editor:* You can always use Notepad if you don't have anything else. A pure text editor generally works best in this situation. Although you can use a product such as Microsoft's Visual Studio or Macromedia's HomeSite, do not use a form layout tool. Doing so will clutter your HTML and require that you manually edit the code to remove any vendor-specific tags. Please keep in mind that you will need to manually insert any Palm-specific meta tags.

- *Query Application Builder:* This tool, shown in Figure 10-1, is provided in the Palm SDK, but is also available from the Palm Web site (http://www.palm.com) as a separate download. The Query Application

Builder converts one or more HTML files along with any linked images into a PQA. I like to think of the Query Application Builder as compiler that takes source HTML and compiles it to a source form that Clipper (which I suppose could be thought of as a Virtual Machine) can recognize and display.[2]

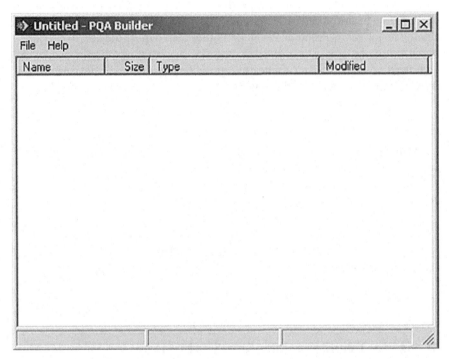

Figure 10-1. The Query Application Builder

After you obtain these tools, you are ready to begin building a Palm Query Application. The process of building the application begins with organizing the HTML files. A PQA can be composed of multiple pages, each of which is defined as a single .htm or .html file. The best way to organize a PQA is to have a central index page to which all subcontent links.

---

[2] The Query Application Builder also compresses the PQA data content to anywhere between 5 and 60 percent, depending on the actual number of images and the content of the HTML pages.

TIP *It is best to try and give users simple and direct access to the sections of the PQA that are most frequently used. In this way, users only need to launch the PQA to start querying for information rather than clicking through a number of pages to find what they are after.*

All of the pages that make up a PQA must fall under the same root directory. However, they can be organized underneath by subdirectories for pages, images, and so on. Keep in mind that from within the PQA, links to pages and images must be relative paths that include whatever subdirectories the information may reside under. It is also a good idea to keep filenames unique, even if they are stored in separate subdirectories, because the Query Application Builder will combine all the pages and images into a single Palm OS database.

Like some other applications, pages that make up the PQA have a limit of 63KB in size. Of course, 63KB of text and images is a very large amount of data. Generally you should limit the use of images in a PQA application, as they do not compress as well as text does.

Building the Hello World PQA

Just as you would when first learning to build an application in any language, you're going to begin with a simple Hello World program. PQA programs should start like any standard HTML document—with a <html> tag, followed by a <head> tag to define the header elements.

Listing 10-1. The Hello World HTML

```
<HTML>
<HEAD>
    <TITLE>PQA Sample</TITLE>
    <META NAME="palmcomputingplatform" CONTENT="TRUE">
    <META NAME="palmlauncherrevision" CONTENT="1.0">
</HEAD>
<BODY>Hello Palm Computing World!</BODY>
</HTML>
```

The text that is contained in the page's <title> tag will appear in the title bar of the Clipper application (see Figure 10-2). This title string should be fairly small, because if it is too long, it will be truncated.

Figure 10-2. The Hello World PQA

Building the Hello World application is very simple. First begin by typing in the Hello World HTML example in Listing 10-1. Next, save the example using the filename Hello.htm.

Open the Query Application Builder and select File | Open Index. Don't be confused by the use of the term "Index," as any HTML page can be considered an index page. Select the Hello.htm file you just created. The newly opened index page will now be displayed in the body of the Query Application Builder. If this index page had contained other pages and images, they would also have appeared in the list (see Figure 10-3).

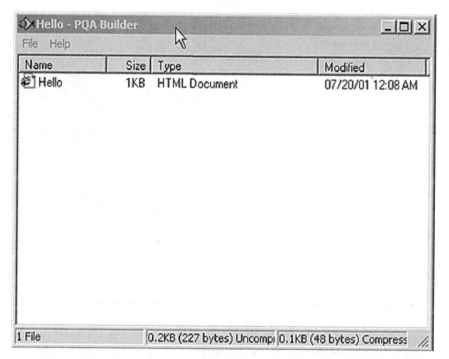

Figure 10-3. The Hello World HTML page, open in the Query Application Builder

The final process of building the PQA application is quite simple. Select File |
Build. When the Build PQA window opens (see Figure 10-4), you will have the
opportunity to supply an icon image. Select an icon and then press the Build button. Now, in the same directory as the Hello.htm file you created, you should see
a file named Hello.pqa.

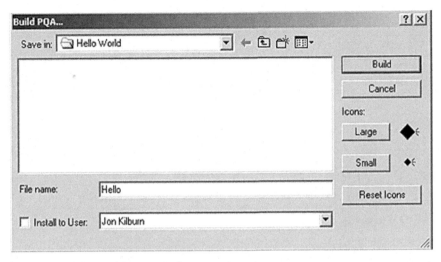

Figure 10-4. The Build PQA window

Formatting Text

You may have noticed that Clipper will display HTML pages using its own type-face. This typeface is called Palm TD. When displayed in normal size, Palm TD looks just like the standard Palm font. Where it differs is that the Palm TD offers support for bold, italic, bold italic, and monospace font.

The sizes available range from 7 to 12, and only certain sizes are available for the <small>, <big>, and <font size=n> HTML tags. What sizes you have available to you can depend on what other formatting may have been applied to the text.

Nuts, Bolts, and PQA Applications

Okay, now you've developed your first PQA application, but it doesn't do a whole lot. So now let's begin to explore the other options you have available to you for developing PQA applications. The first thing I'm going to show you is how to link pages together. Using the standard HTML anchor tag, <a>, you can define links within a local PQA as well as links to other online content.

TIP *You can also use hyperlinks to launch other PQAs and even other Palm applications.*

To mark a specific location in a document, use the anchor tag in association with a name link, as shown in the first example that follows. You can also link to a specific location within the page by using the pound symbol (#) within your link, as shown in the second line.

```
<a name="target page">Link to Another Page</a>
<a name="currentpage.html#target">Link inside the current page</a>
```

By combining the anchor tag with the hyperlink reference marker, you can also create links to other pages:

```
<a href="localpage.html">Link to Local Page</a>
```

Pages located in a subdirectory on the PC can also be referenced, by including the subdirectory in the hyperlink reference:

```
<a href="subdirectory/localpage.html">Link to Local Page</a>
```

The only difference between linking to a local page and a remote Web-hosted page is that you need to include the complete URL in your link, as shown in the following code line. For all remote links, Clipper automatically appends the over-the-air icon to the end of the link text.

```
<a href="http://www.amazon.com">Link to Amazon.com</a>
```

If you need a secured connection via SSL, you can use the same approach—just remember to include the HTTPS prefix, as shown in the following example. In the same fashion as standard remote links, if you are using a secured server link, then Clipper will append the secure over-the-air icon.

```
<a href="https://www.amazon.com/purhcase.asp">Secure Link to Amazon.com</a>
```

NOTE *If you use images for links, you should include the appropriate icons. This will help your pages to maintain the same consistent look and feel of all the other pages.*

Linking can also be accomplished by using a link button instead of a URL. If you use the button suffix appended to a link, as in the code line that follows, Clipper will automatically surround the link text with a Palm OS button, adding the appropriate over-the-air icons to any remote links.

```
<a href="http://www.amazon.com" button>Amazon</a>
```

Linking to Other Applications

As I mentioned earlier, you can also link to other applications using a PQA, and those other applications can be one of two types:

- Another Palm Query Application

- Another application stored on the Palm device

To jump to another PQA application, you simply use the file: prefix and supply the name of the PQA.

```
<a href="file:Another.PQA">Launch another PQA</a>
```

NOTE *Be sure to include the .pga extension after the name of the PQA. Without the extension, Clipper will return an error.*

Linking to a page within the called PQA is also supported:

```
<a href="file:Another.PQA/subpage.html">Launch another PQA</a>
```

Because you are linking to another page within a compiled PQA, any subdirectory information has been removed, so you should code your calls to another PQA as if all the pages were in the original root directory of the application.

There are two supported keywords for launching an application on the current device: palm and palmcall. The differences between the two are not apparent in the syntax for calling them; instead, it is at the OS level that the differences occur. Using the palm syntax will cause Clipper to quit before it launches the requested application, whereas the use of the palmcall will cause Clipper to remain open and running in the background.

```
<a href="palm:memo.appl">Launch Memo Pad</a>
<a href="palmcall:writeprefs.appl">Write Preferences</a>
```

The final piece of information on linking that I'm going to cover involves sending e-mail. You can send e-mail by using the keyword mailto in your supplied URL:

```
<a href="mailto:Jkilburn@Vividsoftware.com">Email Jon Kilburn</a>
```

When a user selects a mailto link, Clipper will automatically launch the iMessenger application to open and display a new e-mail message. Unfortunately, the iMessenger application does not automatically send the e-mail. The user must complete this task.

Building Forms

If you need to collect data from a user in HTML, you generally use the <form> tag. Building a PQA is no different. Through the use of the <form> tag, you can construct simple user interfaces. For example, one of the most commonly used forms is a user login form. Such a form consists of (usually) two elements, a username and a password. In the example that follows, I'm going to add another common feature, a selection combo. When a user logs into this example page, he or she will be prompted to supply a username and password, and to select the property code that he or she is associated with. To accept these inputs in a PQA application, you can construct a simple form as shown in Listing 10-2.

Listing 10-2. The Sample Login Page

```
<HTML>
<HEAD>
<TITLE>Login</TITLE>
    <META NAME="palmcomputingplatform" CONTENT="TRUE">
    <META NAME="palmlauncherrevision" CONTENT="1.0">
</HEAD>
```

```
<BODY>
    <FORM ACTION="http://www.gosomewhere.com" METHOD="GET">
        <TABLE>
            <TR>
                <TD ALIGN="RIGHT">User Name :</TD>
                <TD><INPUT TYPE="TEXT" NAME="USERID" SIZE="15" MAXLENGTH="7"></TD>
            </TR>

            <TR>
                <TD ALIGN="RIGHT">Password :</TD>
                <TD><INPUT TYPE="TEXT" NAME="PWD" SIZE="15" MAXLENGTH="10"></TD>
            </TR>

            <TR>
                <TD ALIGN="RIGHT">Property :</TD>
                <TD>
                    <SELECT NAME="PROPERTY_CODE">
                    <OPTION SELECTED VALUE ="101">AMLI
                    <OPTION VALUE="102">TRAM
                    <OPTION VALUE="103">AMCO
                    </SELECT>
                </TD>
            </TR>

        <TR>
            <TD ALIGN="CENTER" COLSPAN="2">
            <INPUT TYPE="SUBMIT" VALUE="Login">
            </TD>
        </TR>
        </TABLE>
    </FORM>
</BODY>
</HTML>
```

NOTE   *Using HTML comments caused the PQA to not work properly. You should therefore avoid using comments in your HTML.*

There is no law that specifies what tool you have to use to construct your HTML. For the purposes of this example, I used Visual InterDev (see Figure 10-5); however, I could just as easily have used Notepad or any other editor. The reason I chose to use Visual InterDev was for the preview feature offered by the Design tab, which allowed me to get a feel for how the form would look when completed.

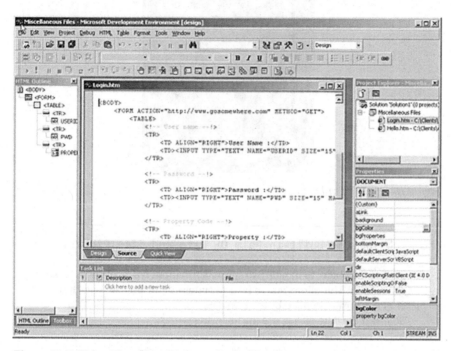

Figure 10-5. Using Visual InterDev to edit the login page

Once the form page has been saved, open the Query Application Builder once more. Select the Login form that you just created and then select the Build PQA menu option. The final application will result in an error because I did not supply a real URL; however, if you look closely at Figure 10-6, you will see that it behaves just like any form created in any of the other programming languages discussed in this book, with the obvious exception that no validation can be performed on this page until the Login button has been pressed.

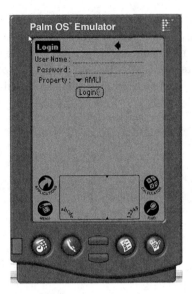

Figure 10-6. The login PQA application

Using the Built-in Palm OS Date and Time Pickers

Clipper has the ability to handle two special form input types: the date picker and time picker. This allows you to take advantage of the built-in date and time picker dialog boxes supplied by the Palm OS.

To insert the date picker, use the following syntax:

```
<input type="datepicker" name="DatePick" value="YYYY-MM-DD">
```

The date picker will display the date using whatever system preferences have been defined. If you omit the value attribute, then the date picker will display the current system date as defined by the Palm device.

Here's the syntax for inserting the time picker:

```
<input type="timepicker" name="TimePick" value="HH:MM">
```

Like the date picker, the time picker will display the time using whatever system preferences have been set by the current user. If you omit the value attribute, then the time picker will display the current system time as defined by the Palm device's internal system clock.

Building Web Clipping Applications

The major difference between a PQA application and a Web Clipping application really occurs on the server end. On the server, an application (generally a CGI-type application) runs to generate the Web Clipping content on the fly. That content can be in the form of data or HTML pages.

Whatever language is used on the server end to generate the Web Clipping content is irrelevant for the purpose of this book. The only concern for the server-side content is that the HTML pages that are generated supply the HTML in the proper format for Clipper to recognize it.

To test an actual PQA Web Clipping application, you have to make a small adjustment to the POSE. Once you have installed one of the wireless supporting ROMs (such as the Palm VII), you need to set up the POSE for PQA testing. Start POSE and then select the Prefs icon. From the menu, select the Wireless option (see Figure 10-7).

Figure 10-7. Selecting the Wireless option from the menu

Once you have selected the Wireless option, the proxy selection screen should appear (see Figure 10-8). The proxy selector trigger in the center of the screen should contain the specific address of a proxy server that Palm.net has set up for testing purposes.

Figure 10-8. The proxy selector trigger

 NOTE   *The current proxy address displayed may or may not be the address that Palm is currently using. You should go to the Palm Web site and confirm this address by visiting the Web Clipping section of the developers zone.*

After you have verified the proxy address, right-click the POSE and select the Settings | Properties menu options to bring up the POSE Property Settings dialog box (see Figure 10-9). This dialog box features a very important option, Redirect Net Lib calls to host TCP/IP, and you must enable this option by clicking the checkbox beside it. Once this option is enabled, the POSE will redirect all the network library calls to your desktop PC's network connection.

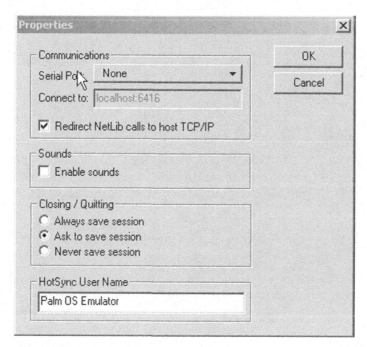

Figure 10-9. The POSE Property Settings dialog box

Once you have the proxy address and the POSE properly configured, PQAs running in POSE should connect to the remote Internet servers as if they were real devices.

Conclusion

In this chapter I've reviewed the techniques required to build both Palm Query Applications (PQA) and Web Clipping applications. Although much more sophisticated applications are possible, I've demonstrated that with little effort (and a bit of knowledge of HTML), you can develop PQA applications quickly and easily.

CHAPTER 11

PDA Utilities

Isn't technology wonderful? Consider this: it's 3 a.m., and I was in New Orleans for a conference. I was scheduled to deliver a session on programming for hand-held devices at 8:30 that morning.

In doing my final research and preparation for this session, I had located what seemed to be a very interesting product for my Palm-sized PC. The problem I had was that it needed a boot image of MS-DOS 6.x in order to run, and I didn't have one with me. Nor, it seemed, did any of the other 25,000 attendees at this conference.

While checking my e-mail, I could see on ICQ that my son, in Sydney, Australia, was online. I was able to make contact with him and have him go through our stash of floppy disks until he found what I was looking for. I sent him a copy of a program that would take an image of the disk I needed, and after running that program against the disk, he then sent me a copy of the image.

I was able to load the image he sent me onto the Palm-sized PC and complete my evaluation of the product in time for my session later that morning.

As you can see, with the appropriate utilities available to me, I was able to take a fairly serious problem and resolve it in a very timely manner. ICQ, the program we used to make an image of the DOS disk, and the products we used to send the requisite files to one another could all be described as utilities in some way. Without utilities, our lives as programmers would be a whole lot tougher than they are.

There are so many other utilities out there for all manner of tasks. Many are very useful in our work as developers of applications. Are there any that you consider indispensable or just plain cool? I've looked at a few, from the perspective of a programmer and just because I like to have a few cool toys.

What follows is by no means exhaustive. It simply represents a small sampling of some of the toys that I find useful. Hopefully it will encourage you to go out and explore the world that these devices—and their applications—can provide to you.

So now, get ready. It's playtime!

Let's Get Physical

I've been using a Palm device of some sort for quite a number of years now. Each of my teenage sons has their own Palm as well. Although I hate to admit it, I even have a couple of broken Palms lying around here, too. For some strange reason, they don't like being dropped, and that is one reason that I switched to a Palm V a couple of years back.

Although the smaller form factor is a real benefit, the solid metal case gives the unit a feeling of robustness that eludes most of the other devices in this market.

This leads me to suggest that, even though you're using your PDA as a development platform, I'd be willing to bet that it's also a near constant companion to you. In keeping with today's busy lifestyles, I'd think it's fair to say that you need to give due consideration to protection.

If you already have a Palm V or similar, then you're probably pretty well set already, but if not, then you need to know that there are a number of good cases and bumper style covers available that will afford your PDA a good measure of protection. While these do not actually fit in with the general software theme of this chapter, I cannot recommend too highly that you ensure that your PDA achieves a level of resistance to the abuse that its life in your pocket (or wherever else you keep it) will inflict upon it.

Palm Utilities

There are a number of utilities that I consider indispensable on my Palm V. A couple of these are just so basic that I consider them to be (almost) a part of the OS itself.

Hacks

HackMaster is probably the first of these sorts of tools that you need to consider. It acts as a sort of "glue" that permits users to customize the basic functionality of the Palm system even more than the designers originally provided for. It was probably the first utility I installed on my Palm Pilot, way back when.

HackMaster has been around for a long time, but there have been few if any updates over the last few years. X-Master, which is said to be fully compatible with HackMaster, brings with it new features, such as a display of details of the hacks installed.

Where applicable, configuration of the hack can be made directly from within X-Master.

By themselves, HackMaster or X-Master don't do all that much. As I said, these are "glue" applications, and it's when you activate some of their extensions that the usefulness of these utilities begins to come to the fore.

The idea is that you install HackMaster, and then you install the HackMaster extensions that you think you might want to use. When you go into HackMaster, you will see a list of the extensions that you have installed. To activate an extension, you simply check its box. To deactivate one, uncheck the box.

You then reset your Palm device to update the current set of hacks. HackMaster is written by DaggerWare (http://www.DaggerWare.net). X-Master comes from LinkeSoft GmbH (http://www.linkesoft.com).

Let's now examine just a few of these extensions.

MenuHack

MenuHack provides true drop-down menu functionality on your Palm device.

Without MenuHack, or when it's disabled, you have access to your drop-down menus only through the menu button on your Palm's silkscreen area.

When MenuHack is enabled, accessing your applications' menus is done either via the menu button on the silkscreen area, or, more intuitively I think, by tapping your applications' caption bar. Recent versions of Palm OS include this modification by default.

MenuHack, like HackMaster, is produced by DaggerWare.

StayOffHack

Some of you will probably identify with this problem: your Palm will be safely stored in your pocket while you're perhaps driving around, or in a meeting, or watching a movie, when without warning it emits a strange noise. The noise sounds something like a cricket chirruping away slowly, and it's just a little more loud than inaudible—certainly loud enough to cause you embarrassment.

What has happened is that an alarm has triggered within your Palm, turning the device on to advise you of that alarm. If not that, then one of the buttons on the device has been inadvertently pressed (possibly as a result of accidental pressure applied to the device while it was in your pocket).

Either way, I find this to be an annoying trait of my Palm, and the Palm V seems to be far more susceptible to this problem. This is no doubt due to the slight protrusion of its accessory buttons, and is exacerbated by the way that the cover folds over and presses directly on those buttons. The buttons on other Palm models don't seem to protrude, and I don't recall this problem in those devices.

StayOffHack addresses this problem, but it also (obviously) disables those accessory buttons that many of us have become so accustomed to. Its use becomes a matter of preference, and which inconvenience you prefer to deal with.

As far as I'm concerned, I can always turn on my device with the power switch, and the Address Book is never more than two buttons away. I can live with that.

StayOffHack can be downloaded from the RGPS site (http://www.rgps.com).

TealEcho

This is a nice extension too, and if your Graffiti skills are less than superb, it can help you improve those as well.

When activated, TealEcho echoes your stylus strokes from the silkscreen area in your Palm's main display. You can see exactly how the Palm is viewing what you are writing, and having that view available can help you work out why it is that your Palm can never understand what you think you're writing.

You can get this extension from TealPoint Software (http://www.tealpoint.com).

CharToBin

An essential tool for programmers, this simple utility asks you to enter a character, and then it displays the equivalent value of that character in binary, hex, and ASCII. The mode is selectable, permitting you to choose how you can enter your character. CharToBin will display the converted results.

If you are binary or hexadecimal challenged but might need to have these conversions available in a field, this utility can be very useful.

CharToBin may be obtained from http://www.jwbfoto.demon.nl/web/.

PDB Reader

This is a simple utility that permits you to view the contents of your PDB (Palm database) files.

Here's how the PDB Reader works: with this utility launched on your desktop system, use the file menu to open the desired Palm database file. After you have selected the file to be opened, PDB Reader will then prompt you to define the record layout. Records can be defined either as a single string (for each record), or alternatively as a set of fields to be applied to each record. After defining the record layout, PDB Reader will then display the contents of the file, starting with the header information for the file, followed by a dump of the records contained within that file (see Figure 11-1).

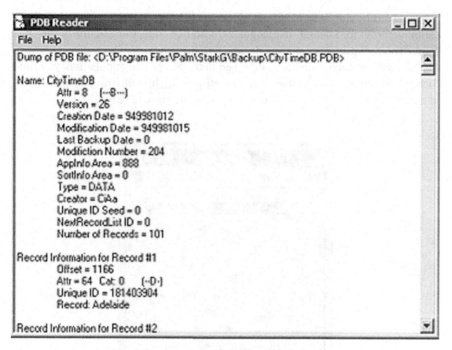

Figure 11-1. The PDB Reader application

Options provided within this application include the ability to save a defined database record layout or a copy of the file report, and to dump the contents of the file into a comma-separated text file.

I can see a weakness in this product in that it expects you to already have detailed knowledge of the record structure of the files that you're looking at. This will not be a problem when it comes to debugging issues that exist within PDB files of your own definition. However, if you have a need (or just a desire) to examine files created by other applications, you will need to experiment a little to find the correct record layout.

Obtain PDB Reader from `http://home.att.net/~sckienle`.

PocketC

I find PocketC to be a very interesting tool. Currently at version 4.1.0, it's the closest thing I've seen to an interpretive version of C, and it's the closest that I've come to finding a tool that permits me to easily write code in C. It provides a complete development tool directly within your Palm OS device.

You start by simply writing your source code in the Palm's MemoPad application. In order for PocketC to recognize the source code, the first line of the source should be a comment line designating the program's filename.

When the source code has been saved in the MemoPad application, you can then launch PocketC. Click the Compile button first; this will bring up a list of all of the source files PocketC can locate on your system (see Figure 11-2).

Figure 11-2. Selecting source code for compilation in PocketC

After successfully compiling your application, you may then select, run, and test it for errors (see Figure 11-3).

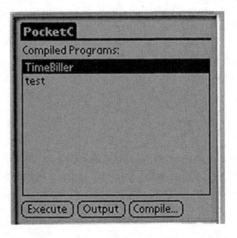

Figure 11-3. Selecting a compiled application to run in PocketC

Apart from being easy to use, PocketC provides a means of distributing just the compiled applet to your end users. Although it still requires a runtime engine in order for your applet to run on the end user's system, this is a freely available application with no runtime license fees. The feature set provided is quite rich, with quite a reasonable group of functions available to the developer.

PocketC also has spawned a number of ancillary tools that make using it even easier than it already might be. These include form designers that operate directly on the Palm system, and libraries of third-party controls that further add to the strength and flexibility of the product.

PocketC is available from OrbWorks (`http://www.orbworks.com`).

Pilot Catapult

If you've ever distributed an application for any of the Windows desktop environments, you are probably familiar with the hassles involved in preparing a complete and accurate distribution set for the application. You need to ensure that all of the correct files are included with the application's distribution set, that they are placed in the correct location, and that the installation routine is made as painless as possible for the end user.

Although the Palm OS platform is nowhere nearly as complex as the Windows platform can be, preparing applications for distribution on the Palm OS platform can be almost as arduous a process. If an application has any degree of complexity, the process will of course be compounded by that complexity.

Beiks LLC (`http://www.beiks.com`) appears to have recognized this problem and has come to the rescue with its Pilot Catapult installation tool. Similar in concept to the Windows installers that we're all familiar with, Pilot Catapult addresses the issues associated with creating a user-friendly set of Palm installation files.

Pilot Catapult runs on your Windows desktop system. It provides three primary dialog boxes into which you enter data relating to the application's properties, the files that need to be installed on the Palm OS device, and the related files that need to be installed on the associated desktop system. See Figure 11-4 for Pilot Catapult's General Properties screen.

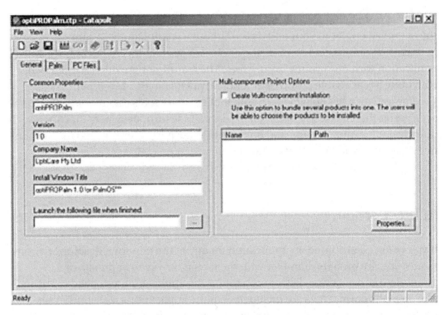

Figure 11-4. The Pilot Catapult General Properties screen

After entering the project details, you will add the files that need to be installed on the Palm system by either dragging and dropping them onto the Palm tab in Catapult, or else by adding them to the project using the Add button on the toolbar. If your application requires companion files to be added to the end user's desktop system, these can be added in the same manner as the Palm system files, but you would drag and drop them onto the PC Files tab.

When you have completed specifying the files that your installation requires, use the Build button on the toolbar to transform the complete installation set into an executable. The executable file created by Pilot Catapult may then be used to distribute your completed application to your end users (see Figure 11-5).

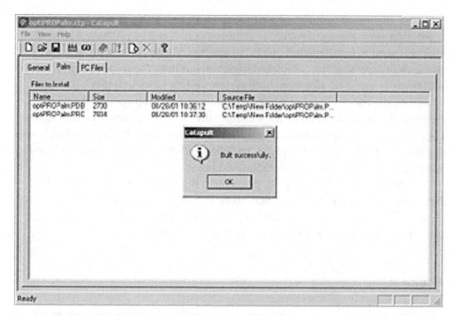

Figure 11-5. The Pilot Catapult Palm tab, showing a successfully completed build of an application

As with its desktop installation tool counterparts, the installation executable created by Pilot Catapult loads as an installation wizard on your end users' systems, and guides them through the installation process before copying the required files into their specified locations.

Pilot Catapult comes in a public (freeware) version, as well as a professional build.

Windows CE Utilities

As for the Palm, there are some utilities for Windows CE devices, and, although the absence of the programs that I am discussing here might not be life threatening, their presence can certainly make your programming tasks a lot more pleasant than they might otherwise be.

ActiveSync

"ActiveSync as a utility?" I can hear the cries now. But yes, Microsoft's ActiveSync program can itself be used as a utility to facilitate other, perhaps less obvious, uses for your handheld.

One oft-missed property of a Windows CE device is that it can also be used as a portable mass-storage device. For instance, consider that you have a large file that you need to transfer from one PC to another. Those two systems are, for some strange reason, not networked together, nor does the source system have a CD burner installed. However, both systems might have ActiveSync installed.

Once the handheld is connected to the source desktop system, the handheld's available storage can be used to store the data that needs to be sent to the target system. Just open up the handheld's file system (use the Explore tool from the toolbar) from within ActiveSync, and drag and drop the file into an appropriate location on the handheld from the desktop system.

Once the file has been copied, disconnect the two devices, and connect the handheld to the target system. Again, using the Explore option from within ActiveSync, locate the file that needs to be copied to the target system, and drag and drop it into the final location on the target system.

PocketC

This PocketC is essentially the same application that I've already described for the Palm OS systems.

Where the Palm OS version relies upon the MemoPad application as the source code editor, the Windows CE version includes its own source code editor. Rather than using a comment line to identify the file, source files are explicitly named and saved to storage in a more familiar Windows manner.

Access to PocketC functionality, such as loading a new file, compiling or executing the currently loaded source file, or jumping to any named function within the current source file, is provided by a typical Windows CE menu bar within the PocketC Editor (see Figure 11-6).

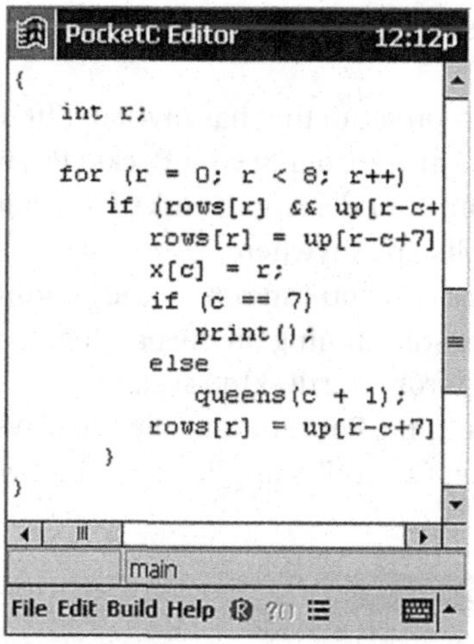

Figure 11-6. The PocketC Editor running on a Compaq iPAQ

Because PocketC relies upon a runtime engine, the issue of distributing different compilations of your Pocket PC applications becomes more of a non-issue. As long as your end users have the appropriate runtime engine for their system installed, you can simply distribute your compiled applet, and it should run across the various Pocket PC processor types without modification.

Transcriber

Microsoft's Transcriber is another one of those programs that I would describe as a must-have.

Transcriber provides Pocket PC users with another method of inputting text via the handheld device's screen, but in a far more usable way. Where the Windows CE Character Recognizer accepts input character by character, Transcriber seems to look at your input both by word and by phrases that have been entered. It then attempts to convert what it understands you to have written to text, and inputs that text into the application that you are using. And even with the poor quality of my handwriting, it seems to do a more than acceptable job of this.

This is one program that has more than just specific use for programmers; I can see it has benefits for all users, and I have no hesitation in recommending it to my users. Transcriber is available at the Microsoft Web site (http://www.Microsoft.com).

Pocket Controller

The Pocket Controller is a program that has myriad different uses. First and foremost, it provides a means of controlling your Pocket PC, while it's connected to your desktop system, from your desktop. Think of it as being the Pocket PC equivalent of something like pcAnywhere.

All of the applications that you can run on the handheld can now be run from the desktop. They're still running on the handheld, of course, but they're now able to be controlled from the desktop system.

When loaded and running, Pocket Controller displays an image of the handheld's screen in the Pocket Controller application window, shown in Figure 11-7.

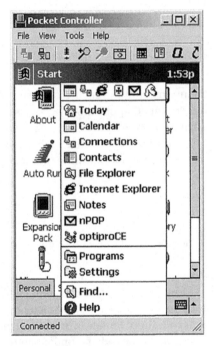

Figure 11-7. The Pocket Controller application

The handheld can be operated from either the device itself or from the desktop, using your mouse and keyboard. For some applications, there will be sufficient benefits derived from the ability to simply use your desktop system's resources for data entry on the handheld, and that will be justification enough to use this program.

In my case, I am frequently called upon to do presentations using the handheld system, and as often as not, these presentations will be done in a group situation, such as in a classroom or perhaps at a trade show. Prior to the advent of Pocket Controller, I had a serious problem in terms of how I was able to demonstrate what was happening on the handheld to the greater group. In a classroom situation, without something like a closed-circuit television system to capture my use of the handheld device, this was a serious challenge.

Because Pocket Controller directly echoes the handheld's display to the desktop system in real time, I can now use the handheld system and, through traditional classroom display equipment, have the classroom view that activity.

I simply cannot overstate the value that I have found of this facility.

Pocket Controller is available at the SOTI Web site (`http://www.soti.net`).

XT-CE

XT-CE creates an 80×86 emulation environment on your Windows CE device; it requires an early version of DOS (I used 6.x) in order to run.

This utility permits you to assign logical DOS device names to the various components of your system, so you can assign and access drive A:, drive C:, and so on. When loaded, it gives you a complete DOS environment within which you can access your system, but in a DOS manner.

And that is where XT-CE becomes very interesting. Because it's running DOS, this means that one can load and run DOS applications within its environment. Here's a partial list of some of the things I've been able to do using XT-CE:

- Load and run copies of my Clipper compiler, my Blinker linker, and my favorite text editor.

- Using those tools, write, compile, link, and run a DOS executable, entirely on the handheld device. I was also able to transfer that same application to a desktop system, and run that application there.

- Share data files between the desktop and handheld system.

- For existing DOS applications with built-in mouse support, copy them across to the handheld, and use them, with the stylus, pretty much as they were designed to be used.

If you have legacy DOS applications, you now potentially have a whole new way of having your clients run these applications. Those applications can now be deployed onto handheld devices and taken directly to where the business problem lies.

Alternatively, you could perhaps write a simple DOS application to solve a transient problem, again harnessing the power and flexibility of a portable device to address those harder-to-solve problems that you sometimes come across in your day-to-day life.

XT-CE can be downloaded from `http://www.xt-ce.com`.

Conclusion

I have recently read that, according to a recent study, almost all PDA owners use their PDA to keep track of contacts, and about 60 percent use their PDA for appointments. That study also contended that although about 15 percent used their PDA for e-mail and 5 percent for surfing the Web, less than 1 percent used any of the massive number of applications that were available for these devices.

I would hope that you are reading this book precisely because you're among the 1 percent that does use your PDA for more than just mundane tasks.

Perhaps you like some of the utilities that I've presented here. You may already be using and enjoying them. Perhaps you know of better variants than those I've listed. If so, great; I'd love to hear of them. Certainly, the small sampling provided here is by no means meant to be exhaustive. Many have been deliberately omitted because I believe that they're already widely in use, or simply because I don't know enough about how to effectively use particular tools to their best advantage.

The important point is that you should take the opportunity to visit some of the Web sites that I've mentioned and download some programs from them. Install them into your handheld device, and explore, experiment, and play with them. I've found that the more I explore, the more I find. The biggest problem I have is simply finding enough hours in the day to do all that I want to with these tools.

Space-Saving Techniques for Palm Databases

Most of us today are accustomed to not worrying about conserving disk space. With 20GB notebooks and 40GB desktops and servers measured in the hundreds of gigabytes or even terabytes—and with all this disk space so inexpensive—we tend to think of space-saving techniques as old-fashioned. Unfortunately, hand-held devices don't currently store gigabytes of data; they will someday, but for now their capacity is limited and space is precious.

To conserve precious disk space, certain database techniques can be used to limit the amount of data that the database requires. We'll examine some of these in the following sections.

 NOTE *The code in the following sections is based on standard Visual Basic, and therefore AppForge. For examples of the compression techniques in NS Basic and CASL, please see the accompanying source code.*

General Storage Techniques

The first issue to be considered in designing a database is how to store certain types of static information. For example, gender is a static set (Male and Female) of possible values, also known as a domain. New genders are not added. Therefore, gender could be indicated as constant value: GENDER_MALE = 0 and GENDER_FEMALE = 1. This constant value could be stored as either 0 or 1, or even M or F. Yet, I have seen databases in which the words *male* and *female* are stored in the tables. Given that *female* is a six-letter word, it consumes six times the amount of disk space as a 0 or a 1.

Likewise, the business rules of an application often dictate limited domains. For example, I have an application that indicates four types of payment schedules all defined by constants as illustrated in Listing A-1.

Listing A-1. An Example of Constants Used for Compressing String Data

```
Const PAY_HOURLY = 0
Const PAY_DAILY = 1
Const PAY_WEEKLY = 2
Const PAY_MONTHLY = 3


Function GetPayFrequency(iStatus As Integer) As String
'-=-=-=-=-=-=-=-=-=-=-=-=-=-=-=-=-=-=-=-=-=-=-=-=-=-=-=-=
'
'   Function    :   GetPayFrequency( iStatus ) -> STRING
'   Params      :   iStatus - Value to Convert to a String
'   Returns     :   STRING  - Converted String Value
'
'   Author      :   Seton Software Development, Inc. - Carl Ganz
'
'   Client      :   Apress
'   Purpose     :   Uncompress String Data
'
'-=-=-=-=-=-=-=-=-=-=-=-=-=-=-=-=-=-=-=-=-=-=-=-=-=-=-=-=
    Dim cResult As String

    Select Case iStatus

        Case PAY_HOURLY
            cResult = "Hourly"

        Case PAY_DAILY
            cResult = "Daily"

        Case PAY_WEEKLY
            cResult = "Weekly"

        Case PAY_MONTHLY
            cResult = "Monthly"

    End Select

    GetPayFrequency = cResult

End Function
```

Here again, the numeric equivalent saves significant space over storing the text. Moreover, if you wish to change the text, you'll need to update every field in the database that contains this text.

Formatting characters are another big waste of space. I often see phone numbers stored as (908)555-1212, which consumes thirteen spaces. Simply by eliminating the parentheses around the area code and the dash, we can save three characters, a savings of 23%. Then, by utilizing the techniques found in the following sections on numeric and date storage, this can be reduced to five spaces, which equals a total space savings of more than 60%.

Be extremely careful in creating large text fields. Users can download an Internet article and paste the text into the database, filling up the Palm device in one motion. Place a limit on the amount of text that can be entered (say, 200 characters). Then, rather than define a free text column as 200 bytes, create a MemoText table that consists of a unique ID, and memo type ID, a line number, and a text field of say, 30 bytes.

Numeric and Date Storage

Both numeric and date storage work from the same principles. The idea is to take a value, say 102372, and reduce it to its ASCII equivalents. In this case, we would store the ASCII equivalents of 10, 23, and 72. This would reduce the six-digit number to a three-character string. (See Listing A-2.) This is not without a few caveats. Consider that we can have the following possible conditions applied to numbers:

- a signed value (I.E. "+" or "-")

- a decimal place

- a single digit (rather than a pair)

These conditions can be easily dealt with. To handle a signed value, we will always store the leading plus (+) or minus (–) sign. So we simply have to check the first character for these values when we decompress, right? Not quite. The plus sign has an ASCII value of 43, and the minus sign has a value of 45. So, to avoid these numbers as potential compressed values, we should "shift" all the compressed values to move them out of the first 47 characters. (These characters are mostly the symbols.)

The next condition to deal with is the decimal place. Because the decimal point has an ASCII value of 46, we can determine that, if a decimal place is present in a compressed string, then we have encountered a decimal for the number and we can include the decimal in the final output.

Finally, how do we deal with single-digit numbers? For example, the value of 1000 would be stored as "10" and "00". The value of "00" would be 0. The trick here is to use values that start at the upper end of the ASCII scale to indicate a value of a compressed single digit. If we start at 147, we are then able to do a value check to determine if this next pair is a single or double compressed pair, and it can then be extracted accordingly.

Listing A-2. Code to Compress Numbers

```
Function CompressNumber(dblData As Double) As String
'-=-=-=-=-=-=-=-=-=-=-=-=-=-=-=-=-=-=-=-=-=-=-=-=-=-=-=-=
'
'    Function    :    CompressNumber( dblData ) -> STRING
'    Params      :    dblData - Value to Compress
'    Returns     :    STRING  - Compressed Value
'
'    Author      :    Vivid Software Inc. - Jon Kilburn
'                     www.Vividsoftware.com
'
'    Client      :    Apress
'    Purpose     :    Compress Data
'
'-=-=-=-=-=-=-=-=-=-=-=-=-=-=-=-=-=-=-=-=-=-=-=-=-=-=-=-=
    Dim cResult     As String    ' Return Result
    Dim cData       As String    ' Converted String Data
    Dim token       As String    ' Compressed Token
    Dim iLen        As Integer   ' Length
    Dim nPos        As Integer   ' Offset Pointer
    Dim nPassCount  As Integer   ' Compression Passes
    Dim strCmp      As String    ' String to Compress
    Dim cWhole      As String    ' Whole Number
    Dim cDecimal    As String    ' Decimal portion of number
    Dim cSign       As String    ' Sign

    ' Convert to String
    cData = CStr(dblData)

    ' Check for a sign
    If Mid$(cData, 1, 1) = "-" Then

        ' Found sign so save it
        cSign = Mid$(cData, 1, 1)
```

```
        ' Remove Sign or decimal
        cData = Mid$(cData, 1)
    End If


' Look for Decimal
nPos = InStr(1, cData, ".", vbTextCompare)
If nPos > 0 Then
    ' We have decimals, so split the string
    cWhole = Mid$(cData, 1, nPos - 1)
    cDecimal = Mid$(cData, nPos + 1)
Else
    ' Whole number
    cWhole = cData
    cDecimal = ""
End If

' Walk each element of the whole number data, compressing
nPassCount = 1

Do While nPassCount <= 2
    ' Initialize Length
    iLen = 1

    ' Compressing whole word or decimal?
    If nPassCount = 1 Then
        strCmp = cWhole
    Else
        strCmp = cDecimal
    End If

    Do While iLen <= Len(strCmp)
        ' Convert Number into Chr() value
        token = Mid$(strCmp, iLen, 2)

        ' Check for single digit
        If Len(token) > 1 Then
            cResult = cResult & Chr(token + nDoubleDigitOffset)
        Else
            ' Single Digit to compress
            cResult = cResult & Chr(token + nSingleDigitOffset)
        End If
        iLen = iLen + 2
    Loop
```

```
          If nPassCount = 1 And Len(cDecimal) > 0 Then
              ' Add in Decimal Place
              cResult = cResult & "."
          End If

          ' Increment Pass Counter
          nPassCount = nPassCount + 1
    Loop

    ' Return Compressed Number (with signage)
    CompressNumber = cSign & cResult

End Function
```

Note that, although this technique works when compressing numbers, it will not work for compressing data such as a Social Security number or a ZIP code. To compress those numbers (if there is a starting zero), we would have to modify the CompressNumber function to accept the number as a string rather than a double. This would then put the burden on the programmer to have converted the data to a string type before passing it to the function. To uncompress the same data is then quite simply a matter of reversing the process. (See Listing A-3.)

Listing A-3. Code to Uncompress String Value

```
Function DecompressNumber(cData As String) As Double
'-=-=-=-=-=-=-=-=-=-=-=-=-=-=-=-=-=-=-=-=-=-=-=-=-=-=-=-=-=
'
'    Function    :    DecompressNumber( cData ) -> DOUBLE
'    Params      :    cData - String to Decompress
'    Returns     :    DOUBLE - Uncompressed Value
'
'    Author      :    Vivid Software Inc. - Jon Kilburn
'                     www.Vividsoftware.com
'    Client      :    Apress
'    Purpose     :    Restore Compressed Data
'
'    NOTES       :    DecompressNumber functions only on those
'                     number values that were previously
'                     compressed using CompressNumber().
'
'                     Example:
'                     cData = CompressNumber(-123.56)
'                     cDblReturn = DecompressNumber(cData)
'
'-=-=-=-=-=-=-=-=-=-=-=-=-=-=-=-=-=-=-=-=-=-=-=-=-=-=-=-=-=
```

```
Dim token       As String   ' Compressed Token
Dim iLen        As Integer  ' Length
Dim nPos        As Integer  ' Offset Pointer
Dim nPassCount  As Integer  ' Compression Passes
Dim strCmp      As String   ' String to Compress
Dim cWhole      As String   ' Whole Number
Dim cDecimal    As String   ' Decimal portion of number
Dim cSign       As String   ' Sign
Dim cResult     As String   ' Uncompressed, assembled String

' Check for a sign
If Mid$(cData, 1, 1) = "-" Then
    ' Found sign so save it
    cSign = Mid$(cData, 1, 1)

    ' Remove Sign or decimal
    cData = Mid$(cData, 1)
End If

' Look for Decimal
nPos = InStr(1, cData, ".", vbTextCompare)
If nPos > 0 Then
    ' We have decimals, so split the string
    cWhole = Mid$(cData, 1, nPos - 1)
    cDecimal = Mid$(cData, nPos + 1)
Else
    ' Whole number
    cWhole = cData
    cDecimal = ""
End If

' Walk each element of the whole number data, decompressing
nPassCount = 1

Do While nPassCount <= 2
    ' Initialize Length
    iLen = 1

    ' Compressing whole word or decimal?
    If nPassCount = 1 Then
        strCmp = cWhole
    Else
```

```
                    strCmp = cDecimal
            End If

        Do While iLen <= Len(strCmp)
            ' Convert Number into Chr() value
            token = Mid$(strCmp, iLen, 1)

            ' Check for single digit
            If Asc(token) >= nSingleDigitOffset Then
                ' Single Digit to decompress
                cResult = cResult & Trim$(Str$(Asc(token) - nSingleDigitOffset))
            Else
                ' Double Digit to decompress

                ' Handle all packed values which are padded
                ' with a 0. For example 01, 02, etc. This check
                ' determines that there were 2 variables packed
                ' so if the value is < 10 then it was a value which
                ' carried a preceeding 0.
                If (Asc(token) - nDoubleDigitOffset) < 10 Then
                    ' Pad with "0"
                    cResult = cResult & "0"
                End If
                cResult = cResult & Trim$(Str$(Asc(token) - nDoubleDigitOffset))
            End If

            iLen = iLen + 1
        Loop

        If nPassCount = 1 And Len(cDecimal) > 0 Then
            ' Add in Decimal Place
            cResult = cResult & "."
        End If

        ' Increment Pass Counter
        nPassCount = nPassCount + 1
    Loop

    ' Return result
    DecompressNumber = CDbl(cSign & cResult)

End Function
```

Dates can likewise be reduced by storing them as the number of days since an agreed-upon base date, say January 1, 1995, or other such date as the business rules permit. Using a maximum of 9,999, we can take the dates out 27 years and 4 months into the future before a fifth digit is required. This four-digit number can then be reduced using the ASCII equivalent technique just discussed. (See Listing A-4.)

Listing A-4. Compressing Dates by Determining the Number of Days Since January 1, 1995

```
' Display Compressed Date
nDiff = CDbl(CDate(cData) - CDate("01/01/1995"))
cData = CompressNumber(nDiff)
MsgBox "Compressed Date : " & cData
```

So, to convert the compressed data back, uncompress the compressed number and then add it to the date January 1, 1995.

Conclusion

Handheld devices continue to become more powerful every day. As such, you may find that, in a few months (maybe even weeks), data compression is no longer needed. Although the technique described here is not the only way to compress data, it is one of the easier methods. I hope that you find it useful.

Index

Symbols

(pound sign)
    for CASL database header records, 223
    for compiler directives, 78
#CDBID header (CASL), 223
#FLDCNT header (CASL), 223
#MAJREV header (CASL), 223
#MINREV header (CASL), 223
#RECCNT header (CASL), 223
#SYNCMODE header (CASL), 223, 224
. . . (ellipsis), 21
^ (caret) for CASL menu shortcuts, 215
3Com, 18
80x86 emulation environment, 365

A

<a> tag, 342–343
about box in CASL, 240–241
Access, 73
    table conversion, 75–78
action buttons, applying actions with
        CASL, 258–260
ActiveSync, 14, 21, 361–362
ActiveX controls. *See also* Ingots in
        AppForge
    Web Clipping and, 335
AFButton control, 63
AFClientSocket Ingot, 56
AFGrid control, 89–90
AFLabel control, 62, 63
AFListBox control, 44
AFScanner Ingot, 56
AFScrollBar Ingot, 56
AFShape control, 63
AFSlider Ingot, 56
AFTextBox control, 62
    and Change event, 105–107
    events supported, 106
AFTimer control, 87
.afx file, 113
Alert function (NS Basic), 142
Alignment property of AFLabel control,
    63

Alliance Program, 24
API calls, AppForge and, 38
AppForge, 3, 37–42. *See also* GolfPro
        application
    advanced functions, 113–114
    building application, 61–70
        calculation code, 64–65
        exit code, 64
        steps for, 45
    compiler directives, 78
    compiler error, 40
        from changing form size, 47
    compiling project, 58–59, 66
        GolfPro application, 110–113
        warnings, 111
    converters, 53–54
        Database Converter, 75–78
        Graphics Converter, 87–88
    Ingots, 51–53
    limitations, 38–39
    and manually resetting POSE, 32
    menu support, 57–60
    Palm Operating System Emulator
        (POSE) and, 42
    Personal Edition, 55
    Professional Edition, 55–56
        converters and viewers, 54
    project creation, 47, 61–63
    Project Manager window, 47
    project properties, 68–70
    running application, 66–67
    VB functions available in, 39
AppForge menu in Visual Basic, 110–111
AppForge Select Target Platform dialog
        box, 48
AppForge Settings dialog box, 68–70
AppForge Universal conduit, 279–292
    conduit creation, 280–281
    DSN (data source name), 282–283
    installing on end user system, 291–292
    name of conduit, 281–282
    sync key selection, 286
    table selection for synchronizing,
        284
application build types in CASL, 206

forums.apress.com

JOIN THE APRESS FORUMS AND BE PART OF OUR COMMUNITY. You'll find discussions that cover topics of interest to IT professionals, programmers, and enthusiasts just like you. If you post a query to one of our forums, you can expect that some of the best minds in the business—especially Apress authors, who all write with *The Expert's Voice*™—will chime in to help you. Why not aim to become one of our most valuable participants (MVPs) and win cool stuff? Here's a sampling of what you'll find:

DATABASES

Data drives everything.

Share information, exchange ideas, and discuss any database programming or administration issues.

INTERNET TECHNOLOGIES AND NETWORKING

Try living without plumbing (and eventually IPv6).

Talk about networking topics including protocols, design, administration, wireless, wired, storage, backup, certifications, trends, and new technologies.

JAVA

We've come a long way from the old Oak tree.

Hang out and discuss Java in whatever flavor you choose: J2SE, J2EE, J2ME, Jakarta, and so on.

MAC OS X

All about the Zen of OS X.

OS X is both the present and the future for Mac apps. Make suggestions, offer up ideas, or boast about your new hardware.

OPEN SOURCE

Source code is good; understanding (open) source is better.

Discuss open source technologies and related topics such as PHP, MySQL, Linux, Perl, Apache, Python, and more.

PROGRAMMING/BUSINESS

Unfortunately, it is.

Talk about the Apress line of books that cover software methodology, best practices, and how programmers interact with the "suits."

WEB DEVELOPMENT/DESIGN

Ugly doesn't cut it anymore, and CGI is absurd.

Help is in sight for your site. Find design solutions for your projects and get ideas for building an interactive Web site.

SECURITY

Lots of bad guys out there—the good guys need help.

Discuss computer and network security issues here. Just don't let anyone else know the answers!

TECHNOLOGY IN ACTION

Cool things. Fun things.

It's after hours. It's time to play. Whether you're into LEGO® MINDSTORMS™ or turning an old PC into a DVR, this is where technology turns into fun.

WINDOWS

No defenestration here.

Ask questions about all aspects of Windows programming, get help on Microsoft technologies covered in Apress books, or provide feedback on any Apress Windows book.

HOW TO PARTICIPATE:

Go to the Apress Forums site at **http://forums.apress.com/**.
Click the New User link.

Printed in the United States
by Baker & Taylor Publisher Services